A Vanished A

Being Some Account of the Jesuits in

1607-1767

R. B. Cunninghame Graham

Alpha Editions

This edition published in 2024

ISBN : 9789362920065

Design and Setting By
Alpha Editions
www.alphaedis.com
Email - info@alphaedis.com

Contents

Preface

Historicus nascitur, non fit. I am painfully aware that neither my calling nor election in this matter are the least sure. Certain it is that in youth, when alone the historian or the horseman may be formed, I did little to fit myself for writing history. Wandering about the countries of which now I treat, I had almost as little object in my travels as a Gaucho of the outside `camps'. I never took a note on any subject under heaven, nor kept a diary, by means of which, my youth departed and the countries I once knew so well transmogrified, I could, sitting beside the fire, read and enjoy the sadness of revisiting, in my mind's eye, scenes that I now remember indistinctly as in a dream. I take it that he who keeps a journal of his doings, setting down day by day all that he does, with dates and names of places, their longitude and latitude duly recorded, makes for himself a meal of bitter-sweet; and that your truest dulcamara is to read with glasses the faded notes jotted down hurriedly in rain, in sun, in wind, in camps, by flooded rivers, and in the long and listless hours of heat — in fact, to see again your life, as it were, acted for you in some camera obscura, with the chief actor changed. But diaries, unless they be mere records of bare facts, must of necessity, as in their nature they are autobiographical, be false guides; so that, perhaps, I in my carelessness was not quite so unwise as I have often thought myself. Although I made no notes of anything, caring most chiefly for the condition of my horse, yet when I think on them, pampa and cordillera, virgin forest, the `passes' of the rivers, approached by sandy paths, bordered by flowering and sweet-smelling trees, and most of all the deserted Jesuit Missions, half buried by the vigorous vegetation, and peopled but by a few white-clad Indians, rise up so clearly that, without the smallest faculty for dealing with that which I have undertaken, I am forced to write. Flowers, scents, the herds of horses, the ostriches, and the whole charm of that New World which those who saw it even a quarter of a century ago saw little altered from the remotest times, have remained clear and sharp, and will remain so with me to the end. So to the readers (if I chance to have them) of this short attempt to give some faint idea of the great Christian Commonwealth of the Jesuit Missions between the Paraná and Uruguay, I now address myself. He who attacks a subject quite fallen out of date, and still not old enough to give a man authority to speak upon it without the fear of contradiction, runs grave risk.

Gentle, indulgent reader, if so be that you exist in these the days of universal knowledge and self-sufficient criticism, I do not ask for your indulgence for the many errors which no doubt have slipped into this work. These, if you care to take the trouble, you can verify, and hold me up to shame. What I do crave is that you will approach the subject with an open mind. Your Jesuit is, as we know, the most tremendous wild-fowl that the world has known. `La guardia nera' of the Pope, the order which has wrought so much destruction, the inventors of `Ciencia media',[1] cradle from which has issued forth Molina, Suarez, and all those villains who, in the days in which the doctrine was unfashionable, decried mere faith, and took their stand on works — who in this land of preconceived opinion can spare it a good word? But, notwithstanding, even a Jansenist, if such be left, must yet admit the claim of Francis Xavier as a true, humble saint, and if the sour-faced sectary of Port Royale should refuse, all men of letters must perforce revere the writer of the hymn.

But into the whole question of the Jesuits I cannot enter, as it entails command of far more foot and half-foot words than I can muster up. Still, in America, and most of all in Paraguay, I hope to show the Order did much good, and worked amongst the Indians like apostles, receiving an apostle's true reward of calumny, of stripes, of blows, and journeying hungry, athirst, on foot, in perils oft, from the great cataract of the Paraná to the recesses of the Tarumensian woods. Little enough I personally care for the political aspect of their commonwealth, or how it acted on the Spanish settlements; of whether or not it turned out profitable to the Court of Spain, or if the crimes and charges of ambition laid to the Jesuits' account were false or true. My only interest in the matter is how the Jesuits' rule acted upon the Indians themselves, and if it made them happy — more happy or less happy than those Indians who were directly ruled from Spain, or through the Spanish Governors of the viceroyalties. For theories of advancement, and as to whether certain arbitrary ideas of the rights of man, evolved in general by those who in their persons and their lives are the negation of all rights, I give a fico — yes, your fig of Spain — caring as little as did ancient Pistol for `palabras', and holding that the best right that a man can have is to be happy after the way that pleases him the most. And that the Jesuits rendered the Indians happy is certain, though to those men who fudge a theory of mankind, thinking that everyone is forged upon their anvil, or run out of their own mould, after the fashion of a tallow dip (a theory which, indeed, the sameness of mankind renders at times not quite untenable), it seems absurd because the progress of the world has gone on other lines — lines which prolonged indefinitely would never meet those which the Jesuits drew. All that I know is I myself, in the deserted missions, five-and-twenty years ago often have met old men who spoke regretfully of Jesuit times, who cherished all the customs left by the company, and though they spoke at secondhand, repeating but the stories they had heard in youth, kept the illusion that the missions in the Jesuits' time had been a paradise. Into the matter of the Jesuits' motives I do not propose to enter, holding that the origin of motives is too deeply seated to be worth inquiry until one has more information about the human mind than even modern `scientists' seem able to impart. Yet it is certain the Jesuits in Paraguay had faith fit to remove all mountains, as the brief stories of their lives, so often ending with a rude field-cross by the corner of some forest, and the inscription `hic occissus est' survive to show. Some men — such is the complexity of human nature — have undergone trials and persecutions for base motives, and it is open for anyone to say the Jesuits, as they were Jesuits, could do nothing good. Still, I believe that Father Ruiz Montoya — whose story I have told, how falteringly, and with how little justice to his greatness, none knows better than myself — was a good man — that is, a man without ulterior motives, and actuated but by his love to the poor Indians with whom he passed his life. To-day, when no one can see good in anything or anybody outside the somewhat beefy pale of the Anglo-Saxon race, I do not hope that such a mere dabbler in the great mystery of history as I am myself will for an instant change one preconceived opinion; for I am well aware that speeches based on facts are impotent in popular assemblies to change a single vote.

It is an article of Anglo-Saxon faith that all the Spanish colonies were mal-administered, and all the Spanish conquerors bloodthirsty butchers, whose sole delight was blood. This, too, from the members of a race who . . .; but `In the multitude of the greyhounds is the undoing of the hare.' Therefore, I ask those who imagine that all Spaniards at the conquest of America were ruffians, to consider the career of Alvar Nuñez, who also struts through his brief chapter in the pages of my most imperfect book. Still, I admit men of the stamp of Alvar Nuñez are most rare, and were still rarer in the sixteenth century; and to find many of the Ruiz Montoya brand, Diogenes would have needed a lantern fitted with electric light. In the great controversy which engaged the pens of many of the best writers of the world last century, after the Jesuits were expelled from Spain and her colonial possessions (then almost half the world), it will be found that amongst all the mud so freely flung about, the insults given and received, hardly anyone but a few ex-Jesuits had any harm to say of the doings of the Order during its long rule in Paraguay. None of the Jesuits were ever tried; no crimes were charged against them; even the reasons for their expulsion were never given to the world at large. Certain it is that but a few years after their final exit from the missions between the Uruguay and Paraná all was confusion. In twenty years most of the missions were deserted, and before thirty years had passed no vestige of their old prosperity remained.

The semi-communism which the Jesuits had introduced was swept away, and the keen light of free and vivifying competition (which beats so fiercely upon the bagman's paradise of the economists) reigned in its stead. The revenues declined,[2] all was corruption, and, as the Governor, Don Juan José Vertiz, writes to the Viceroy,[3] the secular priests sent by the Government were brawlers, drunkards, and strikers, carrying arms beneath their cloaks; that robbery was rife; and that the Indians daily deserted and returned by hundreds to the woods.

All the reports of riches amassed in Paraguay by the Jesuits, after the expulsion of their order proved to be untrue; nothing of any consequence was found in any of the towns, although the Jesuits had had no warning of their expulsion, and had no time for preparation or for concealment of their gold. Although they stood to the Indians almost in the light of gods, and had control of an armed force larger by far than any which the temporal power could have disposed of, they did not resist, but silently departed from the rich territories which their care and industry had formed.

Rightly or wrongly, but according to their lights, they strove to teach the Indian population all the best part of the European progress of the times in which they lived, shielding them sedulously from all contact with commercialism, and standing between them and the Spanish settlers, who would have treated them as slaves. These were their crimes. For their ambitions, who shall search the human heart, or say what their superiors in Europe may, or perhaps may not, have had in view? When all is said and done, and now their work is over, and all they worked for lost (as happens usually with the efforts of disinterested men), what crime so terrible can men commit as to stand up for near upon two centuries against that slavery which disgraced every American possession of the Spanish[4] crown? Nothing is bad enough for those who dare to speak the truth, and those who put their theories into practice are a disgrace to progressive and adequately taxed communities. Nearly two hundred years they strove, and now their territories, once so populous and so well cultivated, remain, if not a desert, yet delivered up to that fierce-growing, subtropical American plant life which seems as if it fights with man for the possession of the land in which it grows. For a brief period those Guaranís gathered together in the missions, ruled over by their priests, treated like grown-up children, yet with a kindness which attached them to their rulers, enjoyed a half-Arcadian, half-monastic life, reaching to just so much of what the world calls civilization as they could profit by and use with pleasure to themselves. A commonwealth where money was unknown to the majority of the citizens, a curious experiment by self-devoted men, a sort of dropping down a diving-bell in the flood of progress to keep alive a population which would otherwise soon have been suffocated in its muddy waves, was doomed to failure by the very nature of mankind. Foredoomed to failure, it has disappeared, leaving nothing of a like nature now upon the earth. The Indians, too, have vanished, gone to that limbo which no doubt is fitted for them. Gentle, indulgent reader, if you read this book, doubt not an instant that everything that happens happens for the best; doubt not, for in so doing you would doubt of all you see — our life, our progress, and your own infallibility, which at all hazards must be kept inviolate. Therefore in my imperfect sketch I have not dwelt entirely on the strict concatenation (after the Bradshaw fashion) of the hard facts of the history of the Jesuits. I have not set down too many dates, for the setting down of dates in much profusion is, after all, an *ad captandum* appeal to the suffrages of those soft-headed creatures who are styled serious men.

Wandering along the by-paths of the forests which fringe the mission towns, and set them, so to speak, in the hard tropical enamel of green foliage, on which time has no lien, and but the arts of all-destroying man are able to deface, I may have chanced upon some petty detail which may serve to pass an hour away.

A treatise of a forgotten subject by a labourer unskilled, and who, moreover, by his very task challenges competition with those who have written on the theme, with better knowledge, and perhaps less sympathy; a pother about some few discredited and unremembered priests; details about half-savages, who `quoi! ne portaient pas des haults de chausses'; the recollections of long silent rides through forest paths, ablaze with flowers, and across which the tropic birds darted like atoms cut adrift from the apocalypse; a hotch-potch, salmagundi, olla podrida, or sea-pie of sweet and bitter, with perhaps the bitter ruling most, as is the way when we unpack our reminiscences — yes, gentle and indulgent reader, that's the humour of it.

    R. B. Cunninghame Graham.

Gartmore,
  March 30, 1900.

Chapter I

Early history — State of the country — Indian races — Characteristics of the different tribes — Dobrizhoffer's book — Various expeditions — Sebastian Cabot — Don Pedro de Mendoza — Alvar Nuñez — His expedition and its results — Other leaders and preachers — Founding of the first mission of the Society of Jesus

With the exception of the French Revolution, perhaps no event caused so much general controversy at the end of the eighteenth century as the expulsion of the Jesuits from Spain and Portugal and their colonial possessions. As no definite charges were ever brought, at least in Spain, against the members of the Company of Jesus (King Charles III. having kept the reasons *ocultas y reservadas* and the proofs *privilegiados*), curiosity is to some extent not satisfied as to the real reason of their expulsion from the Spanish possessions in America.

It is almost impossible to understand nowadays the feelings which possessed the average man in regard to the Jesuits from the middle of the last century till a relatively short time ago. All the really great work done by the Society of Jesus seemed to have been forgotten, and every vulgar fable which it was possible to invent to their prejudice found ready acceptance upon every side. Nothing was too absurd to be believed. From the calumnies of the Jansenists to the follies of Eugène Sue the mass of accusation, invective, and innuendo kept on increasing in intensity. Indiscriminate abuse and unreasoning hatred, mixed with fear, seem to have possessed all minds. Even Pascal confesses (in a postscript to the ninth Provincial Letter) that `after having written my letter I read the works of Fathers Barry and Binet.' If such a man as Pascal could be so grossly unfair as to write a criticism on works which he had not read, what can be expected from the non-judicial and uncritical public which takes all upon trust?

From Japan to the interior of Bolivia there is scarcely a country in which the Jesuits have not laboured assiduously, and in which they have not shed their blood freely without hope of reward, yet it would require much time and a lengthy catalogue to enumerate the list of satirical and calumnious works which have appeared against them in almost every language in Europe. Of these, perhaps the most celebrated is the well-known `Monarquia de los Solipsos',[5] by Padre Melchior Inshoffer, an ex-Jesuit, who describes the company in the worst possible terms. It is interesting chiefly on account of the portraits of well-known people of the time (1615 to 1648), as Pope Clement VIII., Francisco Suarez, Claudio Aquaviva, and others, veiled under easily distinguishable pseudonyms. The object of the writer, as the title indicates, is to show that the Jesuits endeavoured to turn all to their own profit. In this, if it was the case, they do not seem to have been greatly different from every other associated body of men, whether lay or clerical. The celebrated Spanish proverb, 'Jesuita y se ahorca, cuenta le hace', meaning, Even if a Jesuit is hung he gets some good out of it, may just as well be applied to members of other learned professions as to the Jesuits.

The world has rarely persecuted any body of men conspicuous by its poverty, or if it has done so has rarely persecuted them for long. The Inquisition of Spain, violent against the wealthy Jews and comfortable Moriscos, took little notice of the Gipsies; but, then, 'Pobre como cuerpo de Gitano' was and is a common saying in Spain.

As in the case of the Templars, persecution only began against the Jesuits when it became worth while to persecute them. Ignatius Loyola, Francisco Xavier, and Diego Lainez, as long as they confined themselves to preaching and to teaching, were safe enough. Even the annals of theological strife, bloodthirsty and discreditable to humanity as they are, contain few examples of persecutors such as Calvin or Torquemada, to whom, ruthless as they were in their savage and narrow malignity and zeal for what they thought the truth, no suspicion of venal motives is attributed.

Of the Jesuits' intrigues, adventures, rise and fall in Europe, much may be said in attack or in extenuation; but it is not the intention of the present work to deal with this aspect of the question. It was in Spanish America, and especially in Paraguay and Bolivia, where the policy of the Company in regard to savage nations was most fully developed, as it was only the Jesuits who ever succeeded in reclaiming any large number of the nomad or semi-nomad tribes of those countries.

Many excellent works in French, and the celebrated 'Christianismo Felice nel Paraguay' of the Abbate Muratori in Italian, certainly exist. But neither Father Charlevoix, the French historian of the missions, nor Muratori was ever in Paraguay, and both their books contain the faults and mistakes of men, however excellent and well intentioned, writing of countries of which they were personally ignorant. Both give a good account of the customs and regimen of the missions, but both seem to have believed too readily fabulous accounts of the flora and fauna of Paraguay.[6] The fact of having listened too readily to a fable about an unknown animal in no way detracts from the general veracity of an author of the beginning of the eighteenth century, for in all other respects except natural history Charlevoix keeps within the bounds of probability, though of course as a Jesuit he holds a brief for the doings of the Company in Paraguay. Muratori is more rarely led into extravagances, but is concerned in the main with the religious side of the Jesuits, as the title of his book indicates.

Many other French writers, as Raynal, Montesquieu, and Voltaire, have treated of Paraguay under Jesuit rule, but their writings are founded on hearsay evidence. A German, Father Dobrizhoffer, stands alone.[7] His delightful `History of the Abipones, an Equestrian People of Paraguay', is perhaps the most charming book dealing with the subject. A simple and easy style, a keen habit of observation, long acquaintance with the country, a zeal for the conversion of the infidel, not only to Christianity, but to a more comfortable mode of life, to which he adds a faith sufficient to move the Cordillera of the Andes, but at the same time restricted by a common-sense and veracity not always observable in religious writers, render Dobrizhoffer a personal friend after the perusal of his writings.

English is singularly barren in regard to the Jesuits in Paraguay. Father Falconer, an English Jesuit, has left a curious and interesting book (printed at Hereford in 1774), but he treats exclusively of what is now the province of Buenos Ayres, the Falkland Islands, and of Patagonia. As an Englishman and a Jesuit (a somewhat rare combination in the eighteenth century), and as one who doubtless knew many of the Paraguayan priests, his testimony would have been most important, especially as he was a man of great information, much education, an intrepid traveller, and, moreover, only entered the Company of Jesus at a comparatively advanced age.

It is in Spanish, or in Latin by Spanish authors, that the greater portion of the contemporary histories and accounts are to be found.[8] Literatures, like other things, have their times of fashion. At one time a knowledge of Spanish was as requisite as some tincture of French is at present, and almost as universal. Men from Germany, England, and Holland who met in a foreign country communicated in that language. In the early portion of the century Ticknor, Prescott, and Washington Irving rendered Spanish literature fashionable to some degree.

Later the historical researches of Sir William Stirling Maxwell drew some attention to it. To-day hardly any literature of Europe is so little studied in England. Still leaving apart the purely literary treasures of the language, it is in Spanish, and almost alone in Spanish, that the early history of America is to be found.

After the struggle for independence which finished about 1825, some interest was excited in the Spanish-American countries, stimulated by the writings of Humboldt; but when it became apparent that on the whole those countries could never be occupied by Northern Europeans, interest in them died out except for purposes connected with the Stock Exchange. Yet there is a charm which attaches to them which attaches to no other countries in the world. It was there that one of the greatest dramas, and certainly the greatest adventure in which the human race has engaged, took place. What Africa has been for the last twenty years, Spanish America was three hundred years ago, the difference being that, whereas modern adventure in Africa goes on under full observation, and deals in the main with absolutely uncivilized peoples, the conquest of South America was invested with all the charm of novelty, and brought the conquerors into contact with at least two peoples almost as advanced in most of the arts of civilization as they were themselves.

When first Sebastian Cabot and Solis ascended the Paraná, they found that the Guaranís of Paraguay had extended in no instance to the western shore of either of those rivers. The western banks were inhabited then, as now, by the wandering Indians of the still not entirely explored territory of the Gran Chaco. Chaco[9] is a Quichua Indian word meaning `hunting' or `hunting-ground', and it is said that after the conquest of Peru the Indian tribes which had been recently subjugated by the Incas took refuge in this huge domain of forest and of swamp.

Be that as it may, the Chaco Indians of to-day, comprising the remnants of the Lulis, Tobas, Lenguas, Mocobiós, and others, are almost as savage as when first we hear of them in the pages of Alvar Nuñez and Hulderico Schmidel. These tribes the Jesuits on many occasions attempted to civilize, but almost entirely without success, as the long record of the martyrdom of Jesuit missionaries in the Chaco proves, as well as the gradual abandonment of their missions there, towards the second half of the eighteenth century.

Certain it is that at various places in the Chaco, in the quaint old maps the Jesuits have left us, one reads `Mission de Santa Cruz de los Vilelas', `Mission de la Concepcion de los Frontones', and others; but much more frequently their maps are studded with crosses, and some such legend as `Hic occisi sunt PP. Antonius Salinus et Petrus Ortiz Zarate'.[10] It was only when the Jesuits encountered the more peaceful Guaranís that they met with real success.

What was the nature of their success, how durable it was, what were the reasons which caused the expulsion of the order from America, and especially from Paraguay, and what has been the result upon the remainder of the Indians, it is my object to endeavour to explain.

A long residence in the river Plate, together with two visits to Paraguay, in one of which I saw almost all the remnants of the Paraguayan missions and a few of those situated in the province of Corrientes, and in the Brazilian province of Rio Grande do Sul, have given me some personal acquaintance with the subject.[11]

The actual condition of the rich district of Misiones (Paraguay) at the time I visited it, shortly after the conclusion of the great war between Paraguay and Brazil in 1870, does not enable me to speak with authority on the condition of communities, the guiding spirits of which were expelled as far back as the year 1767. The actual buildings of the missions, the churches in a dismantled state, have indeed survived; in many instances the tall date-palms the Jesuits planted still wave over them. Generally the college was occupied by the Indian Alcalde, who came out to meet the visitor on a horse if he possessed one, with as much silver about the bridle and stirrups as he could afford, clothed in white, with a cloak of red baize, a large *jipi-japa* hat, and silver spurs buckled on his naked feet. If he had never left the mission, he talked with wonder and respect of the times of the Jesuits, and at the *oracion* knelt down to pray wherever the sound of the angelus might catch him. His children before bedtime knelt all in a row to ask his blessing. If he had been to Asuncion, he probably remarked that the people under those accursed priests were naught but animals and slaves, and launched into some disquisition he had heard in the solitary café which Asuncion then boasted. In the latter case, after much of the rights of man and the duties of hospitality, he generally presented you with a heavy bill for Indian corn and *pindo*[12] which your horse had eaten. In the former, usually he bade you go with God, and, if you spoke of payment, said: 'Well, send me a book of Hours when you get to Asuncion.'

Of Indians, hardly any were left to judge of, for in the villages in which, according to the reports furnished to Bucareli, the Viceroy of Buenos Ayres at the time of the expulsion of the Jesuits, the population numbered in the thirty towns of the missions one hundred and twenty thousand,[13] a population of at most twenty thousand was to be found. On every side the powerful vegetation had covered up the fields. On ruined church and chapel, and on broken tower, the lianas climbed as if on trees, creeping up the belfries, and throwing great masses of scarlet and purple flowers out of the apertures where once were hung the bells. In the thick jungles a few half-wild cattle still were to be found. The vast *estancias*, where once the Jesuits branded two and three thousand calves a year, and from whence thousands of mules went forth to Chile and Bolivia, were all neglected. Horses were scarce and poor, crops few and indifferent, and the plantations made by the Jesuits of the tree (*Ilex Paraguayensis*) from which is made the *yerba maté*, were all destroyed.

In the vast forests, stretching to the Salto de Guayrá, a few scattered tribes, known as Caaguas, roamed through the thickets, or encamped upon the streams. In the thirty towns, once full of life and stir, in every one of which there was a church, finer, as an old Spanish writer says, than any in Buenos Ayres, there was naught but desolation and despair. The Indians either had returned into the woods, been killed in the ceaseless revolutionary wars, or had been absorbed into the Gaucho populations of Corrientes, Rio Grande, Entre Rios, and of Santa Fé.

It may be that all Indian races are destined to disappear if they come into contact with Europeans; certainly, experience would seem to confirm the supposition. The policy of the Jesuits, however, was based on isolation of their missions, and how this might have worked is matter at least for speculation. It was on account of the isolation which they practised that it was possible for the extravagant calumnies which were circulated as to their rule and riches to gain belief. It was on account of isolation that the first conflicts arose betwixt them and the authorities, both clerical and lay. That the Jesuits were more highly esteemed than the other religious orders in Spanish America in the seventeenth century, the saying current in those days, `Los demas van á uña, los Jesuitas á una' — *i.e.*, The others get all they can, but the Jesuits have one aim (the conversion of the Indians) — seems to show.

It is not my purpose to deal with the probable reasons which induced their expulsion in Europe. Suffice it to say that, whatever crimes or misdemeanours they were guilty of, they were never called on to answer before any tribunals, and that in many instances they were treated, especially in Portugal, with great cruelty and injustice.

The burning, at the age of eighty, of the unfortunate Malagrida in Lisbon under the auspices of Pombal, for a book which it seems improbable he could have written in prison at so great an age, and which, moreover, was never brought into court, only supposed extracts from it being read, may serve as an example. In order clearly to understand the position of the Jesuits in America, and especially in Paraguay and Bolivia, it is necessary to glance briefly at the history of the first conquest of the river Plate.

The discovery of America opened up to Europe, and especially to Spain, opportunities for expansion of national territory and individual advancement which no epoch, either before or since, has equalled. From a cluster of small States, struggling for existence against a powerful enemy on their own soil, in a few years Spain became the greatest empire of the world. The result was that a spirit of adventure and a desire to grow rich speedily possessed all classes. In addition to this, every Spaniard in America during the first few years of the conquest seemed to consider himself, to some extent, not only as a conqueror, but also as a missionary.

Now, missionaries and conquerors are men, on the whole, more imbued with their own importance and sanctity, and less disposed to consider consequences, than almost any other classes of mankind. The conjunction of the two in one disposed the *conquistadores* of America to imagine that, no matter how cruel or outrageous their treatment of the Indians was, they atoned for all by the introduction of what they considered the blessing of the knowledge of the true faith. It will be seen at once that, if one can determine with accuracy which of the many 'faiths' preached about the world is actually the true faith, a man who is in possession of it is acting properly in endeavouring to diffuse it. The meanest soldier in the various armies which left Spain to conquer America seems to have had no doubt about the matter.

Bernal Diaz del Castillo, who, as he himself relates, came to America at the age of eighteen, and therefore could have had little previous opportunity of studying theology, and who, moreover, was unfitted to do so by the want of knowledge of Latin, to which he himself confesses, yet at the end of his history of the conquest of Mexico, one of the most interesting books ever written, has the following passage:

'But it is to be noted that, after God, it was we, the real conquerors, who discovered them [the Indians] and conquered them; and from the first we took away their idols, and taught them our holy doctrine, and to us is due the reward and credit of it all, before any other people, even though they be churchmen: for when the beginning is good, the middle and ending is good, which the curious [*i.e.*, attentive] reader may see in the Christian polity and justice which we showed them in New Spain.

'And I will leave the matter, and tell the other benefits which, after God, by our agency, came to the natives of New Spain.'[14]

One would imagine, on reading the above extract, Bernal Diaz had never killed an Indian in his life, and that he had sacrificed his prospects in coming to Mexico solely to introduce 'a Christian polity and justice' amongst the inhabitants. Yet he was no hypocrite, but a stout sagacious soldier, even kindly, according to his lights, and with a love of animals uncommon in a Spaniard, for he has preserved the names and qualities of all the horses and mares which came over in the fleet from the Havana with Cortes.[15] The phrase, *despues de Dios* (after God) occurs repeatedly in the writings of almost all the *conquistadores* of America. Having, after God, conquered America, the first action of the conquerors was to set about making their fortunes. In those countries which produced gold and silver, as Mexico and Peru, they worked the mines by the labour of the Indians, the cruelties and hardships being so great that, in a letter of Philip II. to the Come de Chinchon, the Viceroy of Peru, dated Madrid, April 30, 1639, written fifty years after the discovery, he says: 'These Indians flee, become ill, and die, and have begun to diminish greatly in number, and they will be finished soon unless an efficient remedy is provided shortly.'

In Paraguay there were no mines, but there were other methods of extracting money from the Indians. At the first conquest Paraguay was not the little country bounded on the west by the Paraguay, on the south by the Paraná, on the north by the Aquidaban, and on the east by Sierra of Mbaracavu, as it is at present. On the contrary, it embraced almost all that immense territory known to-day as the Argentine Confederation, some of the Republic of Uruguay, and a great portion of Brazil, embracing much of the provinces of Misiones, Rio Grande do Sul, Paraná, and Matto Grosso, as well as Paraguay itself. How the little country, twelve hundred miles from the sea, came to give its name to such an enormous territory, and to have the seat of government at Asuncion, demands some explanation. Peru and Chile were discovered and occupied some time before the eastern side of South America. Their riches naturally drew great attention to them; but the voyage, first to Cartagena de Indias, and then across the isthmus, and the re-embarkation again on the Pacific, were both costly and arduous. It had been the ambition of all explorers to discover some river which would lead from the Atlantic to the mines of Peru and what is now Bolivia, then known as Alta Peru. Of course, this might have been achieved by ascending the Amazon, especially after the adventurous descent of it by Orellana, of which Fray Gaspar de Carbajal has left so curious a description; but, whether on account of the distance or for some other reason, it never seems to have been attempted.

In 1526 Sebastian Cabot left Spain with three small vessels and a caravel for the object of reaching the Moluccas or Spice Islands. It was his purpose to reach them through the Straits of Magellan. Being compelled by want of supplies to abandon his route, he entered a broad estuary, and ascended it under the impression that he had discovered another channel to the Pacific. He soon found his mistake, and began to explore the surrounding country. Fifteen years before, with the same object, Juan de Solis had entered the same estuary. On the island of Martin Garcia he was killed by a Chana Indian, and his expedition returned home. Hearing that there was much silver at the head-waters, he had called it the Rio de la Plata. If we take the head-waters of the river Plate to be situated in Bolivia, there certainly was much silver there; but Cabot was unaware that the head-waters were above two thousand miles from the estuary, and he was not destined to come near them. He did go as far as a point on the river Caracara, in what is now the province of Santa Fé, and there he built a fort which he named Espiritu Santo, the first Spanish settlement in that part of America. Whilst at Espiritu Santo, several exploring parties were sent to scour the country. One of them, under a soldier of the name of Cesar, never returned. Tradition, always eager to make up to history for its want of interest, asserted that after marching for years they reached a city. Perhaps it was the mystic Trapalanda of which the Gauchos used to discourse at night when seated round a fire of bones upon the pampa. Perhaps some other, for enchanted cities and Eldorados were plentiful in those days in America, alternating with occasional empires, as that of Puytita, near the Laguna de los Xarayes, Manoa, and the Ciudad de los Cesares, supposed to be situated near Arauco in the Chilian Andes. However, one of the party actually returned after years, and related his adventures to Ruy Diaz de Guzman,[16] the first historian of Paraguay. Thus it was that the stream of adventurers was ever seeking for a channel to the mines of Peru from the Atlantic coast. Cabot appears to have ascended the Paraná to the island of Apipé, and then, returning, entered the river Paraguay. Having ascended past what is now Asuncion, the capital of Paraguay, Cabot encountered Indians from the north who told him of the mines in Peru and in Bolivia, probably unaware that Cabot knew of them already. At this point, encouraged by what he heard, he gave the name of Rio de la Plata to what had previously been known either as La Mar Dulce or El Rio de Solis. Like most names which are wrongly given, it remained to testify to the want of knowledge of the giver. Four years after, Cabot returned to Spain, having failed to attract attention to his discoveries. In the face of the wealth which was pouring in from the Peruvian mines, another expedition started for the river Plate. Its General — for in Spain the title was used indifferently by land and sea — was Don Pedro de Mendoza, a gentleman of Guadix in Almeria, and a member of the household of Charles V.

Don Pedro had seen service in the Italian wars, and seems to have been a man of character and bravery, but wanting in the discretion and the necessary tact essential in the founder of a colony. In 1534 the expedition started, unfortunate almost from the first. In a `certain island', as the historian of the expedition, Hulderico Schmidel, a German or Flemish soldier, calls Rio Janeiro, a dispute occurred between Don Pedro and his second in command, Juan de Osorio. At a court-martial held upon Osorio, Don Pedro appears to have let fall some remarks which Juan de Ayolas, the Alguazil Mayor (Chief Constable), seems to have taken up as an order for instant execution. This he performed upon the spot, plunging his dagger repeatedly into Osorio, or, as Hulderico Schmidel has it, `sewing him up with cuts' (*cosiendole à puñaladas*). This murder or execution — for who shall tell when murder finishes and its legal counterpart begins? — rendered Don Pedro very unpopular with all the fleet; for, as Schmidel has it in his history,[17] `the soldiers loved Osorio.' To be loved by the soldiers was the only chance a Spanish officer had in those times of holding his own. Both Schmidel and Bernal Diaz del Castillo, who had both been common soldiers, and who, curiously, both wrote histories, lose no occasion of vilifying officers who used the soldiers hardly. It is true that Bernal Diaz (who, unlike Schmidel, was a man of genius) does so with some discretion, and always apparently with reason. Schmidel, on the other hand, seems to have considered that any officer who interfered between the soldiers and the Indians was a tyrant, and hence his denunciation of Alvar Nuñez, under whom he served.

In 1535 the expedition entered the river Plate. Here Mendoza, with his usual want of judgment, pitched upon what is now the site of Buenos Ayres as the spot on which to found his colony. It would be difficult to select a more inconvenient place in which to found a town. The site of Buenos Ayres is almost level with the waters of the river Plate, which there are shallow — so shallow that large vessels could not approach nearer than ten to fifteen miles. Without a harbour, the anchorage was exposed to the full fury of the south-west gales, known as `pamperos'. However, if the site was bad the air was good; at least, it seems so, for a captain of the expedition exclaimed on landing, `Que buenos aires son estos!' and hence the name. Here every sort of evil chance came on the newborn colony. The Pampa Indians, whom the historian Schmidel seems to have only known by their Guaraní name of Querandis, at first were friendly. After a little while they ceased to bring provisions, and the General sent out an expedition to compel them under his brother, Don Diego de Mendoza. It does not seem to have occurred to Don Pedro de Mendoza that, had the *cacique* of the Querandis landed in Spain, no one would have brought him provisions for a single day without receiving payment. However, Don Pedro[18] had come to America to introduce civilization and Christianity, and therefore, knowing, like Bernal Diaz and the other conquerors, his own moral worth, was justly indignant that after a day or two the Indians refused him more supplies. In the encounter which took place between the Spaniards and the Indians, Don Diego de Mendoza was slain, and with him several others. Here for the first time we hear of the bolas, or three stones united, like a Manxman's legs, with strips of hide, with which, as Hulderico Schmidel tells us, the Indians caught the horses by the legs and threw them down. After this foretaste of European justice, the Indians besieged the newly-built town and brought it to great straits, so much so that, after three men had been hung for stealing a horse, in the morning it was discovered they had been cut down and eaten. In this desperate state Don Pedro despatched Juan de Ayolas to get supplies. He, having obtained some maize from the Timbu Indians, returned, leaving a hundred of his men in a little fort, called Corpus Christi, close to Espiritu Santo, the fort which Cabot had constructed. The friendliness of the Timbus induced Don Pedro to abandon Buenos Ayres and move to Corpus Christi. There he repaired with about five hundred men, all who remained of the two thousand six hundred and thirty with which he sailed from Cadiz. The horses he abandoned on the pampa; there they became the ancestors of the innumerable herds which at one time overspread the Argentine Republic from the Chaco to Patagonia, and whose descendants to this day stock the *estancias* of that country.[19]

From Corpus Christi Juan de Ayolas was sent out to explore the river, and try to find the long-sought-for waterway to the Peruvian mines. He never reached Peru, and Corpus Christi never saw him return. Mendoza waited a year, and then returned to Spain, leaving his garrison with provisions for a year, the bread[20] `at the rate of (*á razon de*) a pound a day, and if they wanted more to get it for themselves.' On the passage home he died insane. The pious were of opinion that it was a judgment on him for the murder of Don

Juan Osorio. Before he embarked, Don Pedro had despatched a relative, Gonzalo de Mendoza, to Spain to bring provisions and recruits. Gonzalo, having obtained provisions in Brazil, returned to Corpus Christi; thence in company with Salazar de Espinosa he headed an expedition up the river in search of Juan de Ayolas, who had been appointed successor to Don Pedro. With them went Domingo Martinez de Irala, a man destined to play a great part in the conquest of Paraguay.

The expedition went up the Paraguay to a place near Fort Olimpo (21° long., 58° lat.) about a hundred leagues above Asuncion. Here they sent out exploring parties in all directions to seek Ayolas, but without success. Irala remained with one hundred men at Fort Olimpo. Gonzalo de Mendoza on his return, being attracted by the sight of a fine site for a town, landed, and on the fifteenth day of August, 1537, founded Asuncion. Here the Spaniards first met the Guaranís, who were destined in after-years to be the converts of the Jesuits, and be assembled by them in their famous missions.

`At the discovery of America,' says Felix de Azara in his `Descripcion y Historia del Paraguay', `the Guaranís were spread from the Guianas to the shores of the river Plate, and occupied all the islands of the Paraná extending up to latitude 20° on the Paraguay, but without crossing either that river or the river Plate.' They had also a few towns in the province of Chiquitos, and the nation of the Chiriguanás was an offshoot from them. In Brazil they were soon all either rendered slaves or so crossed with the African negro that the pure race has been almost entirely lost, though the language remains under the name of the Lingoa Geral, and many words from it have been introduced into Portuguese spoken by the Brazilians, as *capim*, grass; *caipira*, half-caste, etc. In fact, so great is the number of these words, idioms, phrases, and terms of speech derived from Guaraní, that Dr. Baptista de Almeida, in his preface to his grammar published at Rio Janeiro (1879), computes that there are more words derived from Guaraní than even from Arabic in the Portuguese spoken in Brazil.[21] The Guaranís in Brazil were known either as Tupis, from the word *tupy*,[22] savage, or Tupinambás, from *tupynambá*, literally, the savage or indigenous men.

Jean de Lery, the well-known Huguenot pastor and friend of Calvin, passed a year on the coast of Brazil about 1558, having accompanied the expedition of the famous Villegagnau. In his book (`Histoire d'un Voyage faict en la Terre du Brezil') he always refers to the Indians as Toupinaubaoults, and has preserved many curious details of them before they had had much contact with Europeans. He appears to have had a considerable acquaintance with the language, and has left some curious conversations *en langage sauvage et Français*, in which he gives some grammatical rules. The language of conversation is almost identical with that of Paraguay, though some words are used which are either peculiar to the Tupis or obsolete in Paraguay to-day. His account of their customs tallies with that of the various Spanish writers and explorers who have written on the subject. Tobacco, which seems to have been known under the name of `nicotiane' to Lery, he finds in Brazil under the name of `petun', the same name by which it is called in Paraguay at present. He believed that `petun' and `nicotiane' were two different plants, but the only reason he adduces for his belief is that `nicotiane' was brought in his time from Florida, which, as he observes, is more than a thousand leagues from `Nostre Terre du Brezil'. His experience of savages was the same as that of Azara, and almost all early travellers, for he says: `Nos Toupinambaoults reçoivent fort humainement les estrangers amis qui les vont visiter.'[23] Lery, however, seemed to think that, in spite of their pacific inclination, it was not prudent to put too much power in their hands, for he remarks: `Au reste parcequ'ils chargeyent, et remplisseyent leurs mousquets jusques au bout . . . nous leurs baillions moitié (*i.e.*, la poudre) de charbon broyé.' This may have been a wise precaution, but he omits to state if the *charbon broyé* was *bailli* at the same price as good powder. According to Azara, who takes his facts partly from the contemporary writers — Schmidel, Alvar Nuñez, Ruy Diaz de Guzman, and Barco de la Centenera — the Guaranís were divided into numerous tribes, as Imbeguas, Caracaras, Tembues, Colistines, and many others. These tribes, though apparently of a common origin, never united, but each lived separately under its own chief. Their towns were generally either close to or in the middle of forests, or at the edge of rivers where there is wood. They all cultivated pumpkins, beans, maize, mani (ground nuts), sweet potatoes, and mandioca; but they lived largely by the chase, and ate much wild honey. Diaz in his `Argentina' (lib. i., chap. i.) makes them cannibals. Azara believes this to have been untrue, as no traditions of cannibalism were current amongst the Guaranís in his time, *i.e.*, in 1789-1801. Liberal as Azara was, and careful observer of what he saw himself, I am disposed to believe the testimony of so many eye-witnesses of the customs of the primitive Guaranís, though none of them had the advantage enjoyed by Azara of living three hundred years after the conquest. It may be, of course, that the powers of observation were not so well developed in mankind in the beginning of the sixteenth as at the end of the eighteenth century, but this point I leave to those whose business it is to prove that the human mind is in a progressive state. However, Father Montoya, in his `Conquista Espiritual del Paraguay', affirms most positively that they used to eat their prisoners taken in war.'[24]

Their general characteristics seem to have been much the same as those of other Indians of America. For instance, they kept their hair and teeth to an extreme old age, their sight was keen, they seldom looked you in the face whilst speaking, and their disposition was cold and reserved. The tone of their voices was low, so low that, as Azara says: `La voz nunca es gruesa ni sonora, y hablan siempre muy bajo, sin gritar aun para quejarse si los matan;

de manera que, si camina uno diez pasos delante, no le llama el que le necesita, sino que va á alcanzarle.' This I have myself observed when travelling with Indians, even on horseback.

There was one characteristic of the Guaranís in which they differed greatly from most of the Indian tribes in their vicinity, as the Indians of the Chaco and the Pampas, for all historians alike agree that they were most unwarlike. It is from this characteristic that the Jesuits were able to make such a complete conquest of them, for, notwithstanding all their efforts, they never really succeeded in permanently establishing themselves amongst any of the tribes in the Chaco or upon the Pampas.

The name Guaraní is variously derived. Pedro de Angelis, in his `Coleccion de Obras y Documentos', derives it from *gua*, paint, and *ni*, sign of the plural, making the signification of the word `painted ones' or `painted men'. Demersay, in his `Histoire du Paraguay',[25] thinks it probable that the word is an alteration of the word *guaranai, i.e.,* numerous. Barco de la Centenera[26] (`Argentina', book i., canto i.) says the word means `hornet', and was applied on account of their savageness. Be that as it may, it is certain that the Guaranís did not at the time of the conquest, and do not now, apply the word to themselves, except when talking Spanish or to a foreigner. The word *abá*, Indian or man, is how they speak of their people, and to the language they apply the word *Abanêe.*

In the same way the word `Paraguay' is variously derived from a corruption of the word `Payaguá' (the name of an Indian tribe), and *y*, the Guaraní word for water, meaning river of the Payaguas. Others, again, derive it from a Guaraní word meaning `crown', and *y*, water, and make it the crowned river, either from the palm-trees which crown its banks or the feather crowns which the Indians wore at the first conquest. Others, again, derive it from a bird called paraquá (*Ortolida paraqua*). Again, Angelis, in his work `Serie de los Señores Gobernadores del Paraguay' (lib. ii., p. 187), derives it from Paraguá, the name of a celebrated Indian chief at the time of the conquest. What is certain is that *y* is the Guaraní for water, and this is something in a derivation. *Y* is perhaps as hard to pronounce as the Gaelic *luogh*, a calf, the nasal *gh* in Arabic, or the Kaffir clicks, having both a guttural and a nasal aspiration.[27] It is rarely attempted with success by foreigners, even when long resident in the country. Though Paraguay was so completely the country of the Jesuits in after-times, they were not the first religious Order to go there. Almost in every instance the ecclesiastics who accompanied the first conquerors of America were Franciscans. The Jesuits are said to have sent two priests to Bahia in Brazil ten years after their Order was founded, but both in Brazil and Paraguay the Franciscans were before them in point of time.

San Francisco Solano, the first ecclesiastic who rose to much note as a missionary, and who made his celebrated journey through the Chaco in 1588-89 from Peru to Paraguay, was a Franciscan.[28] Thus, the Franciscans had the honour of having the first American saint in their ranks. It is noteworthy, though, that he was recalled from Paraguay by his superiors, who seem to have had no very exalted opinion of him.

Charlevoix remarks ('History of Paraguay') 'that it seems as if Providence, in granting him miraculous powers, had forgotten the other necessary steps to make them effective.' That he really had these powers seems strange, but San Francisco Solano narrates of himself that, in passing through the Chaco, he learned the languages of several of the tribes, and 'preached to them in their own tongues of the birth, death, and transfiguration of Christ, the mysteries of the Trinity, Transubstantiation, and Atonement; that he explained to them the symbols of the Church, the Papal succession from St. Peter downwards, and that he catechized the Indians by thousands, tens and hundreds of thousands, and that they came in tears and penitence to acknowledge their belief.'

Of course, to-day it is difficult to controvert these statements, even if inclined to do so; but the languages spoken by the Chaco Indians are amongst the most difficult to learn of any spoken by the human race, so much so that Father Dobrizhoffer, in his 'History of the Abipones', says 'that the sounds produced by the Indians of the Chaco resembled nothing human, so do they sneeze, and stutter, and cough.' In such a language the Athanasian Creed itself would be puzzling to a neophyte.

He also says that several of the Jesuits who had laboured for years amongst the Indians could never master their dialects, and when they preached the Indians received their words with shouts of laughter. This the good priest attributed to the presence of a 'mocking devil' who possessed them. It may be that the mocking devil was but a sense of humour, the possession of which, even amongst good Christians, has been known to give offence.

But be this as it may, San Francisco de Solano remained two years at Asuncion, though whilst he lived there his powers of speech (according to the Jesuits) seem to have been diminished, and he held no communication with the Indians in their own languages. It may be that, like St. Paul, he preferred to speak, when not with Indians, five words with his understanding rather than ten thousand in an unknown tongue.

At the time of the first conquest Paraguay was almost entirely peopled by the Guaraní race.[29] It does not appear that their number was ever very great, perhaps not exceeding a million in the whole country. From the writings of Montoya, Guevara, Lozano, and the other missionaries of the time, it is certain that they had attained to no very high degree of civilization, though they were certainly more advanced than their neighbours in the Gran Chaco. It is most probable that they had not a single stone-built town, or even a house, or that such a thing existed south of New Granada, to the eastward of the Andes, for we may take the description in Schmidel's `History of the Casa del Gran Moxo'[30] either as a mistake or as a story which he had heard from some Peruvian Indian of the palaces of the Incas. At any rate, no remains of stone-built houses, still less of palaces, are known to have been found in Brazil or Paraguay.

To-day all the Guaranís who are still unconquered live in the impenetrable forests of the North of Paraguay or in the Brazilian province of Matto Grosso. Their limits to the south extend to near the ruined missions of Jesus and Trinidad. By preference, they seem to dwell about the sources of the Igatimí, an affluent of the Paraná, and in the chain of mountains known either as San Jose or Mbaracayú. The Paraguayans generally refer to them as Monteses (dwellers in the woods), and sometimes as Caaguás. They present almost the same characteristics as they did at the discovery of the country, and wander in the woods as the Jesuits describe them as doing three hundred years ago. Olive in colour, rather thickly set, of medium height, thin beards, and generally little hair upon the body, their type has remained unchanged. The difference in stature amongst the Guaranís is less noticeable than amongst Europeans. Their language is poorer than the Guaraní spoken by the Paraguayans, and the pronunciation both more nasal and guttural. Their numerals only extend to four, as was the case at the time of the discovery.[31]

Like their forefathers, they seldom unite in large numbers, and pay little honour or obedience to their chiefs, who differ in no respect, either in arms, dress, or position, from the ordinary tribesmen.

In Brazil they are confined to the southern portion of the province of San Paulo, and are called by the Brazilians Bugres — that is, slaves. A more unfitting name it would have been impossible to hit upon, as all efforts to civilize them have proved abortive, and to-day they still range the forests, attacking small parties of travellers, and burning isolated farm-houses. The Brazilians assert that they are cannibals, but little is known positively as to this. What has altered them so entirely from the original Guaranís of the time of the conquest, who were so easily subdued, it is hard to conjecture. One thing is certain: that the example given them by the Christian settlers has evidently not been such as to induce them to leave their wild life and enter into the bonds of civilization.

Diaz, in the `Argentina', thinks the Caribs of the West Indies were Guaranís, and the Jesuits often refer to them under that name.[32] This point would be easily set at rest by examining if any Guaraní words remain in the dialect of the Caribs of the Mosquito coast. As to their relative numbers at the time of the foundation of the missions, it is most difficult to judge. At no one time does the population of the thirty towns seem to have exceeded one hundred and thirty thousand.

D'Orbigny in his `L'Homme Américain', estimates the Guaranís of Brazil at one hundred and fifty thousand.

Humboldt cites two hundred and sixty-nine thousand as the probable number of Indians of every kind in the Brazilian Empire.

The Viscount de Itabayana (a Brazilian writer) fixes the number at two hundred and fifty thousand to three hundred thousand.

Veloso de Oliveira puts it at eight hundred thousand; and later statisticians range between one million five hundred thousand and seven to eight hundred thousand.

The numbers given of Indians by the Spanish conquerors are almost always grossly overstated, from the wish they not unnaturally had to magnify the importance of their conquests and to enhance their exploits in the eyes of those for whom they wrote.

Struck by the tractable character of the Guaranís, Mendoza began to build a fort on August 15, 1537 (which is the day of the Assumption), and the name he gave to his fort was Asuncion, which afterwards became the capital of Paraguay.

Espinosa returned to Corpus Christi, and afterwards to Buenos Ayres, where a small force had still remained. This force, tired of the ceaseless battles with the Querandis, or Pampa Indians, embarked for Asuncion.

Irala, after waiting for many months at Fort Olimpo, returned to Asuncion, where he found Ruiz de Galan acting as Governor. A dispute at once arose between them, and Irala, after having been imprisoned, was allowed to return to Fort Olimpo. Here he found the Payaguá Indians in rebellion, and in the battle which ensued he is reported to have slain seven of them with his own hand.[33] He still maintained a fitful search for Juan de Ayolas, but without success.

Galan returned to Buenos Ayres, and, stopping at Corpus Christi, took occasion to fall upon the friendly and unsuspecting Timbú Indians and massacre a quantity of them. Why he did so is quite uncertain, for the Timbues had been in the habit of supplying the fort of Corpus Christi with provisions; it may be that the quality of the provisions was inferior, but neither Ruiz Diaz nor Schmidel informs us on the point. Galan, after his `victory', re-embarked for Buenos Ayres, leaving Antonio de Mendoza in command with a hundred men.

One day, when about the half of the force was hunting, the Indians fell upon it and cut it off to the last man; but for the opportune arrival of two vessels the fort would have been destroyed. However, many Spaniards were slain, and Antonio de Mendoza amongst them.

After this battle, in which Santiago[34] is said to have appeared on the top of the principal tower of the fort dressed in white with a drawn sword in his hand, Galan and Espinosa returned to Asuncion, taking with them the remainder of the inhabitants of Buenos Ayres. At Asuncion they found that Irala had again returned without having discovered traces of Ayolas. Irala was elected Governor under a clause in the royal letters patent which provided for the case of Ayolas not returning. His first act was to order the complete evacuation of Buenos Ayres. An Italian vessel, which was going to Peru with colonists, having been driven into the river Plate, united with the remains of the colonists at Buenos Ayres and proceeded to Asuncion.

Curiously enough, the remnants of several expeditions thus joined to found the first permanent city in the territories of the river Plate; not at Buenos Ayres, but a thousand miles away in the interior of the country, where it seemed little probable that their attempt would prove successful.

To preside over the heterogeneous elements of which Asuncion was composed, Domingo Martinez de Irala was chosen. He was a Biscayan, a member of that ancient race which neither Romans nor Moors were ever able to subdue. Nothing is known about his antecedents. Not improbably he was a son of one of the innumerable small gentlemen with whom the Basque provinces used to swarm. Almost every house in the little towns even to-day has its coat of arms over the door. Every inhabitant claimed to be a nobleman, and in the reign of Charles V. they furnished many soldiers of repute in the wars of Europe and America.

The system of Irala was to conciliate rather than subdue the natives. Isolated from help of every kind, the length of the voyage from Spain precluding all idea of speedy succour in a rebellion, it was the only course he could pursue.

From the very first he encouraged the soldiers to marry women of the country, thus creating ties which bound them to the land.

Two Franciscan friars[35] set about at once to learn the language and preach to the people. They also seem to have endeavoured to reduce the Guaraní language to writing. So, from several circumstances, the early history of Paraguay was very different from that of every other Spanish possession in America. To all the others Spanish women seem to have gone in greater or in smaller numbers. To Paraguay, at the foundation of Asuncion, it seems that hardly any women went.

So there a different state of society arose to that, for example, in Chile or in Mexico. In both those countries few Spaniards ever married native women. Those who did so were either members of the highest class — who sometimes, but rarely, married Indian women of position from motives of policy — or else the lowest class of Spaniards; in this case, after a generation, their children became practically Indians. In Paraguay it was quite the contrary, and the grandchildren of Indian mothers and Spanish fathers were almost reckoned Spaniards, and the next generation always so.

Washburne, in his 'History of Paraguay' (p. 32, cap. i., vol. i.), points out the contrast between the effects of the treatment meted out by Penn to the Indians in Pennsylvania and that by Irala in Paraguay. Where, he asks, are the Indian tribes with whom the celebrated Quaker treated? In Paraguay, on the other hand, at least in the time when Washburne was Minister from the United States to Lopez (from 1861 to 1868), the few remaining Paraguayans of the upper class were almost all descended from the intermarriages of the followers of Irala with the natives.

The tyranny of Lopez, and the effects of the disastrous war with Brazil and the Argentine Republic, have almost extirpated every Paraguayan (of the old stock) with the least pretensions to white descent.

Ruiz Diaz de Guzman, speaking of the mixed race in Paraguay and Buenos Ayres, says:

'They are generally good soldiers, of great spirit and valour, expert in the use of arms, especially in that of the musquet, so much so that, when they go on long journeys, they are accustomed to live on the game which they kill with it. It is common for them to kill birds on the wing, and he is accounted unfit for a soldier who cannot bring down a pigeon. They are such excellent horsemen that there is no one who is not able to tame and ride an unbroken colt.

'The women generally are virtuous, beautiful, and of a gentle disposition.'

If the inhabitants of Paraguay and the river Plate of those days were good marksmen, it is more than can be said of the Gauchos of the Argentine provinces and the Paraguayans of twenty years ago. Without military training, so far from being able to bring down a pigeon on the wing, few could hit the trunk of a tree at fifty paces. The usual method of shooting used to be to cram as much ammunition into the gun as the hand would contain, and then, looking carefully away from the object aimed at, to close both eyes and pull the trigger. Accuracy of aim was not so much considered as loudness of report. As regards their powers of riding, they are still unchanged; and as to the virtue of their women, virtue is so largely a matter of convention that it is generally wisest to leave such matters uncommented on, as it is so easy not to understand the conventions of the people of whom one writes.

Whilst Irala was conciliating the Guaranís in Paraguay, Charles V. had not forgotten that the new settlement of Buenos Ayres had been abandoned. After much search, he selected Alvar Nuñez Cabeza de Vaca to be the new Governor; and, as Alvar Nuñez was perhaps the most remarkable of all the Spanish *conquistadores* of the New World, it may not be out of place to give some facts of his career, as his policy in regard to the Indians was almost that of the Jesuits in after-times.

As he himself informs us in his Commentaries,[36] his `father was that Pedro de Vera who won Canaria,' and his mother `Doña Teresa Cabeza de Vaca, a noble lady of Jerez de la Frontera.' After the Spanish fashion of the time, he used the names of both his parents.

In 1529 he sailed with the ill-fated expedition of Panfilo de Narvaez to Apalache in Florida, was shipwrecked, tried to regain the Spanish settlements in boats, and then cast by a storm absolutely naked, and with only three companions, upon an unknown land. Taken by the Indians, he was made a slave, then rose to be a pedlar, then a doctor, and finally a chief, held sacred for his mysterious powers. At last he made his way on foot into the territory of New Spain, not as a captive, but as the leader of several hundred Indians, who followed him and did his bidding as if he had been born their chief. Rambling about for months, but always followed by his Indians, he at length encountered a Spanish horse-soldier, and, accosting him, found he had almost forgotten Spanish during his ten years' sojourn with the Indians. His first entreaty, when he found Spanish gradually returning to him, was to the Spaniards not to harass his Indian following. Then he besought the Indians themselves to cease their nomad life and cultivate the soil. In neither case was he successful, as the Spaniards, like all other Europeans, held Indians little removed from dogs. And for the Indians, the few remaining are as much attached to their old wandering life as in the days of the discovery of the New World. In all that Alvar Nuñez writes, he shows a grandeur of soul and spirit far different from the writings, not only of the conquerors of the New World, but of the conquerors of Africa of to-day. For him no bragging of his exploits.[37] All that he says he sets down modestly and with excuses (as every now and then, `Me pesa hablar de mis trabajos'), and as befits a gentleman. Lastly, he leaves the reader (when describing his captivity in Florida), by telling him quite quietly and without comment that God was pleased to save from all these perils himself, Alonso del Castillo Maldonado, Andres Dorantes, and that the fourth was a negro called Estevanico, a native of Azimur. But, not contented with his ten years' captivity, after three years at home he entered into a certain *asiento*[38] and *capitulacion*[39] with the King to sail at his own charges with an expedition to succour Don Pedro de

Mendoza, who was hard pressed by famine and the Indians at Buenos Ayres. He agreed to furnish eight thousand ducats, horses, arms, men, and provisions at his own expense, upon condition that he was made Governor and Adelantado of the Rio de la Plata, and General both of its armies and its fleets.

Upon November 2, 1537, he embarked at Cadiz with his fleet, consisting of a caravel and two full-rigged ships. All went well up to the Cape de Verdes. On nearing the equator, it occurred to the `Maestro del Agua' to examine his stock of water, and, out of one hundred pipes which had been put aboard, he found but three remaining, and from these the thirty horses and four hundred men who were on board all had to drink. Seeing the greatness of the necessity, the Governor — for Alvar Nuñez almost always speaks of himself in the third person — gave orders that the fleet should make for land. `Three days,' he says in his Commentaries, `we sailed in search of it'; and on the fourth, just before sunrise, occurred a very notable affair, and, as it is not altogether *fuera de proposito*, I set it down, and it is this — `that, going towards the land, the ships had almost touched on some sharp rocks we had not seen.' Then, as now, I take it, vigilance was not a noticeable quality in Spanish sailors. Just as the vessels were almost on the rocks, `a cricket commenced to sing, which cricket a sick soldier had put into the ship at Cadiz, being anxious to hear its music, and for the two months which our navigation had endured no one had heard it, whereat the soldier was much enraged; and as on that morning it felt the land [*sintio la tierra*], it commenced to sing, and its music wakened all the people of the ship, who saw the cliffs, which were distant almost a crossbow-shot from where we were, so we cast out anchors and saved the ship, and it is certain that if the cricket had not sung all of us, four hundred soldiers and thirty horses, had been lost.' Some of the crew accepted the occurrence as a miracle from God; but Nuñez himself is silent on that head, being a better observer of natural history than a theologian. But `from there, and sailing more than a hundred leagues along the coast, the cricket every evening gave us his music, and thus with it we arrived at a little port beyond Cape Frio, where the Adelantado landed and unfurled his flag, and took possession for His Majesty.' The expedition disembarked at Santa Catalina in Brazil. `There the Governor landed his men and twenty-six of the horses which had escaped the sea, all that remained of forty-six embarked in Spain.' The *odium theologicum* gave the Governor some work at once. Two friars — Fray Bernardo de Armenta and Fray Alonso Lebron, Franciscans — had burnt the houses of some Indians, who had retaliated in the heathen fashion by slaughtering two Christians. The `people being scandalized', the Governor sent for the friars, admonished them, and told them to restrain their zeal. This was the first false step he made, and set all friars and priests throughout America against him. Hearing at Santa Catalina that Buenos Ayres was almost abandoned, and that the inhabitants had founded the town of Asuncion del Paraguay, Alvar determined to march thither by land, and send his ship into the river Plate and up the Paraguay. The two Franciscan friars he told to remain and `indoctrinate' the Indians. This they refused to do, saying they wished to reside amongst the Spaniards in Asuncion. Had they been Jesuits, it is ten to one they had remained and spent their lives `indoctrinating', for the Jesuits alone of all the religious Orders were ever ready to take every risk.

Upon his march the Governor, contrary to all good policy and precedent, ordered that nothing should be taken from the Indians without due payment being made. To insure this being done, he paid for all provisions himself, and served them out to the soldiery. This made him as unpopular with his soldiers as his dealings with the two Franciscans had made him amongst the friars. Surely he might have known that Pizarro, Cortes, Almagro, and the rest, were men who never paid for anything. Still, he persisted in his conduct to the end, and so brought ruin on himself. The Indians seemed to appreciate his method, for he says that `when the news was spread abroad of the good treatment the Governor gave to all, they came to meet the army decked with flowers and bringing provisions in great abundance.' It was, he also says, `a thing to see how frightened the Indians were of the horses, and how they brought them food, chickens and honey to keep them quiet and in good humour, and they asked the Governor to tell the horses not to hurt them.'

After passing the river Iguazú, he sent the two friars ahead to collect provisions, and `when the Governor arrived the Indians had no more to give.'[40]

So having started from the coast upon November 2, 1541, he arrived at Asuncion on March 2, 1542, having accomplished a march of more than two thousand miles with but the loss of a single man and without the slaughter of a single Indian. Hardly had he arrived at Asuncion before he found himself embroiled on every side. The Indians were in full rebellion, the settlement of Buenos Ayres almost in ruins, and the officers appointed by the King to collect the royal dues all hostile to him to a man.

After having consulted with the clergy to find if they thought it lawful to attack the Guaycurús who had assailed the newly-founded town, he received the opinion `that it was not only lawful, but expedient.' Therefore he sent off an expedition against them, to which was joined a priest to require the Guaycurús to become Christians and to acknowledge the King of Spain. The propositions, not unnaturally, did not seem reasonable to the Indians, who most likely were unaware of the benefits which Christianity confers, and probably heard for the first time of the King of Spain. The Governor, who seems to have doubted of the humanity of the clergy, called another council, which confirmed the previous opinion. Strangely enough, this seems to have surprised him, for he probably did not reflect that the clergy would not have to fight themselves, and that the first blood ever spilt on earth was on account of a religious difference.

Just before the expedition started it was found that the two Franciscan friars who had come with him from Santa Catalina could not be found. It then appeared they had started back to the coast accompanied by a bevy of Indian damsels, thirty-five in all. They were followed and brought back, and then explained that they were on their way to Spain to complain against the Governor. The five-and-thirty dusky catechumens remained without an explanation, and the people were once more `scandalized'. The Governor then started out against the Guaycurús. Only those who know the Chaco, or western bank of the river Paraguay, can form the least idea of what such an expedition must have been. Even to-day in the Chaco the change since the beginning of the world can be but slight. As a steamer slips along the bank, nothing for miles and miles is seen but swamp, intersected with backwaters,[41] in which lie alligators, electric eels, and stinging rays. Far as the eye can reach are swamps, swamps, and more swamps, a sea of waving pampa-grass. After the swamps thickets of tacuaras (canes), forests of thorny trees, chañares, ñandubay, jacarandas, urundey, talas, and quebrachos, each one hard enough to split an axe, some, like the black canela, almost like iron; the inhabitants ferocious and intractable as when the Governor himself first saw them; the climate heavy and humid, the air dank with vinchucas[42] and mosquitoes and the little black infernal midget called the jejen; no roads, no paths, no landmarks, but here and there at intervals of many leagues a clearing in the forest where some straggling settlement exists, more rarely still the walls of a deserted Jesuit mission-house or church. Ostriches and deer, tigers,[43] capibaras and tapirs, and now and then a herd of cattle as wild as buffaloes, are seen. Sometimes an Indian with his lance sits motionless upon his horse to watch the vessel pass — a sentinel to guard the wilderness from encroachments from without. So Alvar Nuñez, as he tells us in his Commentaries, started with four hundred men and with one thousand friendly Indians, all well armed and painted, and with plates of metal on their heads to reflect the sun, and so strike terror to their enemies. To save the horses they were put on board,[44] whilst the Indians marched along the bank, keeping up with the ships. Horses at that time in Paraguay and in Peru often were worth one thousand crowns of gold, though Azara tells us that in the last century in Buenos Ayres you could often buy a good horse for two needles, so cheap had they become. Then, as at present, time was of no account in Paraguay, so almost every day they landed the horses to keep them in condition and to chase the ostriches and deer.

Just the kind of army that a thinking man would like to march with; not too much to eat, but, still, a pleasant feeling of marching to spread religion and to make one's fortune, with but the solitary unpleasant feature to the soldier — the system of payment for provisions which the Governor prescribed. All was new and strange; the world was relatively young. Each night the Governor religiously wrote up his diary, now chronicling the death of some good horse, or of an Indian, or commenting upon the fruits, the fish, the animals, the trees, and 'all the other things of God which differ from those in the Castiles.' Occasionally a fight took place with Guasarapos or with Pagayuás, but nothing of much account (*de mucha monta*); always the tales of gold-mines to be met with further on. Eventually the expedition came to a point not far from where is now the town of Corumbá. There Alvar Nuñez founded a town to which he gave the name of Reyes, which has long fallen into decay. He also sent two captains to explore and search for gold, waiting two or three months for their return, and suffering from a quartan ague which confined him to his bed; then, having failed to find the talked-of gold-mines, he set his face again towards Asuncion. Just before starting he gave the final blow to his waning popularity. Some of his followers, having taken Indian girls, had hidden them on board the ships; this, when he knew it, Nuñez at once forbade, and, sending for the fathers of the girls, restored their children to them. 'With this,' he says, 'the natives were much pleased, but the Spaniards rendered angry and desperate, and for this cause they hated me.' Nothing more natural, and for the same cause the Spanish Paraguayans hated the Jesuits who carried out the policy which the wise Governor began.

On April 8, 1543, the Governor returned to Asuncion, worn out and ill with ague. There he found all confusion. Domingo de Irala, a clever, ambitious Biscayan soldier who had been interim Governor before Nuñez had arrived, had worked upon the people, saying that Nuñez wished to take away their property. As their chief property was in Indians whom they had enslaved, this rendered Nuñez most unpopular, and the same kind of allegations were laid against him as were laid against the Jesuits when in their turn they denounced slavery in Paraguay. All the complaints were in the name of liberty, as generally is the case when tyranny or villainy of any sort is to be done.

So Alvar Nuñez[45] tells us in his Commentaries that at the hour of the Ave Maria ten or twelve of the 'factious' entered his house where he lay ill in bed, all shouting 'Liberty!' and to prove they were all good patriots one Jaime Resquin put a bent crossbow to his side, and forced him to get out of bed, and took him off to prison amid a crowd all shouting 'Liberty!' The friends of liberty (upon the other side) attempted a rescue, but the patriots[46] were too strong. So the unpatriotic Governor was thrown, heavily ironed, into a cell, out of which to make room they let a murderer who was awaiting death. 'He' (Alvar Nuñez grimly remarks) 'made haste to take my cloak, and then set off down the street at once, calling out "Liberty!"' That everything should be in order, the patriots confiscated all the Governor's goods and took his papers, publishing a proclamation that they did so because he was a tyrant. Unluckily, the Indians have not left us any commentaries, or it would be curious to learn what they thought as to the tyranny of Alvar Nuñez. Most probably they thought as the Indians of the Jesuit missions thought at the expulsion of the Jesuits from Paraguay, as is set forth in the curious memorial addressed in 1768 by the people of the Mission of San Luis to the Governor of Buenos Ayres, praying that the Jesuits might be suffered to remain instead of the friars, who had been sent to replace them against the people's will.[47] Having got the Governor into prison, the patriots had to elect another chief, and the choice naturally `fell' upon Domingo de Irala, who, having been interim Governor, had never ceased intriguing from the first. He promptly put his friends in office, after the fashion of all Governors, whether they enter office to the cry of `Liberty' or not. The friends of Alvar Nuñez, in the usual Spanish fashion (long sanctified by use and wont), declared themselves in opposition — that is, they roamed about the land, proving by theft and murder that their love of liberty was just as strong as that of those in power. Things shortly came to such a pass that no one could leave his house by night. The marauding Guaycurús burnt all the suburbs, and threatened to attack the town. Nuñez himself was guarded day and night by four men armed with daggers in a close prison. As he says himself, his prison was not `fitting for his health,' for day and night he had to keep a candle burning to see to read, and the grass grew underneath his bed, whilst for the sake of `health' he had a pair of first-rate fetters on his feet. For his chief gaoler they procured one Hernando de Sosa, whom Nuñez had put in gaol for striking an Indian chief. A guard watched constantly at the prison gate, but, still, in spite of this he managed to communicate almost uninterruptedly with his friends outside. His method was certainly ingenious. His food was brought to him by an Indian girl, whom, so great was the fear of the patriots that he should write to the King, they made walk naked into the prison, carrying the dishes, and with her head shaved. Notwithstanding this, she managed to bring a piece of paper hidden between her toes. The party of Liberty, suspecting that Nuñez was communicating with his friends, procured an Indian youth to make love to the girl and learn the secret. This he failed to do, owing, perhaps, to his love-making being wanting in conviction on account of her shaved head. At last Irala and his friends determined to send the Governor a prisoner to Spain, taking care, of course, to despatch a messenger beforehand to distort the facts and prejudice the King. The friends of Nuñez, however, managed to secrete a box of papers, stating the true facts, on board the ship. At dead of night a band of harquebusiers dragged him from his bed (after a captivity of eleven months), as he says, `almost with the candle in his hand' — *i.e.*, in a dying state. As he left the prison, he fell upon his knees and thanked God for having let him once more feel the air of heaven, and then in a loud voice exclaimed: 'I name as my successor Captain Juan de Salazar de Espinosa.' At this one Garci Vargas rushed at him with a knife, and told him to recall his words or he would kill him instantly. This he was stopped from doing, and Nuñez was hurried to the ship and chained securely to a beam. On board the vessel, he says, they tried to poison him; but this seems doubtful, as there was nothing on earth to prevent their doing so had they been so inclined. Still, as a prudent man he took the precaution to provide some oil and a piece of unicorn (*pedazo de unicornio*), with which he tried the food. Unicorns he could not have seen in Paraguay, nor yet in Florida, and he does not explain how he became so luckily equipped.

None the less, of all the discoverers of America he is the man of least imaginative power — that is, in matters appertaining to natural history — so one must conclude he had his piece of unicorn from Spain, where he most probably had bought it from some dealer in necessaries for travellers to the New World.

After a stormy voyage he arrived in Spain to find his accusers just before him. With truly Eastern justice, both accusers and accused were put in gaol, a custom worthy of adoption in other lands. Nuñez was soon released on bail, and, his accusers having all died, in eight years' time he was triumphantly acquitted of all the charges brought against him. To prove, however, that Justice is and always has been blind, the King never restored him to his government in Paraguay, and, as Nuñez says, forgot to repay him what he had expended in his service.[48] With Alvar Nuñez was lost the only chance of liberal treatment to the Indians, for from his time the governors, instead of being men of the world above the petty spite of party differences, were chosen either from officers who, having served in the frontier wars, quite naturally looked on the Indians as enemies, or were appointed by intriguing Ministers at Court. From the death of Alvar Nuñez to the inauguration of the missions by the Jesuits, no one arose to take the Indians' side, and it may be that had his policy prevailed there would have been an Indian population left in the mission territory of Paraguay; for had the civil governors co-operated with the Jesuits, the dispersion of the Indians, which took place at the expulsion of the Jesuits, had not occurred.

Thus was Domingo Martinez de Irala left in sole command in Paraguay. He naturally had all to gain by not communicating with Spain. Had he done so, the part he played in reference to Alvar Nuñez must have been known. He had, however, certain good qualities, courage in abundance, Herculean strength and great endurance, and the power of making himself obeyed. But he had to justify himself to Spain for his position, and the surest way to do so was to discover gold-mines. So, naming Francisco de Mendoza his lieutenant, he started up the Paraguay, taking with him three hundred and fifty soldiers and two thousand Guaranís. After many hardships, he reached the frontiers of Peru, only to find the country already conquered from the Pacific side, and to be met by the messengers of the wise President, La Gasca, who told him to return, and named one Diego Centeno Governor of Paraguay instead of him. Centeno died before he could assume the governorship, so it seemed that fate determined that Irala was to continue in command.

After a year and a half he returned to Paraguay, having found no gold or riches, but bringing many thousand Indians as slaves. It is important to remember that Irala, who was remarkable for his relatively kind treatment of the Indians, on this occasion led so many of them captive. On arriving at Asuncion he found a rebellion going on, as not infrequently occurred when a Spanish Governor left his domains. His lieutenant, Mendoza, had been killed by one Diego de Abreu. After quieting matters in Asuncion, he despatched Nuflo de Chaves (one of his captains) to found a town on the higher waters of the Paraguay.

Like many other captains of those days, the idea of Chaves was to make himself quite independent of authority; so, striking into the interior, he founded the town of Santa Cruz de la Sierra in Bolivia. After many adventures he was killed by an Indian, who struck him with a club whilst he was sitting eating without his helmet.

Irala died at the little village of Itá in 1557, and was buried in the cathedral at Asuncion, which he was building at the time. With him expired the generation of the conquering soldiers of fortune, who, schooled in the wars of Italy, brought to America some of the virtues and all the vices of the Old World. After him began the reign of the half-caste Spaniards who were the progenitors of the modern occupants of the Spanish-American republics. At Irala's death the usual feuds, which have for the last three hundred years disgraced every part of Spanish America, began. Into them it is unnecessary to enter, for with Irala died almost the only Governor of Paraguay who showed the smallest capacity to make himself obeyed.

True indeed that Arias de Saavedra, a native of Paraguay and Lieutenant-Governor under Ramirez de Velasco, the Governor of Tucuman, displayed some traces of ability and of intelligence. He it was who first appealed to Spain for missionaries to convert the Indians.

Whilst Alvar Nuñez and Irala, with Nuflo de Chaves and the other captains, had been conquering and building towns, the Jesuits had been preaching in the wilderness and gathering together the Indian tribes. Not ten years after the foundation of their Order,[49] or about 1550, they had landed at San Salvador de Bahia in Brazil.

In 1554, in the district of Guayrá, on the upper waters of the Paraná, and above the cataract, the towns of Ontiveros, Ciudad Real, and Villa Rica, had been founded by Don Ruy Diaz de Melgarejo.

In 1586 Fathers Alfonso Barcena and Angulo left the town of Santa Maria de las Charcas (Bolivia) at the request of Francisco Vitoria, Bishop of Santiago, who had appealed for missionaries to the Society of Jesus. They reached the province of Guayrá, and began their labours. Shortly afterwards they were joined by Fathers Estezan Grao, Juan Solano, and Thomas Fields; Solano and Fields had already visited some of the wandering tribes upon the Rio Vermejo in the Chaco.

In 1593 others arrived, as Juan Romero, Gaspar de Monroy, and Marcelino Lorenzana. Shortly after this they founded the college in Asuncion. Then Fathers Ortega and Vellarnao penetrated into the mountains of the Chiriguanás, and began to preach the Gospel to the Indians.

In 1602 Acquaviva, seeing the necessity of common action, called all the scattered Jesuits of Paraguay and the river Plate to a conference at Salta to deliberate as to their future policy.[50] In 1605 Father Diego Torres was named Provincial of the Jesuits of Paraguay and Chile, thus proving both the paucity of Jesuits in South America at the time, and the little idea the General in Rome had of the immensity of the countries he was dealing with.

Torres arrived in Lima with fifteen priests, and almost at the same time some others arrived at Buenos Ayres; both parties proceeded to Paraguay. Already the Jesuits found themselves a prey to calumny.

Both in Tucuman and Paraguay they were expected to lend themselves to the enslavement of the Indians. In Chile Father Valdivia was expelled from Santiago, and took refuge at Tucuman. There he found the condition of affairs so intolerable that he went to Madrid to solicit the protection of the King, Philip III., for his Indian subjects.

In 1608 Philip issued his royal letters patent to the Society of Jesus for the conversion of the Indians in the province of Guayrá.

The Bishop and the Governor, Arias de Saavedra (himself a Paraguayan by birth), offered no objection, and the scheme of colonization was agreed upon at once.

Thus the Jesuits obtained their first official status in America.

Fathers Simon Maceta and José Cataldino (both Italians) left Asuncion on October 10, 1609, and arrived in February, 1610, on the banks of the river Paranapané.[51]

There they met the Indians amongst whom Fields and Ortega had begun to labour, and there they founded the Reduction[52] of Loreto, the first permanent establishment instituted by the Jesuits amongst the Guaranís. Thus, in the woods of Paraguay, upon a tributary of the Paraná but little known even to-day, did the Society of Jesus lay the first foundation of their famous missions. But little more than fifty years from the foundation of their Order, thus had they penetrated to what was then, and is perchance to-day, after their missions all are ruined, one of the remotest corners of the world.

There they built up the system with which their name is linked for ever — the system which for two hundred years was able to hold together wandering Indian tribes, restless as Arabs, suspicious above every other race of men — and which to-day has disappeared, leaving nothing of a like nature in all the world.

Chapter II

Early days of the missions — New settlements founded —
Relations of Jesuits with Indians and Spanish colonists —
Destruction of missions by the Mamelucos — Father
Maceta — Padre Antonio Ruiz de Montoya — His work
and influence — Retreat of the Jesuits down the Paraná

It does not seem doubtful but that the work done by Fathers Ortega and
Filds[53] had borne some fruit. Perhaps not quite after the fashion that the
Jesuits believed; but when Maceta and Cataldino arrived at Guayrá and
founded the Reduction of Loreto, their success at first was of a nature that
almost justified the epithet 'miraculous', an epithet which indeed all men
apply to any enterprise of theirs which meets success. Almost from the first
inception of the missions, the Jesuits found themselves in the strange
position of, though being hated by the Spanish settlers, yet recurred to as
mediators when any of the wild tribes proved too powerful for the Spanish
arms. Thus, far from cities, far from even such elementary civilization as
Paraguay should show, almost upon the edge of the great cataract of the
Paraná, the Jesuits founded their first reduction; to which the Indians flocked
in such numbers that a second was soon necessary, to which they gave the
name of San Ignacio, in memory of the founder of their rule.

For the first few years all went well with the Jesuits. The Indians, happy to
escape the persecutions of the Spaniards on the one hand, and the incursions
of the Paulistas[54] on the other, flocked to the reductions, mission after
mission was soon formed, and the wild Indians gathered up into townships
and taught the arts of peace. But though the Guaranís at first entered into
the Jesuit reductions as a refuge against their persecutors, the Portuguese and
Spaniards, soon, as was only natural to men accustomed to a wild forest life,
they found the Jesuit discipline too irksome, and often fled back to the
woods. Then the poor priest, left without his flock, had to take up the trail
of the flying neophytes, follow them to the recesses of the forests, and
persuade them to come back.

As a means to secure the confidence of the Indians, the Jesuits found
themselves obliged to communicate as rarely as possible with the Spanish
settlements. Thus, from the first the policy of isolation, which was one of the
chief charges brought against the Order in later years, was of necessity
begun.[55] Voltaire, no lover of religious Orders, says of the Jesuits:[56]
'When in 1768 the missions of Paraguay left the hands of the Jesuits, they
had arrived at perhaps the highest degree of civilization to which it is possible
to conduct a young people, and certainly at a far superior state than that
which existed in the rest of the new hemisphere. The laws were respected

there, morals were pure, a happy brotherhood united every heart, all the useful arts were in a flourishing state, and even some of the more agreeable sciences; plenty was universal.'

It is, however, to be remembered that Voltaire wrote as a philosopher, and not as an economist, and that his statement most probably would be traversed by those who see advancement rather in material improvement than in moral happiness, for without doubt, in Lima and in Mexico upon the whole, society must have made amongst the Spanish and Spanish-descended citizens greater advances than in the Jesuit reductions of Paraguay. In some respects their almost inaccessible situation close to the cataract of the Paraná was favourable to the early Jesuits, and in quick succession the villages of Loreto, San Francisco Xavier, San José, San Ignacio, San Pedro, and others of less importance, were founded, containing in all about forty thousand souls.[57]

So in the Jesuit reductions of the province of Guayrá was first begun the system of treating the Indians kindly, and standing between them and the Spanish settlers, which made the Company of Jesus so hated afterwards in Paraguay. Little by little their influence grew, so that when, in 1614, Padre Antonio Ruiz de Montoya arrived, he found that there were already one hundred and nineteen Jesuits in Guayrá and in Paraguay. Of all the Jesuits who, during the long period of their labours, appeared in Paraguay, he was the most remarkable; one of the most learned men of the age in which he lived, he yet united in himself the qualities of a man of action to those of scholar and of missionary. Without his presence most likely not a tenth part of the Indians would have escaped after the destruction of the missions of Guayrá in 1630 and 1631 at the hands of the half-civilized hordes known as Paulistas or Mamalucos, who from the city of San Paulo carried fire and sword amongst the Guaranís.

It is easy to understand that the Spanish colonists, who had looked on all the Indians as slaves, were rendered furious by the advent of the Jesuits, who treated them as men.

To-day the European colonist in Africa labours less to enslave than to exterminate the natives; but if a body of clergy of any sect having the abnegation and disregard of consequences of the Jesuits of old should arise, fancy the fury that would be evoked if they insisted that it were as truly murder to slay a black man as it is to kill a man whose skin is white. Most fortunately, our clergy of to-day, especially those of the various churches militant in Uganda, think otherwise, and hold that Christ was the first inventor of the `colour-line'.

At the first settlement of South America great semi-feudal fiefs called *encomiendas* were granted to the conquerors. One of the conditions of their tenure was that the *encomenderos* (the owners of the fiefs) `should see to the religious education of the Indians'. Much the same kind of thing as to enjoin kindness and Christian forbearance upon the directors of a modern Chartered Company. But, in addition to the *encomiendas*, two other systems were in vogue called *yanaconas* and *mitayos*, which were in fact designed to reduce the Indians to the condition of mere slaves.

Herrera[58] says that the `yanaconas were men destined from birth to perpetual slavery and captivity, and in their clothing, treatment, and the conditions of their toil, were differently treated from free men.'

In Paraguay these *yanaconas* were known as `Indios Originarios', and generally were descendants of Indians conquered in war; they, too, were in a condition of serfdom. They lived in the house of the *encomendero*, and could not be sold, and the *encomendero* was (in theory) obliged not only to feed and clothe them, but to instruct them in religious truths. In order to see that these conditions were duly carried out, visitors were sent each year to hear what mutually the *encomenderos* and the Indians had to say.

Herrera[59] describes the Indians under the *mitayo* system by the name of *mitayos tindarunas*, explaining that the word *tindaruna* signifies `forced labour'. The chiefs had to provide a certain number of them every year to work in mines and manufactories, and so well was the labour in the mines known to be fatal, that the Indians upon being drawn for service disposed of all their property, and not infrequently divorced their wives. The *mitayos* were at the beginning Indians who had not fought against the Spaniards, but had submitted to their rule. They were grouped in townships composed of portions of a tribe under a chief to whom the Spaniards gave the position of Alcalde. In the towns thus formed only the men between eighteen and fifty were liable to be drawn for service in the mines; originally their term of service was for only two months in the year, and for the remaining ten months they were in theory as free as were the Spanish settlers. By 1612 the abuses of their system had so diminished the number of the Indians that Don Francisco de Alfaro was named by the Spanish Government to report upon it, and to reform abuses where he found it possible. His report declared that the Guaranís and Guaycurús should not be made slaves of, and it abolished in their favour the forced labour which they had previously endured. The European settlers in Asuncion thought that this was owing to the influence of the Jesuits, and therefore they expelled them from the town. Recalled to Santiago, they founded there a college, and those who remained in Paraguay pushed on the mission-work. Brabo[60] points out that the first twenty reductions founded by the Company of Jesus were settled in the first twenty years from their first appearance in the land,[61] and that from the foundation of the Mission of St. George (the last established of the first twenty towns) to that of San Joaquim, in the wild forests of the Tarumá, they employed a hundred and twelve years. In the interval they chiefly occupied themselves in the consolidation of their first settlements, and in various unsuccessful attempts to institute similar reductions amongst the Indians of the Chaco across the Paraguay.

But whilst the Jesuits were settling their reductions in the province of Guayrá and those upon the Paraná and Uruguay, a nest of hawks looked at their neophytes as pigeons ready fattening for their use. Almost eight hundred miles away, at the city of San Paulo de Piritinanga, in Brazil, a strange society had come into existence by degrees. Peopled at first by Portuguese and Dutch adventurers and malefactors, it had become a nest of pirates and a home for all the desperadoes of Brazil and Paraguay. This engaging population, being in want of wives whereby to propagate their virtues, took to themselves Indians and negresses, and bred a race worse ten times than were themselves, as often happens both in the cases of Mulattos and Mestizos in America. Under the name of Mamelucos[62] (given to them no one knows why) they soon became the terror of the land. Equally at home on horseback, in canoes upon the rivers, or in schooners on the sea, excellent marksmen and courageous fighters, they subsisted chiefly by procuring Indians as slaves for the plantations in Brazil. In a short time they exhausted all the Indians near San Paulo, and were forced to search far in the depths of the unknown interior. Little by little, following the course of the great rivers in their canoes, they reached the Jesuit settlements upon the upper waters of the Paraná, where they burned the towns and the churches, made captives of the converts, and killed the priests. Montoya relates that a Jesuit, having clasped an Indian in his arms to save him, was deluged with his blood, a Mameluco having crept up behind him and plunged his lance into the Indian behind the Jesuit's back. The Mameluco, on being, as Montoya says, `reprehended' by the Jesuit, dogmatically remarked, `I shall be saved in spite of God, for to be saved a man has only to believe,'[63] a remark which showed him clearly an honest opponent of the Jesuits, as they insisted greatly on the doctrine of good works.

Ruiz Montoya and others tell us that the plan of action of the Paulistas was either to attack the Jesuit reductions on Sunday, when the sheep were gathered in the fold listening to Mass, surround the church, murder the priest, and carry off the neophytes as slaves; or else, disguised as Jesuits, enter a mission, gain the confidence of the Indians, and then communicate with their soldiers, who were waiting in the woods. But not content with this, it seems, so often did they practise singing Mass to pass as Jesuits, that on returning to San Paulo, in their orgies, their great diversion was to masquerade as priests. So that the rascals not only profited by their villainy, but extracted much amusement from their wicked deeds.[64] This, in Montoya's opinion, was even more damnable than the actual crime. And so no doubt it was, and we in England, by having made our vice as dull as virtue is in other lands, have gone some way towards morality, for vice and virtue, both deprived of humour, become not so far separated as some virtuous dull folk may think.

Quite naturally, these redoubtable land and river pirates saw in the Jesuit reductions upon the Paranapané, and generally throughout the district of Guayrá, merely an opportunity of capturing more Indians than usual at a haul. In 1629 they first appeared before the Mission of San Antonio and destroyed it utterly, burning the church and houses, and driving off the Indians to sell as slaves. San Miguel and Jesus-Maria shortly suffered the same fate. In Concepcion Padre Salazar was regularly besieged, and he and all the people reduced to eating dogs, cats, rats, mice, and even snakes. At the last moment, when about to surrender, Father Cataldino, hastily arming some Indians with any rude weapons at his command, marched on the place and raised the siege. A worthy member of the Church militant this exploring, fighting, intrepid Italian priest, and one the Company of Jesus should honour, for to him, perhaps as much as to any of these first explorers of the Upper Paraná, is credit due.

But still the Mamelucos ran their course, destroying town after town, so that in the short space of a year (1630-31) they destroyed partially the reductions of San Francisco Xavier, San José, San Pedro, and La Concepcion; and the two first founded, San Ignacio and Loreto, were ruined utterly. The wretched Indians, to whom by law the Jesuits were forbidden to serve out firearms, stood no chance against the well-trained Paulistas, with their horses, guns, and bloodhounds, assisted as they were by troops of savage Indians who discharged poisoned arrows from blowpipes and from bows. Small wonder that, as Montoya, Charlevoix, Lahier,[65] and Filiberto Monero[66] all agree, despair took hold of them, so that in many instances they cursed the Jesuits and fled back to the woods. When one reflects that many of the Indian tribes looked upon baptism as a poison,[67] it is not strange that they should have associated effect with cause, and set down all their sufferings to the influence of the malignant rite to which the Jesuits had subjected them. The isolated Jesuits ran considerable risk from their own sheep, and Padre Mola, after the ruin of San Antonio, was suspected by them of being in league with the Paulistas, and had to flee for safety to another town; and as a touch of comedy is seldom wanting to make things bitterer to those in misfortune, a troop of savage Indians, having arrived to attack the Reduction of San Antonio, and finding it already burning, instantly thought poor Padre Mola had been the instigator, and, starting on his trail, almost surprised him before he reached a refuge from their patriotic rage.

Thus in the greater world reformers of all sorts have not infrequently in times of scarcity and danger been taken by their protégés for the authors of their trials and stoned, whilst the smug Government which caused the ruin, well bolstered up in the affection of its `taxables', chuckled, serenely confident in the unending folly of mankind. Most certainly the Jesuits struggled to do their duty to their neophytes in what they thought they saw was right. On foot and unattended Fathers Maceta and Mansilla followed the fifteen thousand captives to Brazil, confessing those who fell upon the road before they died, and instant in supplication to the Paulistas for the prisoners' release. Father Maceta especially behaved heroically, carrying the chains of those who could hardly drag themselves along, himself half dead with hunger and his constant toil. Especially he strove to effect the release of a captive chief called Guiravera, who had been one of his bitterest enemies, and strove so hard that a Paulista captain, either touched by his zeal or wearied with his pleading, released the chief, his wife and family, and six of the Indians of his tribe. The chief returned to become the Jesuits' best friend, and the two priests on foot followed the captives' train. What they endured on foot without provisions, tortured by insects, and in danger from wild beasts, as well as constant perils from the Paulistas, who now and then pricked them with lances or fired pistols over their heads to frighten them away, none but those who have journeyed in the forests of that forgotten corner of the world can estimate. I see them in their torn and sun-browned cassocks struggling through the *esteros*[68] in water to the knees, falling and rising oft, after the fashion of the supposititious Christian on life's way; pushing along through forest paths across which darted humming-birds, now coming on a dying man and kneeling by his side, now gathering the berries of the guavirami[69] to eat upon the road, and then again catching sight of a jaguar as it slunk beside the trail, and all the time convinced that all their efforts, like the efforts of most of those who strive, would be in vain. So stumbling through the woods, crossing the rivers on inflated ox-skins, baked by the sun upon the open plains, at length the Jesuits reached San Paulo, where they had a college, and without resting set at once to work. In season (and what in cases of the kind is ten times more important), out of season, they besought, pleaded, and preached, and finding as little grace from the Paulista chiefs as a transgressor against some fiery dogma would find from a sour-faced North British dogmatist, they started for Rio de Janeiro to see the Council-General of Brazil. There they were told that the right person to address was the Captain-General of the colony, who had his residence in Bahia, five or six hundred miles away. Not the least daunted, they set out, and found Don Diego Luis Oliveira more or less friendly, but as usual fearful of giving offence to those who had a vested interest in the trade. Then the two Jesuits, hearing that another invasion of the Paulistas was expected in Guayrá, started back on their long journey through the woods, over the plains, across the mountain ranges, and through the dank *esteros* which lay between them and their missions on the Paraná. The Captain-General seems to have been roused to a sense of the position by their words, for on his annual visitation at San Paulo he spoke in public to the colonists against their slave raids, when a shot fired from the meeting ended his speech.[70] The inhabitants then signified to him that, sooner than give up what seemed to them a justifiable and honest means of life, they would be debaptized. How they proposed to debaptize themselves is not related, but perhaps after the fashion of the Guaranís — by sand, hot water, and scraping with a shell; though why the tongue should be thus scarified seems doubtful, for no sect of Christians that is known exacts that people at that sacrament should put out their tongues, and even baptism does little or nothing to increase the power of scandal inherent both in those who have been and those who never were baptized.

About this time (1630) the poor Jesuits were much tormented by the return to paganism of their Indians, and most especially by a hideous dwarf who set himself up as a god, and found a host of worshippers. Good Father Charlevoix thinks that *ce petit-monstre*,[71] despairing of being thought a man, had no resource but to give out he was a god, and remarks that, as even more hideous gods have been adored, it is not surprising that the Indians took him at his word. When stripped of the somewhat strange phraseology of the simple Jesuit, there is nothing really shocking in the incident. People in general, in making gods, endue them with their own least admirable attributes, and logically these poor Indians but followed out the general scheme.

But in the midst of heresies and dwarf-gods, with the Paulistas almost always in the field, a man arose who was to lead the Jesuits and their neophytes out of Guayrá and settle them securely below the cataract in the Misiones of Paraguay. Born probably late in the sixteenth century in Spain, Antonio Ruiz de Montoya was amongst the first of the Jesuit Fathers who came to Paraguay. In 1612 we find him recently arrived from Spain;[72] sent up to the province of Guayrá to the assistance of Fathers Maceta and Cataldino. For thirty years,[73] as he himself informs us in his book, he remained in Paraguay, and in his own pathetic words he tells us how most of his life was spent. `I have lived,' he says, `all through the period of thirty years in Paraguay, as in the desert searching for wild beasts — that is, for savage Indians — crossing wild countries, traversing mountain chains, in order to find Indians and bring them to the true sheepfold of the Holy Church and to the service of His Majesty.[74] With my companions I established thirteen reductions or townships in the wilds, and this I did with great anxiety, in hunger, nakedness, and frequent peril of my life. And all these years I passed far from my brother Spaniards have made me almost a rustic and ignorant of the polished language of the Court.' Travelling as he did continually, few knew the country from Guayrá to Yapeyu[75] so well as he; he tells us that for `all travelling equipment' he took a hammock, and a little mandioca flour, that he usually travelled on foot with either sandals or bare feet, and that for eight or nine years he never once tasted bread.

About the year 1611-12 we find him charged with a mission to the Provincial at Asuncion to disabuse him of a report which had been carried there that the Jesuits of Guayrá were garnering in no fruit from all their labours in the wilds. The rumour had been so much repeated that the superiors in Asuncion were on the point of calling back the missionaries and giving up all hope. Montoya, accompanied by six Indians, set out upon the journey, which by land to-day is enough to appal the boldest traveller. Walking along, he found himself about the middle of his way alone, his Indians having loitered in the rear. Night caught him in the forests, and a storm came on. He passed the night at the foot of a large tree, hungry and wet, and, waking in the morning, found himself so crippled with arthritic pains as to be obliged to continue his journey on his hands and knees. Alone and helpless, he dragged himself to a place called Maracayu, and, failing to obtain a canoe, went on another league, and there lay down to die, his leg being swelled enormously with the rheumatic pains. Then, as he says himself, he prayed to San Ignacio, telling him that from a sentiment of obedience he had set out upon the journey through the waste. Nothing could have been better, for the saint (who must have seen him all the time), flattered, perhaps, that his own chief virtue had been the cause of so much pain, promptly healed him and restored his leg to its usual size, and Montoya went on his way rejoicing to Asuncion. The Provincial heard and was disabused, but was unable to send a single man to help, and poor Montoya set off again back to Guayrá alone, having gained nothing but his sufferings on the road.

Again, in 1614, we find him in Asuncion combating calumnies spread by the Spanish settlers against the Jesuits. In the same year (as he informs us[76]) he was witness in the Reduction of Loreto of a strange circumstance. 'An Indian,' he says, 'of intelligence and pious conduct called me to administer the last Sacraments, and to confess him before he died, and this I did. As there seemed little hope of his recovery, and pressing business called me away, I quitted him after having given orders for his burial. He died in a short time — at least, all those who were with him had no doubt of this; on my return I found the man whom I had charged to stay beside the Indian till his death preparing for his funeral. Toward mid-day they came to tell me that the dead man had come to life, and wished to speak to me. I ran there, and found him with a cheerful face in the middle of a crowd of Indians. I asked him what had happened since I last saw him, and he answered me that the instant that I quitted him his soul had taken its departure from his body; then, at a point which he thought near to his hammock, a devil had appeared, who said to him, "You are my prey," and that he answered it could not be, for he had confessed himself to the best of his ability, and had received the holy

Viaticum before his death; that the devil had sustained that his confession had been incomplete, and that he had forgotten to confess that twice he had been drunk, to which he answered that it was an oversight, and he hoped that God would not remember it. Then, on the devil sustaining that he had committed a sacrilege, St. Peter had appeared, followed by angels, and driven off the fiend. I asked him how he had known St. Peter, and he replied by describing him, though he had never seen an image of the saint. "The saint," he said, "covered me with his mantle, and I felt myself instantly carried through the air. First I perceived a lovely landscape, and further on a great city, from which a shining light appeared. Then the Apostle and the angels stopped, and the first said to me, `This is the city of the Lord; we live here with Him, but the time of your entry is not yet. It is written that your soul shall once more join your body, and in three days you must appear in church.' Then all was dark, and in an instant I woke up alive and well."

`I,' says Montoya, `understood by the last words of St. Peter that the man had to die in three days, and I asked what he thought himself. "I think," said he, "that next Sunday they will carry my body to the church, and I am certain that I only returned to life in order to exhort my relatives and my friends to listen to your instructions." . . . When Sunday came he made his general confession,[77] admitted the two sins the devil had reproached him with, exhorted all to live a Christian life, and a few moments afterwards quietly gave up the ghost.'

This is the sole occasion on which Padre Ruiz Montoya even remotely touches the field of miracles, as he in general relies upon himself, his knowledge of the world, and on his patience, which must have been almost North British in its quality, if he acted up to his own favourite maxim of `by returning thanks for injuries is how wise men conduct their business.'[78]

In 1623 we find him praying Father Cataldino to let him accompany the expedition to Itiranbaru, a mountain wooded to the summit, in which lived several wild tribes. There he so worked upon the Indians as to establish them in a reduction under the title of St. Francis Xavier,[79] and left the mountain, which had been a haunt of savages, as Padre del Techo says in his curious work on Paraguay, `all at the service of the Lord.'

In 1623, whilst preaching, he was suddenly assailed by hostile Indians, and seven of his Indians pierced with arrows at his feet. Undoubtedly, he must have been killed had not an Indian taken his hat and cloak, and run into the middle of the enemy to distract the fire. In the confusion both the heroic Indian and Montoya managed to escape, the latter getting into a canoe which, fortunately, was ready at the river-side. But in the midst of all his occupations he had time to study natural history in the spirit of the time, as the following description clearly shows: `Amongst the other rarities of the land is an amphibious animal. . . . It is like a sheep, with but the difference that its teeth and nails are like a tiger's, which animal it equals in ferocity. The Indians never look on it without terror, and when it sallies from the marshes where it lives (which it does ordinarily in troops), they have no other chance of escape but to climb up a tree, and even then sometimes are not in safety, for this terrible creature sometimes uproots the tree, or sometimes stays on guard until the Indian falls into its jaws.' Thus far Montoya; but Charlevoix informs us that, *en langue Guaranie*, it is known as the `ao', and rather tamely adds, `When one of these animals is slain, the people make a jacket of its skin.'

Again, Montoya tells us of the horse on which the venerable Padre Roque used to ride, which, when he died, refused all food, and wept perpetually, two streams of water running from its eyes. It never allowed an Indian to mount it after its master's death, and finally expired, close to his grave, of grief. A kindly, scholarly, intrepid priest, well skilled in knowledge of the world, and not without some tincture of studies in science, as the above-related anecdotes reveal to us. No doubt the Indians loved him far and wide, and his superiors stood in some little awe of him, as those in office often do of their subordinates when they show that capacity for action which is a sure bar to advancement either in Church or State.

In 1627 Montoya was made head of the missions in Guayrá, which opened up to him the opportunity of showing what kind of man he was. In this year the Spaniards of Villa Rica, the nearest town in Paraguay to the reductions in Guayrá, sent out an expedition to chastize some Indians who had insulted a chief called Tayaoba, whom Montoya had baptized. This was the pretext for the expedition, but Montoya knew well that the real object was to hunt for slaves. He brought before the Governor the edict of the King of Spain forbidding any war to be made upon the Indians without sufficient cause. All was in vain, and the expedition left Villa Rica and plunged into the wilds. Montoya, sore against the Governor's desire, went with the expedition, taking with him Padre Salazar and some well-armed Indians. It was lucky for the Spaniards that he was there, for on the second day a flight of arrows burst from a wood and wounded many of them. The captain of the expedition ordered a retreat, which, situated as they were, exposed on all sides to the fire of an enemy whom they could not see, must have proved fatal. Montoya counselled throwing up earthworks before some huts which stood upon the edge of the woods in which the Indians were; this done, he sent a messenger to Villa Rica for reinforcements. Even behind the earthworks the Spaniards were hard pressed; no one could show himself without being pierced by an arrow. The number of the Indians daily increased, till on the third day they numbered about four thousand, and seemed likely to advance upon the huts. The Spanish captain ordered a rally, and the neophytes wished to decamp, taking Montoya with them, and then gain the shelter of the woods. This he would not allow, and, charging with the soldiers, put the Indians to flight. The Spaniards, far from being grateful for their lives, seeing their hopes of making prisoners had vanished, wished to lay hands upon the Indians whom Montoya had brought, and who had fought beside them in the recent fray. Hearing that in the morning the Spanish soldiers would attack his neophytes, Montoya sent them off by night, and in the morning, when the Spanish captain found him and the other priest alone, he said, 'Thinking you had no other use for the Indians, I advised them to return.' The captain had the grace to say nothing but, 'Then, you gave them good advice, my father.' The two priests waited patiently till the soldiers had retired, and then sent for their Indians and quietly went home. Thus it appears that at necessity Padre Montoya was a true son of San Ignacio.

In 1628 Montoya seems to have met for the first time Padre Diaz Taño, who afterwards was his companion both in the retreat from Guayrá down the Paraná and in his mission to the King. No matter whether a man make his career with Indians in the wilds of Paraguay or amongst the so-called reasoning people in more sophisticated lands, if he once show himself superior to the ordinary run of men, there is something of an invidious character certain to be attributed to him by those who think that genius is the worst attribute that man can have. This, Montoya did not escape from amongst the Spaniards, but the Indians, at least, were less envious, being perhaps less educated, for they believed that the soul of one of their *caciques*,[80] known in his life as Quaratici, had entered into him. The rumour reached at last a chief called Guiravera, known to the Spaniards as the 'Exterminator' from his cruelty, who, hearing that the soul of his late rival had entered into Montoya, came to see him at the head of a large retinue of people of his tribe. Montoya and Maceta were at Villa Rica, and on the chief's approach they happened to be seated in the plaza of the town. As he approached them, followed by his men, and with a threatening air, they remained seated, merely motioning him to take a seat upon a bench. This he did, after making one of his men cover the seat with a tiger-skin and stand behind on guard. What passed between them, most unluckily, Montoya has not set down. What he has told us only makes us wish for more, for it appears that after the usual salutations Guiravera refused to speak, and getting up walked about the town, silently looking at everything. But, as it ever happens, even Montoya was no exception to the general run of history-writers, who usually are occupied alone with facts which seem to them important at the time, forgetting that posterity (for whom they write) can judge of the result as well as they themselves, but thirst for details to complete the chain betwixt them and their predecessors. One thing is set down *in extenso* — not by Montoya, but by another Jesuit — that is, the sermon which Montoya preached to bring the chief into the fold. Considered as a sermon it does not seem out of the common way, and judged by its results was futile at the time, for the chief answered coldly that he would think the matter over, and then retired into the woods. But the seed thus sown in Villa Rica was to bear fruit, for in a year the chief, either tired of his ancestral gods or having pondered on the sermon, came into the fold and was baptized as Paul.

An irruption[81] of the Mamelucos called Father Montoya from baptizing Indians and recovering their souls to the more prosaic, if as useful, task of saving their bodies, which he did at the immediate peril of his own. The Mamelucos had appeared (1628) before the Reduction of Encarnacion, and many of the Indians had already taken refuge in the woods. Those who remained were like a flock of sheep without a shepherd, and knew not what to do. Padre Montoya hastened to the spot, and called on every Christian to take up arms. Under the circumstances he undoubtedly was right; still, in reading history one is puzzled to observe how often and in how many different countries Christians have to resort to arms. But before proceeding to extremities, Montoya sent out Fathers Mendoza and Domenecchi with some of the principal inhabitants of the reduction to parley with the Mamelucos, who, under their celebrated leader Antonio Raposo, were encamped outside the place. Upon arriving within range of the Paulista camp they were greeted with a shower of balls and arrows, which killed several of the Indians and wounded Father Mendoza in the foot. But when, in spite of his wound, the Jesuit advanced towards the camp and insisted on speaking with the leader, the Mamelucos were so struck with his courage that they gave up to him several of the Indians whom they had taken prisoners upon the previous day. Next day Father Montoya, encouraged by the unhoped-for success of Father Mendoza, went out himself, and, facing the Paulistas, somewhat imprudently threatened them with the wrath of Heaven and the King if they did not retire. The wrath of Heaven is often somewhat capricious in its action, and the King of Spain, although as wrathful as he had been an Emperor, was too far away to inspire much terror in his subjects on the Paraná. So that the Paulista treated the wrath of both their Majesties as qualities which he could well neglect, and for sole answer ordered his men to march upon the town. But, whether owing to their hard hearts having been touched by the good Father's eloquence, or the fact that the neophytes were under arms, when the Paulistas arrived close to the town they altered their intentions and filed off into the woods. Profiting by the respite from hostilities, Montoya, in conjunction with Padre Diaz Taño and a Father bearing the somewhat curious name of Padre Justo Vansurk Mansilla,[82] devoted all his attention for the time to the Mission of Santa Maria la Mayor, which was the most flourishing of all the missions of the time, and which to-day still shows the greatest remnants of the Jesuits' work, both in regard to architecture and the remains of Indian population still settled on the old mission lands. But even there the Jesuits did not escape without their trials, for it appears[83] that a quantity of new proselytes arrived with women, whom the good Fathers stigmatized as `concubines', and whom the ignorant Indians in the innocence of their hearts looked on as wives. The order being given to dismiss these concubines (or wives), a few submitted; but the rest, leaving the mission, started cultivating a tract of land in the vicinity.

Then the good Fathers, with Montoya at their head, hit on a stroke of genius. Taking the opportunity when the seceding Indians were away gathering their crops, they set fire to their houses and carried off the children and the women,[84] back to the mission. The recalcitrants appeared next day at Santa Maria la Mayor, and were received again into the bosom of the Church. Heresy, also, now and then made its appearance, for two rascals, having built two temples upon two hills, transported to them the skeletons of two magicians long since dead, and the fickle people left the churches empty, and went to worship at the magicians' shrines. But in this season of sorrow and of care, and whilst the churches in the Mission of Encarnacion were left deserted, Montoya once again showed his determination, and put things right. Not being able to cope alone with the heathen, Father Diaz Taño went to Guayrá, and induced Montoya (still the superior of the reductions in that province) to give his aid. He came, and, having armed some of the faithful, at dead of night attacked the temples and razed them to the ground.

In 1631 Montoya and others came in the forests of Guayrá upon the wild Caaguas. These they strove hard to civilize, but, after labouring long, with all their eloquence were able to induce only eighteen to return with them to the Encarnacion. It was `with difficulty that they were able to give them a sufficient knowledge of the mysteries of our faith to be able to bestow the rite of baptism.' It may be that the Caaguas, not having much to occupy their minds, approached the mysteries of our faith in more receptive attitudes than is attained by those whose minds are full. But, anyhow, Montoya, with true prudence, deferred their baptism till just before their death, for a few months of life outside the forests proved fatal to them all. Faith is a wondrous thing, and able to move most things, even common-sense. One wonders, though, why, when the Jesuits learned from experience that the poor Indians invariably died when exposed to the burning sun upon the plains, they continued in their fatal efforts to inflict baptism on the unoffending people of the woods. If it were necessary, it surely might have taken place in their own homes, and the patients then might have been left to chance, to see how the reception of the holy rite acted upon their lives.

In 1631 the Mamelucos broke into the province of Guayrá. All was confusion, and Montoya sent Father Diaz Taño to Asuncion to beg the Governor, Don Luis de Cespedes, to send them help. He answered that he could do nothing, and thus by leaving the whole territory of Guayrá without defence lost a rich province to the Crown of Spain. Though at the time (1631)

Portugal and Spain were united, yet in the Indies their subjects were at war, and though in Europe Spain was the stronger of the two, in America the Portuguese conquered about that time rich provinces, which to-day form part of the quondam Empire of Brazil.

Upon the failure of Don Luis de Cespedes to render help, Padre Diaz Taño was despatched to Charcas[85] to lay the matter before the Audiencia Real (the High Court of the Indies). The frequent journeys and diplomatic negotiations in which the Jesuits of Paraguay were engaged rendered them far more apt to manage business than members of the other Orders in America. Whilst in Guayrá all was confusion, and the Paulistas swept through the land ruining everything, upon the Uruguay things prospered, and Padre Romero founded two new reductions (1631), known as San Carlos and Apostoles; he also laid the foundation of that territory in which the persecuted neophytes of Guayrá were soon to find a safe retreat. Father Diaz Taño by this time had returned from Charcas with a decree of the High Court, declaring the action of Don Luis de Cespedes in failing to protect Guayrá against the Mamelucos prejudicial to the interests of the King; but as neither he nor the High Court of Charcas possessed any power by means of which to stimulate the Governor to greater zeal, the decree was useless, and Taño and Ruiz Montoya found themselves summoned hastily to meet a new attack. But before they arrived the missions, both of San Francisco Xavier and of San José, had been destroyed. As there were still three reductions undestroyed, Montoya, as Provincial of Guayrá, called all the Jesuits of the province to deliberate as to their chance of making a defence. The debate ran high; some of the priests wished that the neophytes should fight to the end; others, more sensible, pointed out that the ill-armed and quite untrained militia of the missions could do nothing with their bows and arrows against the well-led and well-disciplined Paulistas all armed with guns.[86] Padre Truxillo gave it as his opinion that it would be more prudent to transport the Indians to a place of safety, and pointed out that near the cataract of Guayrá they would be able to cross the river and place it between themselves and the Paulistas in case of an attack. This advice seemed prudent to the rest, and Father Truxillo set out to make his preparation for the march. Few European travellers even to-day have visited the great cataract known as El Salto de Guayrá, or in Portuguese As sete Quedas. Bourgade la Dardye[87] has described it in his book on Paraguay. Situated as it is in the midst of almost impenetrable forests, it has not even now been properly placed upon the map. Bourgade la Dardye inclines to think he was the first to visit it since the expedition sent by the elder Lopez, President of Paraguay, under Lieutenant Patiño in 1861. Before that time it had been left unvisited since 1788, when the Boundary Commissioners sent to determine the dividing line between the Spanish and Portuguese possessions camped near it for a week. Felix de Azara writes about it in his `Historia del Paraguay',[88] but he does little more than reproduce the account given by the Boundary Commissioners. He places it in 24° 4' 27" lat., and refers to it as `a tremendous precipice of water[89] worthy of Homer or of Virgil's pen.' He says the waters do not fall vertically as from a balcony or window (*como por un balcon ó ventana*), but by an inclined plane at an inclination of about fifty degrees. The river close to the top of the falls is about four thousand nine hundred Castilian yards in breadth, and suddenly narrows to about seventy yards, and rushes over the fall with such terrific violence as if it wished to `displace the centre of the earth, and cause thus the nutation which astronomers have observed in the earth's axis.' The dew or vapour which rises from the fall is seen in the shape of a column from many miles away, and on it hangs a perpetual rainbow, which trembles as the earth seems to tremble under one's feet. `The noise,' he says, `is heard full six leagues off, and in the neighbourhood neither bird nor beast is found.' In Azara's time the journey was not too pleasant, for he says: `He who wishes to see this fall must cross the desert for thirty leagues from the town of Curuguaty to the river Guatimi. There he must choose trees to construct canoes. In these he must embark all those who go with him, arms and provisions, and besides, where he embarks, leave an armed escort to secure his base of supplies from the wild Indians' attack. In the canoes he then must navigate the Guatimi for thirty leagues until it joins the Paraná, and always with much care, for in the woods upon its banks are Indians who give no quarter.[90] . . . Then there remain three leagues to sail upon the Paraná, then one can reach the falls either in the canoes or struggling along the woods which fringe the river's bank.'

Azara was, perhaps, of all the travellers of the last century, the man who above all things shines in accuracy, and in point of fact his description of the cataract is the best we have up to the present time. Bourgade la Dardye tells us that not far above the cataract the Paraná expands into a lake almost five miles in breadth, and from the lake the river issues in two great arms, which have forced their way through the mountains known as the Sierra de Mbaracyu.

Dr. Bourgade la Dardye seems to think the circular eddies found in the whirls are the most curious features of the falls. He describes them thus: `They flow in falls varying from fifty to sixty feet in depth; these circular eddies, which are quite independent of one another, range along an arc of about two miles in its stretch. They are detached like giant caldrons yawning unexpectedly at one's feet, in which the flood seethes with incredible fury; every one of these has opened for itself a narrow orifice in the rock, through which like a stone from a sling the water is hurled into the central whirlpool. The width of these outlets rarely exceeds fifteen yards, but their depth cannot be estimated. They all empty themselves into one immense central chamber about two hundred feet wide, rushing into it with astounding velocity. . . . A more imposing spectacle can scarcely be conceived, and I doubt whether abysses such as these exist elsewhere in the world.' He places the falls in latitude 24° 2' 59", but corrects the longitude given by Azara as 56° 55' west of Paris to 58° 18' 8" — that is, 53° 57' 53" west from Greenwich, which certainly has some importance in fixing the breadth of the territory of Paraguay.

But neither Azara nor the French traveller, with their yards and feet, their longitude and latitude, and the rest, give an idea of the grandeur of the place. Buried in the primeval forests, forgotten by the world, known to the wandering Indians who give no quarter (any more to-day than in Azara's time), the giant cataract is a lost wonder of the world. In the ruined missions on the Paraná, two hundred miles away, I have heard the Indians talk of it with awe. They told how through the woods tangled with undergrowth, matted together with lianas, they had hewed a path. Monkeys and parrots chattered at them, and a white miasmatic vapour hung over trees and lakes, burying the clearings in its wreaths, and lifting only at mid-day, to close again upon the woods at night. They talked of alligators, jaguars, the giant ant-eater, and the mysterious bird known to them as the `ipetatá', which in its tail carries a burning fire. In the recesses of the thickets demons lurked, and wild Caaguas, who with a blowpipe and a poisoned arrow slew you and your horse, themselves unseen. Pools covered with Victoria regia; masses of red and yellow flowers upon the trees, the trees themselves gigantic, and the moss which floated from their branches long as a spear; the voyage in canoes, whirled like a cork upon the rapids; lastly the falls themselves, and how they, awestricken at the sight, fell prostrate and promised many candles to the Virgin and the saints on their return, they talked of into the watches of the night.

Somehow, I like those countries which, as the province of Guayrá and Paraguay, appear to have no future, and of which the charm is in the past. It pleases me to think that the sharp business men of times gone by, patting their stomachs (the prison of their brain), predicted great advancement, and were all deceived. For then it seems as if the prognostications of to-day's schemes may also fail, and countries which they have doomed to progress still remain as is Guayrá, their towns deserted, with but the broken spire of some old church emerging from the verdure of the tropics, as the St. Paul's Rocks rise sheer out of the sea. If there is charm in the unknown, there is at least as great a charm in the forgotten, and the Salto de Guayrá is one of the most forgotten corners of the earth. To this wild place Father Mendoza proposed to lead the Indians from the Reductions of San José and San Francisco Xavier, and then unite with them any of the fugitives he could assemble from those reductions which had been destroyed. But even the doglike patience of the Indians was at an end, and they preferred to die or be led captives rather than run the chances of escape in such a solitary place. In their despair, and placed between the Paulistas and the fear of emigration, the neophytes turned, as even more civilized people than themselves will turn, on their best friends, and held the Jesuits responsible for all their woes. Two Indian women, wives of *caciques*, having been taken by the Paulistas, the Indians broke into the church where a Jesuit (Padre Salazar) was officiating, and interrupted him during the Mass with the most bitter insults. One of the Indians menaced him with a lance, another with an arrow, whilst a third tried to snatch the chalice from his hands. He escaped, and ran, holding the chalice, out into the woods, followed by two little Indian boys. Wandering about, he fell in with the other Jesuits, all like himself outcasts, without a church, and almost deserted by the Indians. Padre Ruiz Montoya alone possessed a shadow of authority, and he advised the outcasts with the remnant of their flocks to retire into the woods, and sow a crop of maize for food, whilst he endeavoured to get help from Paraguay. Hardly was this done, when news was brought him which made him alter all his plans. Two messengers came to inform him that an army of Paulistas was marching on Villa Rica, and that a strong detachment of them was advancing from the south. Then Padre Montoya took a supreme resolve, and ordered the evacuation of the two principal reductions (San Ignacio and Loreto) which yet remained intact. They were the first which had been founded in Guayrá, and were as important as any of the Spanish towns in Paraguay. The churches, all the Jesuit writers, as Montoya, Charlevoix, Mastrilli, and Lozano, are agreed, were finer than any in the land. The Indians were, according to Montoya, far better Christians than the inhabitants of the Spanish settlements, and their faith and innocence were above all praise. They cultivated cotton and had large herds of cattle, so that the most bitter enemies of the Jesuits must allow that much had been accomplished in the short space of two-and-twenty years. In 1609 the Jesuits came to Guayrá, and found it absolutely untouched; and when in 1631 they left it, it was upon the road to become one of the most flourishing American provinces of the Spanish throne. The other missionaries imagined that nothing would persuade the Indians to depart from their homes, where for so many years they had been happy; but after Montoya explained to them his plans, they all assented to them as with a single voice.

The plan by means of which the Jesuit Moses led his sheep out of the wilderness of Guayrá was most remarkable. The river Paraná forms a great artery between Brazil and Paraguay; upon each side of it a network of rivers disembogue. The Paranapané, on which most of the missions of Guayrá were situated, flows from the east, and falls into the Paraná, not much more than fifty miles above the cataract. After the last of the once-flourishing six Jesuit reductions had been evacuated at the orders of Montoya, he collected all the boats, rafts, and canoes, and after much persuasion got all the Indians persuaded to follow him to seek for safer habitations lower down the Paraná.

The population of the six reductions has been estimated at about one hundred thousand souls; but of these, during the years of 1629 and 1630, thousands had been led captive to San Paulo, and thousands had dispersed into the woods. Still, assembled on the banks of the Paranapané, there was a multitude of Indians of every sex and age. Fortunately or unfortunately, no record by an eye-witness exists,[91] except that written by Montoya, and he is modest to a fault about all details, and absolutely silent as to the part he played himself. He tells us that at the starting-point were gathered two thousand five hundred families, and this in spite of the dispersions and the efforts made by the Spanish settlers in the town of Ciudad Real,[92] who feared, with cause, to be exposed to the full fury of the Paulistas without allies. It appears the Indians were in a state of spiritual exaltation, for some young men having remarked the Jesuits were packing up a Christ and an image of the Blessed Virgin, which in happier times had been miraculous, they declared that to affront exile, and even death, in such good company was a foretaste of heaven.

Montoya, in opposition to the modern style, tries to shift the burden of the praise on to the shoulders of the Provincial, Padre Francisco Lopez Truxillo,[93] but with indifferent success. This matter of bearing your own praise will require regulation in the future, when an advance of civilization has opened people's eyes to the perception that praise is just as disagreeable to the sufferer as is blame. The sentinel whom they had placed to warn them of the enemy's approach gave the alarm. Montoya sent at once to Ciudad Real for help, but the Spanish settlers were too hard pressed themselves to give assistance. Nothing remained but to make a portage of all their rafts, boats, and canoes, and then to re-embark and sail down the Paraná out of the reach of the Paulistas. Montoya passed in review his boats, and found he had seven hundred, and that twelve thousand people had embarked with him on leaving the Paranapané. When the Paulistas found the Jesuits had evacuated all their towns, they burnt the churches, on the principle, perhaps, that, the nests once pulled down, the rooks would not return. They turned the Jesuit cells into barracks for themselves, taking, as Montoya says with horror, 'infamous women' into those chaste abodes, where never woman had passed through the doors. The Paulistas then entered into a rigorous examination[94] of the Jesuits' private lives, hoping to find some scandal to bring against them. Especially they questioned the Indian women, giving them presents to discover everything they knew. All was in vain, the discipline of the Order, or the strict conscientiousness of the individual members of it, not having given scandal any hold.[95] The most difficult part of the great exodus was now to come. The rapids and the cataracts of the Paraná extend to nearly ninety miles, and the whole country is a maze of tangled forest interspersed with rocks. No paths exist, the place is desert, and over the dank mass of vegetation the moisture from the clouds of vapour thrown up by the falling water descends in never-ending rain.[96] In order to endeavour to save the trouble of reconstructing new rafts and canoes at the bottom of the cataract, Montoya launched three hundred empty boats (sending an Indian in advance) to see if any of them would arrive safely at the bottom of the falls. Not one escaped; and so the pilgrimage began, almost without provisions and without arms, in the middle of a country quite uncultivated, and where game was scarce.[97] To make things worse, intelligence was brought that, a few miles below the beginning of the falls, the Spaniards of Guayrá had built a wooden fort, surrounded with a strong stockade, hoping to intercept the retreating Indians, and make slaves of any who might fall into their hands. Montoya himself, dressed as an Indian, went out to observe the enemy, and on his return the whole immense assemblage silently plunged into the woods, leaving so little traces of its passage that the Spaniards in the fort were still expecting them when they were far beyond their reach.

Each Indian had to take his bundle on his back; even the children carried bundles in proportion to their strength. The missionaries carried what was held most sacred, as altar-plate and images of saints. In front a band of men armed with machétes (cane-knives) opened the way through the dense woods and pathless jungle of the bank; and as they marched along, Montoya says they sang hymns which the Jesuits had taught them, and at the sound of them fugitives who had been hiding in the woods came out and joined their march. Especially those from the out-station of Tayaoba joined them; their priest, Pedro de Espinosa, had met his death 'with a good chance of his eternal welfare,' as Montoya says.[98] But after the second day the hymns no longer sounded through the woods, nor did they play upon the harps and other instruments, whose strings being all broken and the wood unglued, 'they left them on the rocks, being too sad to look at them.' All through the weary journey Montoya seems never once to have despaired, and sets down in his book the adventures of each separate day, never forgetting to chronicle anything strange or pathetic as it occurred to him. On the fourth day he sent off Fathers Diego, Nicolas Hennerio, and Mansilla into the province of Itatines to found a mission there, acting upon orders which had just reached him from the Provincial of the Order shortly before he had started from Guayrá. They took with them 'bells, images, and everything suitable for the foundation of a mission'; but the first two were martyred by the wild Indians, and the third just fled in time to save his life. It took the fugitive Indians eight weary days of marching to reach the lower end of the cataract, where once again the Paraná was navigable. On their arrival they hoped to find provisions and more boats; but none were there, their own stores were almost done, and the people too exhausted to march on. Fever broke out, and many of them died; and others, lost in the forests, without a guide, wandered about till death released them from their march. A weaker man than Padre Montoya might have despaired of ever issuing from the woods. However, he set the Indians to work to make canoes, and others[99] to cultivate patches of maize for food, working himself alternately with axe and hoe to give example to the neophytes. Others, again, cut down the enormous canes, which in that region grew to fifty feet in height, to make them into rafts.

So, after a considerable time, all was in readiness for a new start, and luckily provisions from the reductions on the Paraná arrived. So they embarked again, and on the journey a raft in which a woman and two children were sitting upset, to Montoya's agony, as he knew that 'in that river there are fish that the people call culebras,[100] which have been seen to swallow men entire, and throw them out again with all their bones broken as if it had been done with stones.' He says: 'I confess I suffered infinitely, and, turning my eyes to heaven, I blamed my sins as having been the cause of so much misery, and said, "O Lord, is it possible that for this Thou hast brought these people out of their country, that my eyes should endure the spectacle of so much misery, and my heart break at so much suffering, and then to let them die devoured by savage fish!"' As the good man was praying, the Indian woman's head appeared above the water, and Montoya himself, aided by Indians, drew her and the children in safety to the land. But his trials were not at an end, for many of the hastily constructed rafts and canoes sank before his eyes, and the mortality of Indians was great. Eventually they found a temporary refuge in the Reduction of the Nativity upon the Acaray, and at Santa Maria la Mayor upon the Iguazú. Then famine raged, and the arrival of so many people increased the scarcity, so that six hundred of the new arrivals died in one reduction, and five hundred in the next. At last the scarcity became so great that the poor Indians had to roam about the forests to gather fruit, and many of them died in the recesses of the woods.

Seeing no hopes of saving the remainder, Montoya led them further on to the banks of a little river called the Jubaburrús,[101] and there he once again founded two reductions, which he named Loreto and San Ignacio, after the two the Mamelucos had destroyed. He bought ten thousand head of cattle out of the money the King allowed to the Jesuits of Guayrá, and from the sale of some few objects saved from the general destruction of the towns, and settled down his Indians, who in Guayrá had been all agriculturists, to a pastoral life. Thus did he bring successfully nearly twelve thousand people a distance of about five hundred miles through desert country, and down a river broken in all its course by rapids, landing them far from their enemies in a safe haven at the last. Most commonly the world forgets or never knows its greatest men, while its lard-headed fools, who in their lives perhaps have been the toys of fortune, sleep in their honoured graves, their memory living in the page of history, preserved like grapes in aspic by writers suet-headed as themselves. But though this Hegira was the most stirring episode of

Montoya's life, he yet had work to do, and in the province of diplomacy rendered as great, or even greater, services to the Indians, whom he loved better than himself, as in the memorable journey when he led them down the Paraná.

Chapter III

Spain and Portugal in South America — Enmity between Brazilians and Argentines — Expulsion of Jesuits from Paraguay — Struggles with the natives — Father Mendoza killed — Death of Father Montoya

In the province of Guayrá the Spaniards who had looked with disfavour on the Jesuits, and had enslaved the Indians when they were able, were in sore straits. The Mamelucos, finding no more Indians to enslave, fell on the two towns of Villa Rica and Ciudad Real, destroyed them utterly, and forced the inhabitants to flee for refuge into Paraguay. Thus Guayrá went the way of Matto Grosso and several other provinces of Spain, and became Portuguese. Strangely enough, most of these losses happened when Spain and Portugal were joined under one crown. At home the Spaniards and the Portuguese, however much they detested one another, were forced to keep the peace. In America they were always at war, which ended invariably to the detriment of Spain.[102] The strife begun by the Papal Bull of 1493, in which Pope Alexander VI. divided the territories discovered and to be discovered between Portugal and Spain, went on, till bit by bit Spain was stripped of the provinces of Matto Grosso, Rio Grande, and Guayrá, and found herself drawn into the numerous disputes about the Colonia del Sacramento, which cost so much blood to both contending Powers. Perhaps the most curious and interesting incident of the long struggle was the Three Years' War, which began in 1750, after the marriage of Ferdinand VI. of Spain with Doña Barbara of Portugal. By the treaty entered into at this marriage, seven of the most flourishing of the missions situated on the left bank of the Uruguay were ceded to Portugal in exchange for La Colonia del Sacramento on the river Plate. The towns resisted change of sovereignty, as Portugal to them was typified by the Paulistas, their most inveterate enemies. The Marquis de Valdelirios in his curious despatches touches much upon this war, but perhaps the best account is to be found in the curious memoir of the Irish Jesuit Father, Tadeo Hennis,[103] who was the backbone of the resisting Guaranís.

The ancient enmity of the two nations has been continued in their descendants, the Brazilians and the Argentines and Uruguayans, and little by little Brazil is absorbing all the northern portion of the Republic of Uruguay. After the retreat under Montoya down the Paraná, the Jesuit missions, especially in Paraguay and what is now the province of Corrientes, for some time enjoyed a period of peace and of repose, and the strange policy of the Jesuits was developed, and township after township arose amongst the Guaranís (1630-31). But there was still no rest for Ruiz Montoya, who was of those who rest but in the grave. In 1632, at the instance of the Governor and magistrates of the township of Jerez, Montoya sent Fathers Jean Rançonier and Mansilla to the north of Paraguay to found a mission amongst the Itatines, a forest-dwelling tribe. Their territory was marshy and the climate bad, and woods of indiarubber-trees covered all the land. Fathers del Techo and Charlevoix both speak of the 'rebounding balls' with which they played, which, thrown upon the ground, start up again as if they were filled with air. This is, perhaps, one of the first times that indiarubber is mentioned, though in some places Jean de Léry[104] seems to indicate he was acquainted with its use.

The Jesuits found that to make progress was not easy with these Indians, who willingly enough listened to their preaching, but refused to alter their social habits, to which the Jesuits ascribe the fact that even then their numbers were diminishing. Like most of the Indians of America, they were polygamists, which custom in their race operates differently to polygamy amongst the negroes: for whereas they seem to increase and thrive, the Indians even at the conquest often tended to become extinct. When a headman amongst the Itatines died, a number of his followers jumped down precipices to accompany him upon his journey to a better world. This custom and polygamy gave much trouble to the Jesuits, but their most admirable patience and knowledge of mankind helped them to overcome them by degrees. All was about to flourish in the mission, when one Acosta, a Brazilian priest, appeared. Perhaps he was in league with the Paulistas, or perhaps was jealous of the Jesuits, for he tried hard to lead a number of the Indians to San Paulo to show them (as he said) how they should follow the true law of God.[105]

The Itatines, either suspecting that Acosta's true law was false, or tired of his preaching, rose and killed him; but the effect was bad, and there grew up amongst those infidels a coldness even towards the Jesuits themselves. Had it not been for two miraculous events which happened opportunely, as such things should happen if they are to be turned to good account, much harm might have been done. A chief, having cursed a priest, was seized at once with a malignant ulcer in the throat, which shortly killed him. The Itatines did not apparently think anything of the influence of the unhealthy climate in which they lived, and set the occurrence down to the act of God.

But more was still to come. Another chief having so far forgotten himself as to jeer at a priest, a thunderbolt fell so close to him that he was knocked senseless, and lay as dead. These two events confirmed the Jesuits' power, and things began to flourish in their four new missions. But the Great Power, so careful of the individual effort of His priests, seems to have been most unaccountably remiss of their success considered as a whole. In the same year (1632) the Mamelucos appeared and ruined all the four missions, so that the efforts of the Jesuits and the miracles were lost.

In 1633 the first skirmish took place between the Bishop of Paraguay and the Jesuits. This skirmish little by little grew into a war, kept up for more than a hundred years, and ended finally in the expulsion of the Jesuits from Paraguay. The Governor, Don Luis de Cespedes, having called upon the Indians of the Jesuit missions for personal service, a proceeding quite against both the King's orders and the Papal Bulls, the Bishop thought the moment opportune to press for tithes. This, too, was equally forbidden both by a Bull and by an order of the Council of the Indies. Padre Romero went to Asuncion and displayed his Bulls and his orders of the Council, and the Governor withdrew his claims. The Bishop, after some opposition, withdrew likewise, and the Provincial of the Order arrived at Asuncion, bringing with him an order from the King signifying that the Indians of the reductions were to be left entirely to the Jesuits. So for the present the Jesuits scored a victory, though in the future it was to cost them dear. But the Governor of Paraguay having returned apparently to his design of exacting personal service from the Indians of the missions, the Provincial checkmated him with a royal order from Philip IV. The order was addressed to the Viceroy of Peru, the fourth Count of Chinchon. The missive, dated at Madrid in 1633, condemned in the strongest terms all personal service (that is, forced labour) amongst the Indians, not only of the Jesuit missions, but of Peru and Mexico. With a touching confidence in his own powers, and absolute right Divine, the well-meaning King added to his orders a paragraph commanding all to be done as he had ordered within six months. Strange to find Philip IV., whom Velasquez has immortalized and shown us as he sat upon his horse ineffable, so far away from the Museo del Prado, where alone he ever seems really to have lived. But foolish Governors and Bishops were not the Jesuits' worst enemies in Paraguay. In 1634 the Provincial, Father Boroa, was shipwrecked in a voyage up the Uruguay, and only saved by the devotion of his neophytes.

Sometimes the cruel treatment of the natives by the Spanish settlers was avenged upon the Jesuits. This was the case with a band of Guapalaches, who, coming on Father Espinosa in a wood, attacked and massacred him and all his Indians, and, having cut his body into pieces, left it for the wild beasts to eat. Upon another occasion Father Mendoza fell into an ambuscade, from which he might have escaped had not his horse sunk in a miry stream. Long he defended himself with an Indian shield, but at length was stretched upon the ground and left for dead. During the night he revived, and dragged himself up to some rocks; but the Indians in the morning, following up his trail, came on him praying in a loud voice. They told him that he served a blind God, or at best a powerless God, as He did nothing to defend His servant; then, after torturing him cruelly, they despatched him, and, taking out his heart, said: 'Let us see if his soul will take the road to heaven.' These savages do not seem to have been genuinely interested in finding out what became of the soul after the dissolution of the body, for they sat down and made a hearty meal of two young Indians who accompanied the unlucky priest. But they had heard their victim say that when he baptized them it purified their souls, and the last words of Father Mendoza had been to recommend his soul to God. I often wonder if the Christians of to-day, their creed so firmly fixed by the martyrdoms of simple folk, who held their faith without perhaps much reasoning on it, know what they owe to men like Father Christopher Mendoza, slain by the Indians in the Paraguayan woods. Your ancient martyr, fallen out of fashion and forgotten by the Christians of to-day, should have his homage done to him, if only by the chance writer, who in his studies for some subject of no interest to the general world comes on his trail of blood; for martyrdom, no matter how obscure, forgotten by the people of the faith for which the martyr suffered, is a slur not only on the faithful, but on the faith itself. In 1636 occurred the second invasion of the Paulistas, which induced Father Montoya, accompanied by Father Diaz Taño, to go to Europe to seek protection for the Indians both from the King of Spain and from the Pope.

The Mamelucos burst into the province of Tapé,[106] and, as the mission of Jesus-Maria (one of the few left undestroyed at the former invasion) was most exposed, Father Romero asked permission of the Governor of the River Plate[107] to make some trenches to defend the place. The Governor consented, but the storm burst on the mission before the defences were in a fit state to defend. The mission priests Antonio Bernal and Juan Cardenas were in the front ranks encouraging the Indians, and both were badly wounded. Fathers Mola and Romero went about ministering to the wounded, but escaped themselves. At last, the Mamelucos having set fire to the church, capitulation became inevitable, and the chief part of the Indians were led away in chains. The same fate would have overtaken the mission of San Cristobal, where father Romero had retreated with some fugitives from Jesus-Maria, had not the people and their priest retreated hastily upon the mission of Santa Ana. But even there they were not long in safety, and had to undertake another perilous journey down the river Iguai. Here a party of passing Mamelucos fell into an ambuscade, and were hewn in pieces, presumably before the Lord. The Mamelucos pushed their advance so far that Father Montoya had given orders that all the missions of that province should be burned. The inhabitants, who trusted him quite blindly, were just about to begin to burn their houses, when an order from the Provincial stopped them from doing so till he himself appeared upon the scene. He arrived, and, gathering up the scattered Indians as far as he was able, left them for safety in some of the missions which had not been destroyed, and set off himself to ask for help from the Governor of Paraguay.

Finding no help either from him or from the Governor of the River Plate, he went to Corrientes, and was received almost with contumely. Then, desperate, he equipped an army of the mission Indians, and advanced to fight the Mamelucos; but they had retreated into Brazil, and were beyond his reach. Seeing that nothing was to be hoped from the Spanish Governors, he sent a box of papers in a ship going to Portugal, and laid his case before the Council of the Indies. Montoya and Charlevoix relate that the box was thrown into the sea near Lisbon by some enemy of the Jesuits, but providentially was washed up by the tide, and, being found miraculously, was taken to the King of Spain. Whether this happened as it is written, who shall say? But, in distress, when have good men (before the time of the encyclopædists) been without a miracle to sustain their cause? In the next year (1637) Father Montoya and Taño started upon their mission to Europe, and a new field was opened to Montoya in which to show his talents on the Indians' behalf.

Whilst Father Montoya was in Spain, the Provincial appointed Father Alfaro to take his place. He fell on troublous times, for the Mamelucos were preparing to attack the three remaining missions in the province of Guayrá.[108] As they were not defensible, it was agreed to evacuate them, and to retreat into the provinces upon the Uruguay. When they were just about to start from Santa Teresa, where the inhabitants of the other missions had been collected, the Mamelucos appeared just before Christmas. The Indians were driven off as slaves, and the Mamelucos, with their usual sense of humour, attended Mass as penitents on Christmas Day, with candles in their hands, and listened to the sermon in an edifying way. The priest reproached them for their cruelty, and they, after listening devoutly, gave him the liberty of two choir boys, and quietly left the church.

At length the Jesuits, rendered desperate by the perils to which the mission Indians were exposed, armed several bands of Indians and attacked the Mamelucos. But, as was to be expected, the half-armed Indians were always worsted by the well-armed and disciplined Paulista bands, and then the Jesuits took the supreme resolve to evacuate Guayrá entirely, and place the Indians in safety between the rivers Paraná and Uruguay.

Formed into three great companies, the Indians started on their second exodus. Although the difficulties were less than in the voyage down the Paraná, still, to march several thousand Indians just emerged from savagery, accompanied by their women and children, and charged with all their possessions, through a wild country, where they were exposed to the attack of a well-armed enemy upon the way, was not an easy task. Father Christobal Arenas formed them into three divisions, leading the first himself; but the Provincial seems to have done most of the organizing, for Charlevoix says that 'to his courage, prudence, and inalterable kindness,' the success was due.[109]

Courage and prudence and inalterable kindness are the three virtues which have most moved the world; perhaps the last has been most efficacious, and one would hope that in the future it would be the only one of the whole three required.

Twelve thousand Indians, not counting women and children, were thus led into a territory[110] between the rivers Uruguay and Paraná, rich, fertile, and, as the distance between the rivers is not above some five-and-twenty miles, defended in some measure, and easily rendered almost impregnable.

No one can see the heart of man, and, even if God sees it, He never tells us what is there, so that we are obliged to judge of actions as we find them, and leave the search for motives to omniscients. On the face of it, the Jesuits, both those who led the Indians down the Paraná and those who headed them in this migration to the Mesopotamia between the Uruguay and Paraná, were not impelled by thought of gain; and if a Jesuit must of necessity have some dark scheme behind the smallest action of his life, these men concealed it so deep down within their souls that all the researches of their keenest enemies have not been able to throw light on it. But, even settled in their new homes, the Indians were defenceless against the Mamelucos, as it was a state maxim of the Spanish court that the Indians should never be allowed the use of guns. This was a wise enough precaution, without doubt, for the Indians of the Encomiendas, who lived amongst the Spaniards and owed them personal services; but arms for the Indians of the missions were a necessity of life. Therefore, before he started for Madrid, the Provincial impressed upon Montoya to approach the Council of the Indies and the King, and represent to them that it was impossible to guarantee the existence of the reductions against the Mamelucos unless the Indians were allowed to provide themselves with arms. So Father Montoya, though he was charged to press for various reforms, was most especially impressed upon this point. He was to tell the King that the Indians were not to be allowed to keep their arms themselves, but that they would be kept by the Jesuits, and served out to the Indians in case of an attack; then, that the arms would not cost a penny to the treasury, but be all paid out of the alms collected for the purpose by the Company; lastly, and this was a true stroke of Jesuit policy, that, to instruct the Indians how to shoot, they would bring from Chile certain Jesuits who in the world had served as soldiers. One sees them brought from the frontiers of Araucania, and from the outposts of the trans-Andean towns, half sacristan, half sergeant, instant in prayer, and yet with a look about them like a serious bull terrier — a fitting kind of priest for a frontier town, and such as could alone be found amongst the Jesuits.

About this time (1639) the third invasion of the Mamelucos took place, and Father Alfaro, who had been left in charge of the missions on the Uruguay and Paraná, was shot by a Mameluco with a crossbow, and fell dead from his horse. The Governor of Paraguay, on hearing of it, marched with an army, and, having killed two or three hundred of the Mamelucos, took the rest prisoners, and carried them back to Asuncion. There, to the disgust of all the Jesuit historians, he menaced them with the wrath of Heaven and let them go. The feelings of a churchman, when his own privilege is thus usurped, may be compared to those of a strict game-preserver who sees his coverts poached. It is not so much the damage that is done as the personal insult and the humiliation which he suffers in his pride.

In this year, too, the Indians of the missions rendered their first armed service to the State which afterwards so often drew on them in its necessity and treated them so ill.

The Governor of Buenos Ayres, Don Pedro Estevan Davila, was setting out upon an expedition against a tribe of Indians who had taken refuge in the islands of the Lake Yberá. Eighty of the Indians were sent, and, being well led and armed, contributed considerably towards success. Next year a second contingent was required by the Governor of Tucuman, and duly sent to his assistance. History seems to repeat itself, and foolish soldiers and others never to gain experience; for the Governor (Padre del Techo in his `Historia Paraquaiæ' tells us), having made war in Flanders, could never be dissuaded that the same system was not suitable for warfare in America. Accordingly, he set out in good order, but neglected to send out scouts, and consequently fell into the middle of the Calchaquis strongly entrenched within a marsh, attacked them with a rush, lost heavily, and had to retire to Tucuman. But all this time Father Montoya and Diaz Taño were striving in Rome and at Madrid with the Pope and with the King.

Urban VIII., at that time God's vicegerent for the Christian portion of the world, received Diaz Taño kindly, listened to all he had to say with interest, promised him his help, and gave him a Papal letter menacing the Mamelucos with the wrath of God. From Rome Father Taño went to Madrid, and thence to Lisbon, whence he sailed armed with the protection of the Pope and accompanied by a fresh band of zealous priests. Arrived in Rio de Janeiro, he published the Papal letter, and fixed it on the doors of the Jesuit College and on those of their church. He seems on this occasion to have been wanting in the chief Jesuit virtue, prudence, or at the least he seems to have mistaken the character of the people amongst whom he was. Most of the colonists having relations with the Mamelucos were indignant, and a mob broke in the doors both of the college and of the church. The riot grew so serious that the Governor convoked a council, and cited Father Taño to appear. He came and spoke, and in the eyes of the chief people of the place made out his case; but the multitude, caring not much for reason (and nothing for philanthropy), became more furious, but was appeased at last by a petition being sent in protest to the Pope.

But if these things passed in Rio de Janeiro (which Del Techo refers to as *oppido sanctorum*), what was the fury of the people in San Paulo, the very centre of the Mamelucos, when the Vicar-General published the brief by order of Don Pedro Albornoz! The people rose immediately, and menaced the Vicar-General with instant death unless he instantly withdrew the brief. This he refused to do, although forced on his knees and with a naked sword held at his throat. His courage quieted them, and they drew up an appeal which they tried hard to make him sign, but he again refused. The mob, having demanded the brief, was told it was in the college of the Jesuits. Thither they went post-haste, and were met upon the steps by the Superior, dressed in canonicals and holding the holy wafer in his hand. He spoke, and most of them fell prostrate on the ground before the Body of our Lord. Others stood upright, and said that, whilst they adored the Holy Sacrament with their whole souls, they would not suffer that their slaves, who were their chiefest property, should be set free. An atheist (or some kind of Protestant) cried out to fire upon the priest, but he had no support. The Superior then gave them a copy of the brief, and they returned to the Vicar-General to ask for absolution for any censure of the Church they might have incurred; but he for the third time was obdurate, and let them welter in their sin.

The news of the revolution which liberated Portugal from Spain having just reached the town, the Jesuits had to retreat from it, leaving the inhabitants enraged against them and more determined than before to push their forays into Paraguay. But the time was past for their incursions, for Father Ruiz Montoya had prospered at Madrid, and secured even more than he had hoped for when he started on his quest. On arriving at Madrid, which he did after a prosperous journey of four months, he waited on the King (Philip IV.), and laid before him and commissaries chosen from the Indies and Castile the following points:

1. That the law of 1611, which provided that no Indians, unless taken in a just war, should be reduced to slavery, should be put into effect.

2. That the Pope should be approached to confirm the briefs of Paul III. and Clement VIII., which contained the same provisions.

3. That those who did not conform to these instructions should be handed over to the Inquisition to be judged.

4. That the Indians who had been enslaved by the Paulistas should be at once set free and the aggressors punished.

The King after deliberation granted every point, and, further, regulated the tribute which the Indians were to pay.[111] All this was easy to enact, but, like most other laws, not quite so easy to put into effect. Moreover, as the revolution which separated Portugal from Spain had just occurred, all Spanish thunder against the Mamelucos was of but small account. Montoya then pressed the demand for license to use firearms in self-defence against the Mamelucos. The King after deliberation granted this last point, and from that time the incursions of the Mamelucos ceased in Paraguay and generally throughout the mission territory. Then also there was set on foot that Jesuit militia which rendered such good service to the crown, but was the cause of so much murmuring, as it protected the mission Indians both from the Paulistas and from the inroads of the Spanish colonists.

Father Montoya never returned to Paraguay, where he had fought so long and done so much for the poor Indians. Apparently it was not written that he should see the results of all his efforts, for, having embarked at Seville for Peru, he was detained at Lima on business of the Order. From thence he went to Tucuman, and, having returned to Lima, died aged seventy. The Viceroy and the chief members of the Audiencia (with whom he had struggled all his life) accompanied his body to the grave, and it is said that several miracles showed forth the glory he enjoyed in heaven.

That may be so, and if they happened (as they well may have done, for, after all, a miracle[112] really exists for those who credit it), if Heaven has honoured him, 'tis more than man has done: for even in Paraguay his name is not remembered, though it remains enshrined in the neglected pages of many a dusty Latin or a Spanish book.

But all the time that Fathers Montoya and Diaz Taño were in Europe a serious danger to the Jesuits was growing up. At the discovery of the New World, the Franciscans had been the first of all the Orders to go out. Some had accompanied Columbus, some were with Cortes in Mexico. Almagro and Pizarro's hosts had their Franciscan chaplains. In his commentaries, Alvar Nuñez relates how he met some of the Order in Brazil. Lastly, the first of all the saints of the New World was a Franciscan.

In 1638 the Franciscans in the province of Jujuy[113] disputed with the Jesuits the right to certain missions, accusing them, as Padre del Techo says, `of putting their sickle into their ripening corn.'[114] What could be more annoying if it were true? As if a Wesleyan mission in the Paumotus Group should, after having shed its Bibles and its blankets like dry leaves, suddenly find an emissary from Babylon itself arrive and mark the sheep!

But from Jujuy the dissensions spread to Paraguay, where the Franciscans had several missions extending from Yuti to Cazapá, thus being almost within touch of the Jesuit Gospellers in Santa Maria, upon the eastern bank of the Tebicuari, which bounds their territory. These jealousies might have gone smouldering on, and never burst out into fire, had not the appointment of a Franciscan to the see of Paraguay caused the flames to flare out fiercely.

Had a firebrand been wanted to stir up strife, none better could have been found than Don Bernardino de Cardenas, who was just then appointed to the bishopric of Paraguay.

Chapter IV

Don Bernardino de Cardenas, Bishop of Paraguay — His
labours as apostolic missionary — His ambitions and
cunning — Pretensions to saintliness — His attempts to
acquire supreme power — Quarrels between Cardenas and
Don Gregorio, the temporal Governor

Don Bernardino de Cardenas first saw the light in the town of La Plata,[115]
capital of the province of Charcas in Bolivia, or, as it was then called, Alta
Peru. The date of his birth is uncertain, but it would appear to have been in
the early years of the seventeenth century. At an early age he entered the
Franciscan Order.

As the Franciscans had had the honour of having furnished to the calendar
the first saint canonized in the New World, it seems to have been the dream
of Cardenas from his earliest youth to emulate him. In this desire he seems
to have acted in good faith, and all his life the dream of saintship haunted
him. Charlevoix[116] says 'he made a rather superficial study of theology,
and then engaged in preaching, in which, with memory, assurance, and
facility, he found it easy to succeed in a country where brilliant gifts are more
esteemed than solid learning.' Certainly a preacher without assurance,
memory, and facility would scarcely have succeeded in any country; and in
what country in the world is brilliancy not far esteemed above the deepest
scholarship? Besides, 'he was a man of visions (*homme à visions*) and
revelations, which he took good care to publish.' Visions are generally, in the
case of saints, confined to the soul's eye, and revelation to the inward ear; if,
therefore, the recipient of them does not make them known, they run the
risk of being lost. In a word, according to Charlevoix,[117] he was 'one of
the most complete and dangerous ecstatics that ever lived.' 'His first
successes' (whether as preacher or ecstatic are not specified) caused his
superiors to name him guardian of their college of La Plata. They soon
repented of their choice. No sooner was he named Superior than he sought
to qualify himself for saintship by a sort of royal road. Saints are of several
classes, and, in looking through the calendars, it strikes one how different
seem to have been the methods by which they severally attained their goal.

Prince Juan Manuel, in the preface to his 'Fifty Pleasant Stories of Patronio',
says that, 'amongst the many strange things our Lord God made, He thought
good to make one marvellous in special — that is, that, of the numberless
men who are on earth, not one entirely resembles any other in his face.' He
might have said the same of saints and of their ways. One, like St. Francis of
Assisi, treats his father (as it seems to me) but scurvily, and yet to every other
created man and all the animals he is a brother. The saint of Avila founds

convents, mingles with men of business, and has visions in the intervals of her journeying through Spain upon an ass. Again, another preaches to the Indians or the Japanese, gives up his substance, begs his bread from door to door, and leaves the devil's advocate scarcely a quillet or a quiddity against him. Lastly, you find against the names of some merely the docket `virgin' or `martyr', as their case or sex may serve.

Don Bernardino adopted none of these methods of procedure. Carrying a heavy cross, with ashes on his head and shoulders bared, followed by all his priests, he sallied out one day to discipline himself in public. This plan did not succeed with all the world, for his superiors ordered him to remain inside his convent gates. There he remained, and, as his Life informs us, profited by his retreat to study Holy Scriptures, and to such good effect that, the next time he preached, he charmed his hearers by his eloquence. Soon after this the Archbishop of La Plata held a provincial council, with the object of reforming the morals of the Indians in his diocese. Cardenas, being a fluent speaker, was chosen for the post of Apostolic Missionary. From this time dates the beginning of his fame.

In those days all the Indians of the Charcas, and generally of all Peru, were sunk in misery, but little removed from slaves, and their religion was a mixture of Christianity and paganism — just the kind of folk a fluent preacher of the style of Cardenas could work upon. All through the province he made his apostolic progress, preaching, converting, and confessing, everywhere preceded by his fame as seer of visions, miracle-worker, and recipient of celestial light. He took his way, dressed like a pilgrim, on foot, carrying a wooden cross, and followed by a multitude of Indians from town to town.

Religion in America (Catholic or Protestant) has always tended to revert to the original Eastern form, from which, no doubt, it sprung. The influence of the vast plains and forests, and the great distances to travel, have introduced the system of camp meetings amongst the Protestants, whereas the Catholics have often held a sort of ambulatory mission, the people of one village following the preacher to the next, and so on, in the same fashion as in Palestine the people seem to have followed John the Baptist.

Soon the news was spread about that the Indians who followed Cardenas had told him of rich mines, on the condition that he would not divulge the secret to the Spaniards. At that time the search for mines was carried almost to madness in Peru. Even to-day, in almost every mining town, a mysterious, poverty-stricken man sometimes approaches you with great precaution, and, drawing from his pocket an object wrapped in greasy paper, declares with oaths that it is *rosicler* (red silver ore), and that he knows where there are tons and tons of it. In Mexico the curious class of miners known as *gambusinos* rove through the valleys of the Sierra Madre armed with pick and pan, passing their lives in hunting mines, as pigs hunt truffles. If they come upon a mine, they never try to work it, but sell the secret for a trifling sum, and, drinking out the money, start on again to find the mines worked by the Aztecs, till an Apache bullet or arrow stops them, their El Dorado still ahead, or they are found beside their pick and shovel dead of thirst.

Neither in Mexico nor in Peru do things grow less in telling, and we may well suppose the stories of the mines the Indians told to Cardenas became colossal; for at last the Alcalde of Cochabamba wrote on the subject to the Count of Salvatierra, the Viceroy of Peru.

As Charlevoix says, `it seemed as if it all worked to the advantage of the holy missionary, who, not content with saving souls, did not forget the interests of his native land.' In the middle of his triumphs, being recalled to Lima, no one doubted that it was in order to confer with the Viceroy about the supposititious mines. Others, again, imagined that a mitre was destined for the successful evangelist, and therefore many, even quite poor people, pressed forward to offer funds to help him on his way. With quite apostolic assurance, he took all that was offered to him, being certain, as some think, that, the mines being real, he could some day repay with usury all he had borrowed, or, as others said, being indifferent about the matter, and trusting to repay in that better country where no usury exists and where no gold corrupts.

The Viceroy, being a man of little faith, sent to investigate the supposititious mines, but found them non-existent.

The superiors of Cardenas, as judicious as the higher officers of the Franciscan Order often proved themselves throughout America, informed him that he had given offence to many by his public scourgings and processions carrying a cross, and, most of all, that in his sermons propositions had escaped him of a nature likely to bring him under the censure of the Holy Office. A convent in Lima was assigned to him as a retreat and place of meditation on the virtues of submission and obedience.

As we may well believe, no man who felt he had the stuff within himself to make a saint ever cared much for obedience or submission, except in others; so in his convent, instead of meditating on his faults, he passed his time in writing a memorial to the Council of the Indies, setting forth his views on the way in which to spread the gospel amongst the Indians. Nothing was better calculated to win him favour. Every Indian baptized was so much yearly gain to the Spanish Government.

Conversion and taxation always went hand-in-hand, and therefore Indians who, unbaptized, brought nothing to the treasury, having received the

Gospel truths, were taxed so much a head to show them that from thenceforth they were Christians. Thus, we find that in the Paraguayan missions each Indian paid a dollar every year as a sort of poll-tax, and most of the disputes between the Viceroys of Paraguay and the Jesuits arose from the number of the Indians taxable. The Viceroys always alleged that the population of the missions never increased, on account of the Jesuits returning false numbers to avoid the tax.

Cardenas specially inculcated, in his memorial to the Council of the Indies, that it was not expedient to place the Indians under the regular clergy, a theory of which he himself was destined to become a great antagonist. Promotion, as we know, cometh neither from the east nor from the west; so it fell out that during his retreat, through the influence of his friend Don Juan de Solorzano, a celebrated lawyer, who had heard him preach when Governor of Guancavelico, he found himself named Bishop of Asuncion del Paraguay. This piece of luck opened the doors of his convent to him, and he repaired at once to Potosi to wait the arrival of the Papal Bull authorizing him to take possession of his bishopric. There he appeared in the habit of his Order, a little wooden cross upon his breast, and a green hat upon his head, a costume which, if not quite fitting to his new dignity, was at least suited to the Indian taste.

His biographer informs us that, without a word to anyone, he began to preach and hear confessions. Being absolutely without resources, he was reduced to distribute indulgences and little objects of piety, and at the end of every sermon to send his green hat round the audience. His talent for preaching stood him in good stead, and after every sermon gifts were showered upon him, and a crowd accompanied him home.

The priest of Potosi being just dead, Don Bernardino took his place without permission, and set himself up in the double character of parish priest and Bishop to hold a visitation throughout the diocese.

Some people took this conduct as evidence of his saint-like humility in condescending, though a Bishop, to officiate as a mere priest. The Archbishop had a different opinion, but, as Don Bernardino had a great following, he thought it best to dissemble his resentment. Cardenas himself, by his imprudence, furnished the Archbishop with an excuse to get him out of the bishopric.

A rich Indian, whom Cardenas confessed upon his death-bed, left him ten thousand crowns. Not content with that, he influenced one Diego Vargas to change his will and leave him money. On this the Archbishop wrote to him, requesting that he would go and govern his own see. He had to go, but left the town, which he had entered without a farthing, with a long train of mules carrying his money, plate, and furniture. Why he did not instantly go to

Asuncion is not quite clear, for in America it was the custom, owing to the great distance from Rome, that Bishops, on receipt of the royal order of appointment, got themselves chosen by the chapter of their diocese to govern provisionally. Instead of doing that, he went to Tucuman, and thence to Salta, where he arrived in 1641.

In Salta, his first visit was to the Jesuit college, where he laid his case before the Jesuit fathers, and showed them several letters, one from the Cardinal Antonio Barberini dated in 1638, and another from the King without a date, naming him Bishop of Asuncion. On the strength of these two letters he asked the Jesuits if he could get himself consecrated without the Papal Bulls. Charlevoix alleges that they dared not refuse to answer in the way he wished. Why this was so is not so easy to make out, as, even with his green hat and wooden cross, he could not at that time have been a formidable personage. Their written opinion he sent at once to the rector of the Jesuit college at Cordova, asking for his opinion and that of the doctors of the university. The answer reached him in Santiago del Estero, and was unfavourable. On reading the letter, Cardenas fell into a most unsaint-like fury, and tore it up without communicating it to anyone, not even to the Bishop of Tucuman, Don Melchior Maldonado. This was not strange, as he had counted on this Bishop to consecrate him.

Notwithstanding what was at stake, he went on in the diocese of Tucuman just as he had done in that of Charcas, preaching, confessing, and celebrating Mass. Don Melchior Maldonado, a quiet man of no pretensions, wrote him a letter in which he said: `You came into my diocese like a St. Bernard; such is the reputation you have for holiness and preaching that my people pay me no respect, and only look on me as a man of common virtue and mediocre talents. Although I hope I am not jealous, still, I must remind you that you act as if you were St. Paul.'

A Bishop of common virtue and of mediocre talents is, of course, a Bishop lost, and one can well conceive that poor Don Melchior Maldonado was placed in an unpleasant position during the stay of Cardenas in his diocese. Such were Don Bernardino's powers of persuasion that at last the Bishop consecrated him. The ceremony was hardly over, when a letter arrived from the Rector of the University of Cordova advising Bishop Maldonado against the consecration. Unluckily for Paraguay, it was too late to undo the action, and Cardenas was now in a position to take possession of his see. Poor Melchior Maldonado, Bishop of Tucuman, had, as it happened, laid hands a little hastily upon the candidate. The Council of Trent pronounced upon the case, and found `that the consecration of the Bishop of Paraguay had been a valid one as touching the sacrament (ordination), and the impression of the character, but that it had been void as regards the power of discharging the functions attaching to the dignity, and that the Bishop and his consecrator had need of absolution, which the same holy congregation thinks ought to be accorded with the good pleasure of the Pope.' As the same holy congregation had previously declared the taking possession of the diocese by Cardenas had been illegal, it is difficult for ordinary minds to grasp their real opinion of the case.

Finding that he had failed with the University of Cordova, Don Bernardino took his way to Santa Fé, from whence he wrote an insulting letter to the poor rector. The letter was conceived in such outrageous terms that the Bishop of Tucuman wrote in expostulation, saying he expected to see something extraordinary happen in Paraguay if he gave way to such excess of passion.

Don Bernardino's usual luck attended him in Santa Fé. This town then formed part of the diocese of Buenos Ayres, though situated about four hundred miles from the metropolis. It happened that the see of Buenos Ayres was vacant, and the chapter of the cathedral invited Cardenas to visit that portion of the diocese through which he had to pass. Cardenas was, of course, delighted to show his talents for preaching, as he had done before in Charcas and in Potosi. When he arrived at Corrientes the enthusiasm for his holiness and talents was extraordinary. In Corrientes, Don Bernardino seems to have felt, for the first time, his calling and election really sure. At the time he landed (1642) the land was sunk in ignorance and superstition. Even to-day in Corrientes (the city of the seven currents), situated just at the junction of the rivers Paraná and Paraguay, close to the celebrated missions of the Jesuits, the inhabitants, living in a country almost tropical, are half Indians in type.

What Corrientes looked like in Don Bernardino's time is matter of conjecture. Perhaps it was not greatly different from some remote Spanish-American frontier towns some five-and-twenty years ago, save for the groups of Spanish soldiery, with their steel morions, trunk hose and heavy arquebuses lounging about, and in the matter of the scarcity of horses in the streets. No doubt the self-same listless air hung over everything, and in the place of the modern blue and white barred flags with a rising sun or cap of liberty stuck like a trade-mark in the corner, the blood and orange Spanish colours with the quarterings of castles and of lions flapped heavily against the flagstaff of the fort. The Indian women dressed all in white, their hair cut square across the forehead and hanging down their backs, sat with their baskets of fruit and flowers in the market-place. The town, as now, built chiefly of adobes, with a few wooden huts dotted about, was semi-oriental in design. On every church were cupolas after the eastern fashion, flat roofs on every house, and everything shone dazzling white against the dark, metallic-looking foliage of the trees. The streets, as now, were sandy water-courses, crossed here and there with traverses of rough-hewn stone to break the force of the water in the season of the rains.

At night the fireflies glistened amongst the heavy leaves of the mamayes and the orange-trees, whilst from the Chaco rose the mysterious voices of the desert night, and from the outskirts of the town the wailing Indian Jarabis and Cielitos sung in a high falsetto key to the tinkling of a cracked guitar, but broken now and then by the sharp warning cry `Alerta centinela!' of the soldiers on the walls. Could one have landed there, one would have felt much as a sailor feels, dropped on the beach of Eromango or on some yet unbemissionaried island of the Paumotus Group.

Embarking from Corrientes up the river Paraguay, the Bishop met two vessels sent from Asuncion to do him honour. When night approached he put in practice one of the manœuvres which in Peru had stood him in good stead. On every side a swarm of launches and canoes accompanied the ship to see the Bishop, whom already many believed a saint. He asked them all to retire a little from his ship. All did so but the guard of honour sent from Asuncion. Towards the middle of the night the sound of scourging wakened them. It was their Bishop trying to prepare himself for the duties that awaited him. Every succeeding night the same thing happened. During the day he celebrated Mass pontifically upon the deck. Voyages upon the river Paraguay before the days of steamers took a considerable time, especially as every night the custom was to anchor or to make fast the vessel to a tree. Soon the rumour reached Asuncion that a second St. Thomas was on his way to visit them. St. Thomas, as is said, once visited Paraguay, and a cave in the vicinity of a town called Paraguari, where he once lived, exists to-day to prove the passage of the saint.

Fate seemed determined that the Bishop should always meet the Jesuits, no matter where he went.

Becoming weary of the slow progress of the ships, he disembarked four leagues below Asuncion, at a farm belonging to the Company. He managed to dissemble his resentment so perfectly that no one knew he had a grudge against them. Arrived at the capital, he went at once to the church of San Blas, then to the Cathedral, where he celebrated Mass and preached, his mitre on his head. After service he dismissed the people to their homes to dine, saying, however, that he himself was nourished by an invisible food and by a beverage which men could not perceive. `My food' (he said) `is but to do the work and will of Him who sent me.' Therefore he remained in prayer and meditation until vespers, and that office finished, he retired to the palace accompanied by a shouting crowd.

In his position his conduct was most adroit, for, as his Bulls had not arrived, he must have known he had no legal status, and that, in default of that, he had to conquer public sympathy. The chapter never doubted that Don Bernardino would place himself entirely in their hands as his Bulls had not arrived. He, however, seems to have thought that the act of celebrating Mass pontifically in the Cathedral had put him in possession of his powers. So he named one Cristobal Sanchez as his Vicar-General. Two of the members of the chapter, Don Diego Ponce de Leon and Don Fernando Sanchez, remonstrated, but a considerable portion of the chapter sided with Cardenas. The stronger party left the Cathedral and celebrated Mass in the church belonging to the Jesuits, thus giving Cardenas a second cause of offence against the Company.

The Bishop, not being secure of his position, had recourse to every art[118] to catch the public eye: fasting and scourging, prayers before the altar, two Masses every day, barefoot processions — himself the central figure, carrying a cross — each had their turn. Along the deep red roads between the orange-gardens which lead from Asuncion towards the Recoleta and the Campo Grande, he used to take his way accompanied by Indians crowned with flowers, giving his benediction as he passed, to turn away (according to himself) the plague and to insure a fertile harvest. Not being content with the opportunities which life afforded, he instituted an evening service in a church in order to prepare for death.

Soon, as was to be expected in such a country, this service proved the occasion of much scandal, and, instead of showing people how to leave the world, became the means of introducing many into life in a clandestine way. The rector of the Jesuit college thought it his duty to inform the Bishop; but he, like all good men, thought nothing bad could spring from anything that he himself originated. No doubt he put it down to malice, as good people will when worldlings put the finger on the weak spot of a religious institution; but anyhow, regardless of the scandals, he continued his nocturnal rites.

The Governor of Paraguay at that time was one Gregorio de Hinostrosa, an officer born in Chile, an honest, pious, wooden-headed man, and much beloved by the inhabitants of Paraguay. On his arrival Don Bernardino tried to conciliate him. Unluckily, a friendship with the Bishop was impossible without a blind submission to his will. In the beginning all was flattery; when Don Gregorio attended Mass, the Bishop used to meet him at the church door. Not to be outdone, the Governor returned the Bishop's politeness in a similar way, but went so far in his complaisance that Don Bernardino ceased to respect him. Soon there arose bickerings and jealousies, and at length they hated one another fervently.

Nor was the Bishop more successful with his clergy. Some of them laughed at his pretensions to be a saint, and called him an ambitious schemer. Again, amongst the laity, many did not quite understand his habit of celebrating two

Masses every day. He answered that he never celebrated without releasing a soul from purgatory, and that there had been saints who celebrated nine Masses every day, and, moreover, that he was Pope in his own diocese. This cut the ground from under the feet of his detractors, for in a town of the calibre of Asuncion the people looked on a service in a church as a welcome means of getting through the day, and had he celebrated a dozen masses they would but have been more delighted with their new Bishop.

Under the pretext that there were not enough priests to serve the churches, he, by degrees, took several parishes into his own hands, and went from church to church to celebrate his Mass in each, whilst not forgetting to draw the various stipends for his work. But, not content with this, he began to ordain young men who knew no Latin, and even criminals, setting forth the view that ordination was a sort of second baptism, which purged all crimes — a most convenient theory, and one which is not half enough insisted on in these degenerate days.

The position of Asuncion gave him an opportunity of an almost unique kind to show his talents in another sphere. Across the river Paraguay, there about one mile broad, extends the country called the Chaco, a vast domain of swamp and forest, inhabited in those days, as at present, by tribes of wandering Indians. From the city walls, whilst listening to the church-bells, one can see the smoke of Indian encampments across the river only a mile away.

Of all the Indian tribes in the time of Cardenas, the most ferocious were the Guaycurús. The Jesuits had laboured almost in vain amongst them. Missions had been founded, and all gone well for months, and even years, when on a sudden, and without reason, the Guaycurús had burned the houses, killed the priests, and gone back to the wilds. From Santa Fé up to the province of Matto Grosso they kept the frontier in a turmoil, crossing the river and feeding like locusts on the settlements in Paraguay.

Not long before his arrival the Guaycurús had intimated their intention of holding a conference with Don Gregorio Hinostrosa. Don Bernardino thought the chance too good to lose, and at once declared that, as a Bishop, it was his place to carry on negotiations with the barbarians. Dressed in his robes and with an escort furnished by the Governor, he met the chiefs — who no doubt looked on him as a new kind of medicine-man — preached to them through an interpreter, curiously being without the gift of tongues, but notwithstanding that a reasonable number of them were baptized. On his return, he wrote to the King that by his efforts he had appeased the most ferocious Indians within his Majesty's domains.

Within a week the Guaycurús surprised and burned a settlement a little higher up the stream. Not content with this Caligulesque apostolate to the

Guaycurús, the Bishop longed for serious occupation, and caused it to be rumoured about the city that he did nothing except by the direct authority of the Holy Ghost, an allegation hard to confute, and if allowed, likely to lead to difficulties even in Paraguay.

Some years before the advent of Don Bernardino the Dominicans had built a convent in Asuncion. As they had no license to build, they were in the position of religious squatters on the domain of God. The citizens had applied to the Audiencia of Charcas, the supreme court on all such matters in South America, situated, with true Spanish unpracticality, in one of the most secluded districts of the continent. The Audiencia had refused the license, but had taken the matter *ad advisandum* for ten years. To take a matter into consideration for ten years, even in Spain or South America, where the law's delay is generally more mortal than in any other country, was as good as giving a permission. So the Dominicans construed it, and no one dreamed of now molesting them.

One day the Bishop, dressed in his robes, proceeded from his palace to the convent, informing the Governor that he wanted him to meet him there. Entering the convent church, he took the sacrament from off the altar and stripped the church of all its ornaments, setting a gang of workmen to demolish both the convent and the church. When the work was over, he went to a neighbouring church, and then and there, without confession, celebrated Mass, remarking to the faithful that there was no need for him to make confession, as he was satisfied of the condition of his conscience. Some murmured; but the greater portion of the people, always ready to take a saint at his own valuation, were delighted with his act. Doubts must have crossed his mind, as shortly afterwards he wrote to Don Melchior Maldonado, Bishop of Tucuman, for his opinion. That Bishop answered rather tartly that his zeal appeared to him to savour more of the zeal of Elias than of Jesus Christ, and that in a country where churches were so few it seemed imprudent to pull down rather than to build. 'However,' he added, 'my light is not so brilliant as the light your lordship is illumined by.'

When once a man is well convinced that all he does comes from the Holy Ghost, there is but little that he cannot do with satisfaction to himself. Self-murderers, according to the custom of those times, were not allowed admission into holy ground, as if the fact of having found their life unbearable debarred them from the right to be considered men. Such a man a few years previously had been buried at a cross-road. It now occurred to Cardenas to have a special revelation on the subject; and, curiously enough, this special revelation was on the side of common-sense. 'This body,' said the Bishop, 'is that of a Christian, and I feel pretty sure his soul is now in bliss.' He gave no reason for his opinion, as is the way of most religious folk, but, as he had special means of communication with heaven, most people were contented. Incontinently he had the corpse dug up and buried in the church of the Incarnation, himself performing all the funeral rites.

Although a miracle or two would have shocked nobody, still, in the matter of the suicide he had gone too far for the simple people of the place. They murmured, and for a moment the Bishop's prestige was in jeopardy; but in the nick of time his Bulls arrived, brought by his nephew, Pedro de Cardenas, who, like himself, was a Franciscan friar. This saved him, and gave the people something new to think of, though at the same time he incurred a new anxiety.

In the Bulls there was a passage to the effect that, if at his consecration any irregularity had been incurred, he was liable to suspension from all his functions. This the Jesuit who translated the documents into Spanish for the purpose of publication drew his attention to. However, Cardenas was not a man to be intimidated by so small a matter, but read the translation to the people in the Cathedral, and intimated to them that the Pope had given him unlimited power in Paraguay, both in matters spiritual and temporal.

Though Don Gregorio, the Governor, was present at the ceremony, he made no protest at the assumption of temporal power by Cardenas. He had remarked it, though, and secretly determined to show him that his pretensions were unfounded. His nephew, Don Pedro de Cardenas, furnished the occasion. This young man had been despatched to Spain to get the Bulls. Upon the voyage he seems to have conducted himself with scant propriety. On his return, when passing Corrientes, he took on board a lady whom Charlevoix, quite in the spirit of the author of the Book of Proverbs, describes as 'une jeune femme bien faite'. Having some qualms of conscience, he put on a secular dress, and on nearing Asuncion put his religious habit over it. In such a climate this double costume must have been inconvenient, and why he should have worn one dress above the other does not appear. His uncle, in his delight at the forthcoming of the Bulls, most probably paid little attention to his appearance. He lodged him in the palace, and assigned him a prebendary which was vacant. Where the 'jeune femme bien faite' was lodged is not set down, and the people of Asuncion no doubt looked leniently on such affairs, as does society to-day in England. After his usual fashion, the Bishop set all down to calumny.

About this time the Governor had put in prison one Ambrosio Morales, a sub-official of the Inquisition, who had had a quarrel with an officer. Cardenas, being informed of this, could not lose so good a chance of exercising the power he arrogated in temporal affairs. Holding a monstrance in his hands, he went to the prison and asked for the prisoner, placing the monstrance on a table at the prison gate. The rector of the Jesuit college came and expostulated with him, saying that it was not fitting to expose the body of Jesus Christ in such a place, and that it was not decent that the Bishop himself should stay there. Considering his position, and the times in which he lived, it seems the rector was judicious in his expostulation. Cardenas replied that he would stay there till the prisoner was released. The rector, knowing him to be as obstinate as a male mule, went and begged the Governor to let Morales out. This he did at once, and then the Bishop, cross in hand, returned in triumph to the palace with the rescued Inquisitor following amongst his train. The people, whose lives were dull, snatched at the opportunity for some amusement, and said that it was good luck the Governor and Bishop were not always of one mind, for that their agreement had caused the demolition of a church and convent, and their quarrel the setting of a prisoner free.

This little triumph emboldened the Bishop to go further. He admitted Morales into minor orders, gave him the tonsure, and thus, having placed him above the temporal power, enabled him to brave the Governor openly. The Bishop's nephew, taking the Governor's kindness for weakness, broke publicly into insulting terms about him. The Governor's brother, Father Hinostrosa, pressed him to vindicate his dignity, but he refused, saying he wanted peace at any price. This policy the Bishop did not understand, for all concessions he set down as weakness, and they encouraged him to fresh exactions and more violence.

Dining with the Governor, the Bishop chanced to see upon the table a fine pair of silver candlesticks. To see and to desire with Cardenas was to ask, and so he intimated to the Governor his wish to have them. The Governor, thinking, perhaps, to wipe out the remembrance of the difficulty about Morales, sent them to the palace with his compliments. The Bishop took the present, and, turning to the man who brought them, said, `I should now be quite content if I only had the silver ewer and flagon which I noticed in your master's house.' The Governor, we may suppose, on hearing this made what the Spaniards call `la risa del conejo'; but sent the plate and a message, saying all his house contained was at the Bishop's service. Don Bernardino, who, though he may have been a saint, as his friends proclaimed, was certainly far from a gentleman, sent for the flagon and the ewer, which he received at once, together with a friendly message from the Governor.

But even this free-will offering brought no quiet, for a new quarrel soon arose between the Bishop and the unlucky wielder of the temporal power. The Society of the Holy Sacrament enjoyed an *encomienda* at or near Asuncion. The Bishop, no doubt thinking he was most fitted to indoctrinate the Indians, endeavoured to persuade the Governor to get the Society of the Holy Sacrament to make their Indians over to himself. The Governor, who knew his fellow-countrymen, flatly refused, and upon this Don Bernardino fell into a fury, and reproached him with such bitterness that Don Gregorio, too, overstepped the bounds of prudence, and threw the conduct of his nephew with the `jeune femme bien faite' into the Bishop's teeth.

Hell has been said to have no fury equal to a woman scorned, but a Bishop thwarted makes a very tolerable show. Don Bernardino was one of those who think an insult to themselves carries with it a challenge to God, an outrage on religion, and generally conceive the honour of Heaven is attacked by any contradiction of themselves. To animadvert upon the actions of a Bishop's nephew is as bad as heresy — far worse than simony — and the man who does it cannot but be a heretic at heart. So, at least, Don Bernardino thought; for, with candle, bell, and book, and what was requisite, he excommunicated the poor Governor, and declared him incompetent to bear the royal standard in a religious festival which was shortly to take place. Excommunication was at least as serious then as bankruptcy is now, though in Spanish America it did not carry with it such direful consequences as in European States.

Not wishing to use force, the Governor yielded the point, and did not trouble the procession. His moderate conduct gained him many partisans, and put many people against the Cardenas. The nephew, Pedro de Cardenas, thought it a good occasion to insult the Governor in public; so one day in the street he followed him, casting reflections on his mother and his female relatives. Don Gregorio, who was a man of tried courage, having served for years against the Indians of Arauco, the bravest race of all the Indians of America, controlled his temper, and, turning to the young Franciscan, said, `Go with God, my father; but do not try me any more.' It was not to be expected that in those times and such a place a man like Don Gregorio de Hinostrosa, who had passed his life upon the frontiers, and who held supreme authority, would quietly submit to such a public insult; so one night he appeared at the Bishop's palace, accompanied by soldiers, to arrest Don Pedro. Out came Cardenas, and excommunicated the Governor and all his soldiers on the spot, and Don Pedro pointed a pistol at his head. He, seeing himself obliged either to make a public scandal or retire, being for peace at any price, retired, and the triumphant Bishop published his edict of excommunication, which he extended with a fine of fifty crowns to every soldier who had been present at the scene. On reflection, thinking, perhaps, it was unwise to excommunicate so many soldiers, who might be needed to repel an Indian attack, he sent and told the Governor he was ready to absolve him upon easy terms. The Governor, who had made light of the first excommunication, was rather staggered when he found the second posted at the Cathedral door. And now a comedy ensued; for Don Gregorio went to the Bishop, and on his knees asked for forgiveness. He, taken unawares, also knelt down, and, when the Governor kissed his hand, wished to return the compliment, and would have done so had the rector of the Jesuit college not prevented him.

As Charlevoix says, `to see them on their knees, no one could have imagined which one it was who asked the other's grace.' The Bishop granted absolution to the Governor; but the soldiers' action had been flat sacrilege at least, for every one of them was forced to pay the fine.

Two excommunications in a week were almost, one would think, enough to satisfy a Pope; but having nominated one Diego Hernandez, a Portuguese, to the post of Alguacil Mayor of the Inquisition, and given him the right to wear a sword in virtue of his office, the Governor, meeting the man in the street wearing a sword against his regulations, made him a prisoner. At once Don Bernardino launched another excommunication. But this time he had gone too far; the Governor laughed at his thunder, and condemned the prisoner to be hanged. At his wits' end, the Bishop sent a servant to the man, and told him to fear nothing, for that, if he suffered death, he was a martyr, and that he himself would preach his funeral sermon. The Governor, who was perhaps a humorist, laughed at the message, which, he said, was not consoling, and then himself let Hernandez out of prison under heavy bail. The excommunication was then taken off, and peace once more reigned in Asuncion.

As well as being not given to wine, it is essential that a Bishop shall know how to keep his own counsel — as Lorenzo Gracian expresses it,[119] `not to lie, but not for that to speak out always the whole truth.' Everyone who knew the Bishop and his hasty temper was astonished at his behaviour to the Jesuits. No one imagined he had forgotten the attitude the rector of the University of Cordova had assumed towards his consecration, and still the Bishop seemed to show more favour to the Jesuits in Asuncion than to the members of the other religious communities. Perhaps he felt the want of partisans amongst the educated classes, for his quarrel with the Governor had lost him many friends. Certainly in Asuncion it was of great importance that the Jesuits should not declare against him openly.

He praised them fulsomely both in the pulpit and in conversation, went in procession to their church, and treated them in public with marked consideration. As a contemporaneous Jesuit has left a record, they were not his dupes, but still endeavoured to live up to the praises he dispensed to them. He went so far as in a letter to the King, Philip IV., to say that the Jesuits only in all Paraguay were really fitted to have the care of Indians, and he advised the King to transfer the Indians who were under other religious bodies, as well as those under the secular clergy, to the care and guidance of that Order. No doubt in this the Bishop was right, even if not sincere. One of the qualifications the Jesuits had for the care of Indians was that the Indians did not look on them as Spaniards.

As in the same way that in Matabeleland, perhaps, a German, Frenchman, or Italian is less hateful to the natives than an Englishman, so in Paraguay the Indians liked the Jesuits better than the other Orders, for there were many foreigners amongst their ranks. The Jesuits soon comprehended that the Bishop wished to make them odious to the public by overpraise. To set to work in such a manner almost requires an early training in a seminary, and that such tactics should have been put in force against such skilled diplomatists as were the Jesuits argues no ordinary capacity for diplomatic work in Cardenas. With him, however, the Spanish proverb, 'Betwixt the word and deed the space is great', had little application. The vicar of a place called Arecayá, close to Asuncion, had fallen into disgrace; the Bishop removed him from his parish, and asked the rector of the Jesuit college to send a priest to take his place. The answer he received was politic, and to the effect that there was no Jesuit who could be spared, and even if there was it ill-befitted any Jesuit to infringe upon the duties of the secular clergy; but that, if Cardenas intended to found a new reduction with all the privileges that the King had always given to that kind of establishment, the rector himself would ask permission from his Provincial to undertake the work. A splendid answer, and one which proved that the man who gave it was a man wasted in Paraguay, and that his place by rights was Rome or, at the least, some court.

Don Bernardino, who in matters such as these was quite as cunning as the rector, thanked him, and said he did not want a saint, but a priest to take the duty of another priest for a short time. The rector, seeing his diplomacy had failed, told Father Mansilla, who was at Itatines, to transfer himself to Arecayá, and, writing to the Bishop, told him that he had no doubt Mansilla would do all that was fitting in the case. The Bishop, who had gained his point and saw no further use for diplomacy, said: 'Of that I am quite sure, and if he does not I shall excommunicate him, and lay the district of the Itatines under an interdict.' Nothing appeared to give Don Bernardino such unmitigated pleasure as an excommunication; on the slightest protest he was ready, so that during his episcopate someone or other in Asuncion must have always been under the ban of Holy Mother Church. The rector felt instinctively that Don Bernardino had not done with him. This was the case, for soon another order came to send two Jesuits to undertake the guidance of a mission near Villa Rica. As at the time the Jesuits had no missions near Villa Rica, the order was most unpleasant to him. Firstly, the two who went — Fathers Gomez and Domenecchi — had to leave their missions and undertake a lengthy journey in the wilds. On reaching Villa Rica, they found not only that the inhabitants looked on them with great disfavour as interlopers, but that the Indians, whom they were sent to guide, were under the *encomienda* system, thus forcing them to wink at that which they disapproved. The resolution that they took did them great honour; it was to leave the town of Villa Rica and live out in the forests with the Indians.

The Jesuits of the college at Asuncion felt the situation keenly. People began to murmur at them for their invasion of the spiritual domains of others, and the rector, in despair, sent to the Bishop, and begged him not to praise them in his sermons. Nothing cost Cardenas so little as to promise, so he promised not to mention them again, and next time that he preached he spent an hour in telling of the wonders that the Jesuits had done in saving souls, not only amongst Catholics, but also amongst the infidels and Turks. The tactics of the Bishop were so marked that at last a rumour reached Don Melchior Maldonado, the Bishop of Tucuman, of whom Don Bernardino always stood in dread. His letter somehow became public, and as in it he spoke most warmly of the Jesuits, and praised the rector, the public turned again upon their side. Just at this time, however, the sleeping feud between the Bishop and the Governor broke out anew with so much fury that attention was directed from the Jesuits for the time being; but on them the situation still was hung, and both sides made advances to them for support.

Chapter V

Renewal of the feud between the Bishop and Don Gregorio — Wholesale excommunications in Asuncion — Cardenas in 1644 formulates his celebrated charges against the Jesuits — The Governor, after long negotiations and much display of force, ultimately succeeds in driving out the Bishop — For three years Cardenas is in desperate straits — In 1648 Don Gregorio is suddenly dismissed, Cardenas elects himself Governor, and for a short time becomes supreme in Asuncion — The Jesuits are forced to leave the town and to flee to Corrientes — A new Governor is appointed in Asuncion — He defeats Cardenas on the field of battle — The latter is deprived of his power, and dies soon after as Bishop of La Paz

The Governor, like a prudent soldier, was biding his time. The Bishop, not yet strong enough to walk alone, dared not break openly with the Jesuits. Don Pedro Cardenas still following up his evil courses, poor Don Gregorio Hinostrosa, accustomed all his life to deal with `officers and gentlemen', thought fit to bring this under his uncle's notice. The Bishop spoke to his nephew in a paternal fashion, enjoining certain penances upon him, and amongst others that he was to kiss the earth. Although Don Pedro Cardenas was not a man accustomed to lavish kisses on things inanimate, he complied, but, though complying, still pursued his vicious course.

Quite in the manner of King Charles (of pious memory), the Governor determined to arrest the recalcitrant with his own hand. Armed to the teeth, and with a band of musketeers accompanying him, he appeared before the convent of St. Francis, where Father Cardenas had taken refuge, and, dragging him from his bed, haled him incontinently to the river's bank, and left him gagged and bound, a prey to flies and sun, for two whole days, dressed in his drawers and shirt. On the third day he was embarked in a canoe for Corrientes, with a small quantity of jerked beef for all provision, and a woman's cloak wrapped round his shoulders to shield him from the cold. Not quite the guise in which a clergyman would care to appear before the eyes of his superiors, even in Paraguay. Naturally, the Bishop, having nothing else to do, got out his excommunication in his usual style, but no man marked him.

Meantime Asuncion was in confusion, the Bishop and the Governor keeping no measure with the other man of sin. One tried to obtain possession of the other's person to throw him into prison; the other strove to animate the preachers in the various churches to consign his rival's soul to hell. In the deserted streets drums thundered, whilst in the air bells jangled, and the quiet, sleepy town was rent in twain by the dissensions of the opposing powers. The churches closed their doors, and the consolations of religion were withdrawn from those who wanted them.

To add to the confusion, Don Pedro Cardenas escaped from Corrientes, and, having taken to himself a companion — one Francisco Sanchez de Carreras — raged through the city like a devil unchained. In his extremity, the poor Bishop went to the Jesuits for advice, informing them he could not stand the scandals that were taking place, and that he intended to leave the city after launching an interdict of excommunication upon all. Placed in the position of declaring openly either for Bishop or for Governor, the Jesuits refused an answer, knowing that anything they said would be brought up against them. All their advice to him was, `to trust in God, to persevere in his good efforts, to resign himself to divine will, which will, as the Bishop knew full well, worked sometimes in a mysterious fashion for the welfare of the soul.' The Bishop answered this advice `fort sèchement',[120] taking it for a reproach, and as a sort of thing not to be tolerated amongst professionals — as if one lawyer, having gone to another for his advice upon a private matter, had received for answer a lecture on conveyancing or a short treatise upon Roman Law.

Still, the occasion called for something to be done; so, calling an Indian servant, he stripped to the waist, and, to the horror and amazement of the public, appeared with naked feet and shoulders, dressed in a sack and armed with a heavy scourge. At the first blow he gave himself some canons of the Cathedral begged him to desist; but he, after prayer, replied that he intended, so to speak, to act as his own Pascal lamb, and wipe out the affront done to St. Francis in his unworthy blood.

A naked Bishop in a sack is almost sure to attract some observation even in Paraguay. Religious women not unfrequently have been attracted by such a spectacle, and so it proved on this occasion. Although the Jesuits and the saner portion of the population blamed the Bishop's action, he made himself a host of partisans amongst the women of all classes, who followed him as they have often followed other thaumaturgists in times present and gone by.

His friend Don Melchior Maldonado, hearing what had passed, wrote to reprove him for his inconsiderate zeal. In his epistle he observed that, though some of the Apostles had scourged themselves, it was not their habit to appear half naked before a crowd of women; that our Lord Himself had not of His own accord taken off His garments for the scourger; that saints who scourged themselves had, as a general rule, chosen a private place for their self-discipline. This was quite reasonable, but the advice was little to the taste of the recipient, who hated criticism when levelled at himself.

If crosses make a saint, about this time Don Bernardino had his full share of them. News came from Itatines, where the two Jesuits had been marooned, that both of them were ill. Cardenas, who, we may remember, was *homme à visions*, called in the rector of the Jesuit college to inform him that the Company of Jesus had a new martyr in their ranks. Though martyrs (even to-day) enter the ranks of General Loyola's army pretty frequently, it still seemed strange that the Bishop should know of this particular recruit before the rector. Pressed for an explanation, he replied that a pious person who was vouchsafed communication with the Lord in prayer had seen Father Domenecchi in heaven shining in glory and with a halo round his head.

Nothing could be more satisfactory. All the essentials of a well-attested miracle had been complied with. A man was dead, another man had seen the dead man in an ecstasy of prayer, and, to make all complete, refused to testify himself, sending the Bishop as a sort of pious phonograph. No true believer in such a case could doubt, and all went well till it appeared a man from Itatines, charged with a message to the Jesuit college, had passed the night before he gave his message at the Bishop's house. In Holy Writ we read the wicked man shall have no rest; if this is so, it is as it should be, though generally the good seem just as troubled in their lives as the most erring of their brethren. He who would be a saint must be a-doing, year in, year out, just like a common workman, and Cardenas was no exception to the rule.

The pseudo-miracle not having been quite a success, he turned to other fields, and summoned all the inhabitants of Paraguay to attend at the Cathedral upon a certain day. The Governor, thinking there was a revolution likely to break out, fixed a review of all the troops for the same date. A Jesuit priest waited upon the Bishop to persuade him that the crowds which would assemble might break the peace. The Bishop reassured him, and sent him to the Governor to say that his intention was to preach to the people and explain to them the faith; further, that he intended on that day to raise his excommunication and be reconciled: only he asked him to allow the troops to attend and hear his sermon. The crowd was great; the Bishop mounted the pulpit, and, extending his forefinger in the attitude of malediction so dear to Bishops, straight began to preach. For a time all went well. The Governor, presumably, was waiting for the circulation of the hat — that awful mystery which makes all sects kin — when to his horror Cardenas began to enumerate all his offences: he was anathema, was excommunicated, a disbeliever, and had endeavoured to cast down that which the Lord Himself had set on high. The Bishop then informed the crowd that God was angry with the Governor, talked about Moses, and dwelt with unction on the fact that the great lawgiver had been swift to slay.

In a peroration which, no doubt, went home to all, he called upon his hearers, under penalty of a heavy fine and his displeasure, to seize the Governor, adding that if there was resistance 'he should kill his brother, his friend, or his nearest relative.'[121] After these words he seized a banner from the hands of the astonished officer who stood nearest to him, and stood forth, like another Phineas, surrounded by his clergy, all of whom had arms beneath their cloaks.

A most dramatic scene, and probably almost successful, had but the Bishop only reckoned with two things: Firstly, he had forgotten that the Governor was an old Indian fighter, and ready for surprises; and, secondly, he had not taken into account the usual apathy of the common people when their leaders fight. Dumbly and quite unmoved the people stood, staring like armadillos at a snake, and made no sign. Then word was brought that the Governor had left the church and was assembling a force of arquebusiers.

Surrounded only by clergymen, Don Bernardino had to yield, and yielded like a Levite, with a subterfuge. He sent a priest to beg the magistrates to come to the Cathedral and reason with him. After a consultation this was done, and Cardenas consented to abate his fury and exhale his wrath. He said that Holy Writ itself gave leave to recur to force in self-defence (but did not quote the text), and that the Governor had meditated a like enterprise against himself; moreover, that, he being an excommunicated man, it became lawful for God's vicegerent to lay hold on him.

After the scene was over, and the Bishop was escorted back to his palace by the magistrates, a second letter came from Tucuman making plain his conduct to him after the manner of a friend. The rector of the Jesuits also thought fit to remonstrate, and say that Cardenas had gone too far in attempting to assume the temporal power. This sufficed to further strain the relations between the Bishop and the Jesuits.

As, even in Asuncion in 1643, it was unusual that the Governor should remain for ever under the ban of Holy Mother Church, arbiters were chosen to discuss the matter, and provide means whereby the Bishop could conveniently climb down. The arbiters absolved the Governor on the condition that he paid a fine of four thousand arrobas[122] of *yerba maté*, which in money amounted to eight thousand crowns. Quite naturally, the Bishop refused to abide by the decision, replaced his adversary under the ban, and recommenced to preach against him with considerable force.

The higgling of the market not having proved effectual in the adjustment of the sum to be paid by the Governor, a priest, one Juan Lozano, who had been condemned to imprisonment by his superiors for his loose life, and who had taken refuge with the Bishop, hit on a stroke of veritable genius. At a conference which took place between the Bishop and several notables of the place, including the rector of the Jesuits, Lozano gave it as his opinion that, if the Governor refused to pay, a general interdict should be proclaimed.

The rector of the Jesuits retired indignantly, and `Père Lozano, retroussant sa robe le poursuivit en criant à pleine tête, et s'exprimant en des termes peu seans à sa profession.'[123] By this time Asuncion must have been like a madhouse, for no one seems to have been astonished, or even to have thought his conduct singular. The Bishop, always ready to take the worst advice, got ready for his task, and on Easter Eve embarked upon the river, leaving his Vicar-General under orders to proclaim the general ban. This was done, and the edict so contrived as to catch the luckless Governor in every church. The practical effect was to close all the churches, for to whatever church the Governor went the priest refused to celebrate the Mass. Several other persons were mentioned in the ban, which was posted up below a crucifix in the choir of the Cathedral. As Don Bernardino had omitted to state the particular offences for which they were condemned, the general confusion became intense, and no one attended Mass, so that the churches were deserted. After a little some of the churches opened in a clandestine manner, others remained closed, and the followers of the Bishop and the Governor alternately assembled in a rabble, and threw stones at all the churches, dispensing their favours quite impartially. The various religious Orders, not to be behindhand, also took sides, the Jesuits giving as their opinion that the Governor, not having a war upon his back, was really excommunicated; the Dominicans holding that the Bishop, in the general interest, ought to absolve him. He, armed with the opinion of the latter Order, marched to the dwelling of the Bishop's Vicar-General, and, having nailed up both doors and windows, sent a trumpeter to tell him he should not leave his house till absolution had been granted. Still nothing came of it, and then the Governor did what he should have done at first: he sent a statement of the whole proceedings to the high court at Charcas. This high court (Audiencia) was situated right in the middle of what is now Bolivia, miles away from Lima, half a world from Paraguay, at least two thousand miles from Buenos Ayres, and separated from Chile by the whole Cordillera of the Andes. Even to-day the journey from Paraguay often exceeds a month.

The Bishop, not to be outdone, also prepared a statement, in which he accused his adversary of all the crimes that he could think of, and confirmed his statement with an oath. The chapter, thinking things were in an impossible condition, besought that the fine laid on the excommunicated folk should be raised or lessened, as it appeared to them there was not money in the town to satisfy it. Cardenas refused, and thus four months elapsed. Soon after this arrived one Father Truxillo, of the Order of St. Francis, who came from Tucuman as Vice-Provincial. Cardenas, thinking, as they were both Franciscans, that Truxillo must needs be favourable to his cause, made him his Vicar-General, with power to bind and to unloose — that is, to free the excommunicated folk from all their disabilities if, on examination, it seemed good to him. Truxillo, who was quite unbiassed as to matters in

Asuncion, looked into everything, and declared the Governor and everybody ought to be absolved. He further gave it as his opinion that, the affair having gone to the high court at Charcas, he could do nothing but give an interim decree. Don Bernardino heard the news at Itati, an Indian village a few miles outside Asuncion. From thence he went to a somewhat larger village called Yaguaron, and shut himself up in a convent, after declaring everyone (except the superior clergy) under the severest censure of the Church if they should dare approach. Not a bad place for prayer and meditation is Yaguaron. A score or two of little houses, built of straw and wood and thatched with palm-leaves, straggle on the hillside above the shores of a great camalote-covered[124] lake. Parrots scream noisily amongst the trees, and red macaws hover like hawks over the little patches of maize and mandioca planted amongst the palms. Round every house is set a grove of orange-trees, mingled with lemons, sweet limes, and guayabas. Inside the houses all is so clean that you could eat from any floor with less repulsion than from the plates at a first-class hotel. A place where life slips on as listless and luxuriant as the growth of a banana, and where at evening time, when the women of the place go to fetch water in a long line with earthen jars balanced upon their heads, the golden age seems less improbable even than in Theocritus. To Yaguaron the higher clergy flocked to intercede for the good people of Asuncion, all except Father Truxillo, who, knowing something of his Bishop, did not go. That he was wise, events proved shortly. Two canons — Diego Ponce de Leon and Fernando Sanchez — he imprisoned in their rooms, calling them traitors to their Bishop and their Church. Deputations came from the capital to beg for their release, but all in vain. The Bishop answered them that he had set his mind to purge his diocese of traitors; and the two canons remained in prison. After a detention which lasted forty days, they escaped and fled to Corrientes, which must have looked upon Asuncion as a vast madhouse. Truxillo, who seems to have been a man not quite so absolutely devoid of sense as the other clergy, endeavoured to organize a religious *coup d'état*; but, most unfortunately, a letter he had written to some of the saner clergy fell into the Bishop's hands. Excommunications now positively rained upon the land. The Governor, the Jesuits, the Dominicans, each had their turn; but, curiously enough, the poorer people still stood firm to Cardenas, thinking, no doubt, a man who treated all the richer sort so harshly must do something for the poor. Nothing, however, was further from the thoughts of Cardenas, who thought the whole world circled round himself. The Bishop's nephew having returned to Corrientes and his former naughty life, Don Bernardino, casting about for another secretary, came on one Francisco Nieto, an apostate from the Order of St. Francis, and living openly with an Indian woman, by whom he had a son. Him the Bishop made his chaplain, then his confessor; and poor Nieto found himself obliged to send his Indian wife away in spite of all his protests and his wish to live obscurely as he had been living before his elevation to the post of secretary. A veritable beachcomber Father Francisco Nieto seems to have been, and the type of many a European in Paraguay, who asks no better than to forget the tedium of our modern life and pass his days in a little palm-thatched hut lost in a clearing of a wood or near some lake.

So in Asuncion things went from bad to worse. Such trade as then existed was at a standstill, and bands of starving people swarmed in the streets, whilst the incursions of the savage Indians daily became more frequent. In fact, Asuncion was but a type of what the world would be under the domination of any of the sects without the counterpoise of any civil power. The Governor, seeing the misery on every side, determined, like an honest man, to pocket up his pride and reconcile himself with Cardenas at any price. So, setting forth with all his staff, he came to Yaguaron. There, like a penitent, he had to bear a reprimand before the assembled village and engage to pay a fine before the rancorous churchman would relieve him from the ban. The weakness of the Governor had the effect that might have been expected, and heavy fines were laid on all and sundry who had in any manner displeased the Bishop or leaned to the other side in the course of the dispute.

Right in the middle of the struggle between the clerical and lay authorities, a band of over three hundred Guaycurús appeared before the town. Unluckily, all the chief officers of the garrison were excommunicated, and thus incapable of doing anything to defend the place. Foolish as Cardenas most indubitably was, his folly did not carry him so far as to leave the capital of his diocese quite undefended. Still, he would not give way first, and only at the moment when the Indians seemed prepared to attack the town, at the entreaty of a `pious virgin', he raised the excommunication on the Governor and his officers for fifteen days. The Governor, instead of, like a sensible man, seizing the Bishop and giving him to the *cacique* of the Guaycurús, led out his troops and drove the Indians off. That very night he found himself once more under the censure of the Church, and the conflict with his opponent more bitter than at first. The Viceroy of Peru, the Marquis of Mancera, indignant at the weakness of the Governor, wrote sharply to him, reprimanding him and telling him at once to assert himself and force the Bishop to confine himself to matters spiritual. On the Governor's attempt to reassert himself, the answer was a general interdict laying the entire capital under the Church's ban. On this, he marched to Yaguaron with all his troops, resolved to take the Bishop prisoner; but he, seeing the troops approach, went out at once, fell on the Governor's neck, and straightway absolved him.

After the absolution came a banquet, which must have been a little constrained, one might imagine, and even less amusing than the regulation dinner-party of the London season, where one sits between two half-naked and perspiring women eating half-raw meat and drinking fiery wines with the thermometer at eighty in the shade. Thus disembarrassed from the Governor, Don Bernardino turned his attention to the Jesuits, and signified to them that he intended to take the education of the young out of their hands. This was a mortal affront to the Jesuits, as they have always understood that men, just as the other animals, can only learn whilst young. Hard upon this new step, Cardenas issued an edict forbidding them to preach or hear confessions. As for the Governor, the Bishop did not fear him, and the poorer people of Asuncion had always inclined to the Bishop's party, either through terror of the Church's ban or from their natural instinct that the Bishop was against the Government.

But Cardenas saw clearly that, to deal as he wished with the Jesuits, he must entirely gain the Governor's confidence. This he tried to do by sending to him one Father Lopez, Provincial of the Dominicans. This Lopez was an able and apparently quite honest man, for he told the Governor that the wish of Cardenas was to expel the Jesuits from Paraguay, and from their missions, warning him at the same time not to allow himself to be made use of by the Bishop in his design. From that moment the two adversaries seemed to have changed characters, and Don Gregorio became as cautious as a churchman, whereas the Bishop seemed to lose all his diplomacy.

To all the protestations of friendship which were addressed to him, the Governor answered so adroitly that the Bishop fell into the trap, and thought he had secured a partner to help him in the expulsion of the Jesuits. Finally, at Yaguaron, during a sermon, he formulated his celebrated charges against the Jesuits, which, set on foot by him in 1644, eventually caused the expulsion of the whole Order from America, and, though refuted a thousand times, still linger in the writing of all those who treat the question down to the present day. The charges were seven in number, and so ingeniously contrived that royal, national, and domestic indignation were all aroused by them. The first was that the Jesuits prevented the Indians from paying[125] their annual taxes to the crown. Secondly, that the Jesuits kept back the tithes from Bishops and Archbishops.[126] Thirdly, he said the Jesuits had rich mines in their possession, and that the product of these mines was all sent out of the country to the general fund at Rome. This the Jesuits disproved on several occasions, but, as often happens in such cases, proof was of no avail against the folly of mankind, to whom it seemed incredible that the Jesuits should bury themselves in deserts to preach to savages, unless there was some countervailing advantage to be gained. Even the fact that at the expulsion of the Company of Jesus from America no treasure at all was found at any of their colleges or missions did not dispel the conviction that they owned rich mines. The fourth charge was that the Jesuits were not particular about the secrets of the confessional, and that they used the information thus acquired for their own selfish ends. Further, that Father Ruiz de Montoya had acquired from the King, under a misapprehension, a royal edict,[127] giving the territory of the missions to the Jesuits, thus taking the fruits of their conquest from the Spanish colonists. Fifthly, that the Jesuits entered Paraguay possessed but of the clothes upon their backs, that they had made themselves into the sovereign rulers of a great territory, but that he was going to expel them, as the Venetians had expelled them from Venetia.[128] Sixthly, that even the Portuguese of San Paulo de Piritinanga had expelled them.[129] His last assertion was that he himself, together with the Bishop of Tucuman and others, had secret orders from the King to expel the Jesuits from their dioceses, but that the other Bishops lacked the courage which he (Cardenas) was then about to show. He wound up all by saying that, once the Jesuits were gone, the King would once again enjoy his rights, the Church be once again restored to freedom, and, lastly, that there would be plenty of Indians for the settlers to enslave. Quite possibly enough, the public, ever generous to a fault with other people's goods, cared little for the rights of a King who lived ten thousand miles away; and as for the Church, it seems most probable they failed to see the peril that she ran. But when the Bishop spoke of enslaving the Indians, they saw the Jesuits must go, for from the conquest the Jesuits had stood between the settlers and their prey. All things considered, Don Bernardino made a remarkable discourse that Sunday morning in the palm-thatched village by the lake, for the echo of it still resounds in the religious world against the Jesuits.

Like other men after a notable pronouncement, it is most probable that Cardenas was unaware of the full import of his words. Perhaps he thought (as speakers will) that all the best portions of his sermon had been left unsaid. Be that as it may, he shortly turned his thoughts to other matters of more direct importance to himself. In judging of his life, it should not be forgotten that, by his sermon at Yaguaron, he placed himself upon the side of those who wanted to enslave the Indians. Perhaps he did not know this, and certainly his popularity amongst the Indians outside the missions was enormous. His next adventure was to try and eject the Jesuits from a farm they had, called San Isidro. The Governor having forbidden him to do so, he armed an army of his partisans to expel the Jesuits from their college in the capital.

Outside Asuncion the Lieutenant-Governor, Don Francisco Florez, met the Bishop's secretary, Father Nieto, who informed him of the enterprise, exhorting him to enlist the sympathies of the Governor in so good a cause. Florez, a better diplomatist than his commanding officer, seemed to approve, and naturally deceived poor Father Nieto, who, like most hypocrites, became an easy prey to his own tactics when used against himself.

Florez informed the Governor at once, and he sent to the Jesuits, and put them on their guard. Next day he met the Bishop, and told him that his enterprise could not succeed, as the Jesuits were under arms. No doubt he learned these artifices in his campaigns against the Indians of Arauco, or it may have been that, like others who have had to strive with churchmen, he learned to beat them with their own controversial arms. The Bishop fell completely into the snare, and, thinking the Governor was a fast friend, confided all his plans to him for the expulsion of the Jesuits and the conquest of the mission territory. Just then Captain Don Pedro Diaz del Valle came from La Plata, and gave Don Bernardino a new decision of the High Court of Charcas, telling him to live in peace with all men, and govern his diocese with zeal. He certainly was zealous to an extraordinary degree, if not judicious. Therefore, the very mention of the word `zeal' must have been peculiarly offensive to such a zealous man. The letter went on to say that all the fines he had exacted were illegal, and commanded him to give back the *yerba* which he had extorted from his involuntary penitents, and in the future live on better terms with all around him. To all of this he paid no notice, as was to be expected, but, to avoid returning the *yerba*, sent a letter to his officers to have it burned. This letter, which he denied, was subsequently produced against him in the High Court at Charcas.

Seeing the Governor was bent on frustrating or on deceiving him, he tried to get from Don Sebastian Leon, who held an office under the Governor, an edict of the Emperor Charles V., which he had heard was in the archives, and which provided that, in case a Governor should die or be deposed, the notables of the place had power to appoint an interim Governor to fill his place. If such a paper ever existed, it must have been a very early document given by Charles V. at the foundation of the colony, for nothing was more opposed to the traditions of Spanish policy throughout America. Don Sebastian Leon having informed the Governor, the latter saw that things were coming to a crisis, and that either he or the Bishop would have to leave the place. Not being sure of all his troops, and the Bishop having the populace upon his side, he sent to the Jesuit missions for six hundred Indians. Thus the supremacy of the royal government fell to be supported by men but just emerging from a semi-nomad life, who owed the tincture of civilization they possessed to the calumniated Jesuits.

On many occasions armies of Indians from the Jesuit missions rendered important services to the crown of Spain: not only against the Portuguese, but against English corsairs, and in rebellions, as in the case of Cardenas; or as when, in the year 1680, Philip V. wrote to the Governor of Buenos Ayres to garrison the port with a contingent of Indians from the Jesuit reductions; in 1681, when the French attacked the port with a squadron of four-and-twenty ships; and at the first siege of the Colonia, in 1678, when three thousand Indians marched to the attack, accompanied by their Jesuit pastors, but under the command of Spanish officers.[130]

An army from the Jesuit missions consisted almost entirely of cavalry. It marched much like a South American army of twenty years ago was wont to march. In front was driven the *caballada*, consisting of the spare horses; then came the vanguard, composed of the best mounted soldiers, under their *caciques*. Then followed the wives and women of the soldiers, driving the baggage-mules, and lastly some herdsmen drove a troop of cattle for the men to eat. When Jesuits accompanied the army, they did not enter into action, but were most intrepid in succouring the wounded under fire, as Funes, in his `Historia Civil del Paraguay', etc.,[131] relates when speaking of their conduct at the siege of the Colonia in 1703. For arms they carried lances, slings, *chuzos* (broad-pointed spears), lazos, and bolas, and had amongst them certain very long English guns with rests to fire from, not very heavy, and of a good range. Each day the accompanying Jesuits said Mass, and each town carried its particular banner before the troop. They generally camped, if possible, in the open plain, both to avoid surprises and for convenience in guarding the cattle and the *caballada*. In all the territories of South America no such quiet and well-behaved soldiery was to be found; for in Chile, Peru, Mexico, and Guatemala, the passage of an army was similar to the passing of a swarm of locusts in its effect.

Don Bernardino, on his side, was occupied in animating the populace against the Jesuits with all the fervour of an Apostle. Naturally, he first commenced by launching his usual sentence of excommunication against them, and having done so returned again to Yaguaron. This village, like other Paraguayan villages, many of which in times gone by have been the scenes of stirring episodes, retains to-day but little to distinguish it. Nature has proved too powerful in the long-run for men to fight against. On every side the woods seem ready to overwhelm the place. Grass grows between the wooden steps of the neglected church; seibos, lapachos, espinillos de olor, all bound together with lianas, encroach to the verges of the little clearings in which grows mandioca, looking like a field of sticks. All day the parrots scream, and toucans and picaflores dart about; at evening the monkeys howl in chorus; at night the jaguar prowls about, and giant bats fasten upon the incautious sleeper, or, fixing themselves upon a horse, leave him exhausted in the morning with the loss of blood.

When Cardenas used the place as a sort of Avignon from which to safely utter his anathemas, it must have worn a different aspect. No doubt processions and ceremonies were continual, with carrying about the saints in public, a custom which the Paraguayans irreverently refer to as `sacando á luz los bultos'.[132] Messengers (*chasquis*), no doubt, came and went perpetually, as is the custom in countries such as Paraguay, where news is valuable and horseflesh cheap. Thereto flocked, to a moral certainty, all the broken soldiers who swarmed in countries like Peru and Paraguay, with

Indian *caciques* looking out for work to do when white men quarrelled and throats were to be cut. Priests went and came, friars and missionaries; and Cardenas most certainly, who loved effect, gave all his emerald ring to kiss, and made those promises which leaders of revolt lavish on everyone in times of difficulty.

When the Indian contingent arrived, the Governor marched upon Yaguaron, although the air was positively lurid with excommunications. The Bishop, rushing to the church, was intercepted by the Governor, who seized his arm and tried to stop him. Cardenas struggled with him, and declared him excommunicated for laying his hand upon the anointed of the Lord. But, most unfortunately, there was no Fitz-Urse at hand to rid the Governor of so turbulent a priest. A mulatto[133] woman rushed to the Bishop's aid, together with some priests. This gave him time to gain the altar and seize the Host, which he exposed at once to the public gaze, and for the moment all present fell upon their knees. Turning to the Governor, he asked what he wanted with armed men in a church. The Governor replied he had come to banish him from Paraguay, by order of the Viceroy, for having infringed upon the temporal power. Cardenas, taken aback, replied he would obey, and, turning to the people, took them all for witnesses. The Governor, no doubt thinking he was dealing with an honest Araucan chief, retired. The Bishop immediately denounced the Governor in a furious sermon, after which he left the church, carrying the Host in full procession, accompanied by the choir singing the `Pange Lingua', followed by a band of Indian women with their hair dishevelled, and carrying green branches in their hands. He then returned to the church, and from the pulpit denounced the Governor, who, standing at the door surrounded by a group of arquebusiers blowing their matches, answered him furiously.

The honours, so to speak, being thus equally divided, it remained for one side or the other to negotiate. Cardenas, knowing himself much abler in negotiations than his adversary, proposed a conference, in which he bore himself so skilfully that he made the Governor consent to dismiss his Indians, and allow him six days to make his preparations for the road. This settled, at dead of night he set out for the capital. Arrived there, he showed himself in public in his green hat, having upon his breast a little box of glass in which he bore the Host. A band of priests escorted him, all with arms concealed beneath their cloaks, in the true spirit of the Church militant. The bells were rung, and every effort strained to raise a tumult, but all in vain. He had to throw himself for refuge into the convent of the Franciscans.

At once he set about to fortify the place to stand a siege. In several places he constructed embrasures for guns, and pierced the walls for musketry. But, thinking that his best defence lay in the folly of the people — as public men always have done, and do — he sent to the Cathedral for a statue of the

Blessed Virgin, and another of San Blas, and placed them at the gate. Then, remembering that calumny was a most serviceable weapon, he put about the town a report that the Indians from the missions had pillaged Yaguaron, and that they even then were marching on the place. Again recurring to the edict of Charles V., which he pretended to have found, he issued a proclamation that, as the present Governor was excommunicated, and therefore could not govern, the office being vacant, he intended to nominate another in his stead. His subsequent behaviour shows most clearly that he wished to nominate himself.

Again both sides sent off a relation of their doings to the High Court of Charcas. Don Bernardino wrote in his that the Jesuits had offered the Governor thirty thousand crowns, and placed a thousand men at his command, if he would expel the Bishop from the country, under the belief that he (Don Bernardino) knew of their hidden mines in the mission territory. His witnesses were students and priests, and one of these proving recalcitrant, the Bishop had him heavily chained, and then suspended outside the convent of the Franciscans.

This drastic treatment had the desired effect, as torture always has with reasonable men, and the poor witness signed, but afterwards protested, thus giving a good example in himself of the truth of the Spanish saying, `Protest and pay'.[134]

By this time the patience and long-suffering of the Governor were quite exhausted. He therefore sent to the Bishop to say a ship was ready to take him down the river, and at the same time reminded him of his promise at Yaguaron to obey the order of the Viceroy of Peru. He sent the message by the royal notary, Gomez de Coyeso, who accordingly repaired to the convent of San Francisco. At the door a priest appeared, armed with a javelin, who three times tried to wound the notary, on which the Governor stationed a band of fifty soldiers at the convent gate, in spite of the presence of the statues of the Blessed Virgin and San Blas. Then, having published an edict that the Bishop was deposed, he proceeded to elect another in his stead.

One of the canons, Don Cristobal Sanchez, who had governed the diocese during the interregnum before the advent of Don Bernardino, still lived in retirement near the town. The Governor approached him with the request that he would once more take the interim charge until the King should send another Bishop to replace Cardenas. Sanchez consented, on the understanding that the Governor would guarantee his personal safety. This being done, Sanchez was taken to the Jesuit college as the securest place.

So it fell out that everything concurred to strengthen the hatred of the Bishop to the Jesuits. To the Jesuit college came the Governor and all the notables, and, having taken Sanchez in procession through the streets, they placed him on the Bishop's throne in the Cathedral, and invested him with all the power that he had held before the coming of Don Bernardino Cardenas. The proclamation set forth by the Governor alluded to the informality of the consecration of Don Bernardino, and to his actions during his time of power.

At last the Bishop saw that he must go. So, after launching a supreme anathema, and after having expressed his great unwillingness to tarry longer in a city where half the population had incurred the censure of the Church, and marked with a cross those churches where he permitted Mass to be celebrated, he went on board the ship. Before embarking, he drew a silver bell from underneath his cloak, and to the sound of it he solemnly proclaimed the town accursed. The bells of the Franciscan convent and the Bishop's palace, according to his orders, all tolled loudly. This caused so much confusion that, in order to appease the tumult, the authorities ordered the bells of all the churches in the town to ring.

Entering the vessel, Don Bernardino sat himself upon the poop on a low stool, with all the clergy who were faithful to him grouped about the deck. With him he had the sacred wafer in a glass box, and not far off a group of sailors on the forecastle lounged about smoking and drinking *maté* whilst they played at cards. Someone reminded him it was not fitting that God's Body should thus be seen so near to sailors, and therefore the Bishop, according to the custom of the Church in cases of accident or desecration, consumed the offended wafer, and peace descended on the ship.

Thus, in 1644, he took his first departure from the place where for the last two years he had brought certainly rather a sword than peace. His friends assured the public that, at the moment he stepped on board the ship, stars were seen to fall from heaven towards the church of St. Luke, and passed from thence to the episcopal palace and disappeared; that at the same time a slight shock of earthquake had been experienced; that stones had danced about, and several hills had trembled. The sun, quite naturally, had appeared blood-red; trouble and desolation had entered every heart, and animals had prophesied woe and destruction, predicting ruin and misfortune to the town till the good Bishop should return once more.

The events of the past two years in Paraguay had not been favourable to the conversion of the Indians. Not only in the missions, where the neophytes had seen themselves obliged to furnish troops against their Bishop, but in the territory of Paraguay itself, the Indians had not had a good example of how Christians carry out the duties of their faith. As a general rule, the Indian (unlike the negro) cares little for dogma, but places his belief entirely in good works. Perhaps on this account the Jesuits, also believers in good works, have had the most success amongst them. Be that as it may, the Jesuits, after the departure of the Bishop, found that many of their recent converts had fallen away and gone back to the woods.

Whilst Jesuits in Paraguay were seeking to convert the Indians, and whilst the Governor, no doubt, was thanking his stars for the absence of his rival, in Rome the question of the Bishop's consecration filled all minds. From May 9, 1645, to October 2 of the same year no less than four congregations of the Propaganda had been held about the case. The Pope himself was present at one of them. Nothing was arrived at till 1658, when finally the consecration was declared in order, but not until Don Bernardino was appointed to another see.

Just about this time (1644-45) a rumour was set on foot that the Jesuits had discovered mines near their reductions on the Paraná. These rumours were always set about when there was nothing else by means of which to attack the Jesuits. An Indian by the name of Buenaventura, who had been a servant in a convent in Buenos Ayres, on this occasion was the instrument used by their enemies. For a short time everyone believed him, and excitement was intense; but, most unluckily, Buenaventura happened at the zenith of his notoriety to run away with a married woman, and, being pursued, was brought to Buenos Ayres, and then in public incontinently whipped. In any other country Buenaventura after his public whipping would have been discredited, but a letter arrived from the Bishop of Paraguay, telling the Governor of Buenos Ayres that the mines really existed. At that time a new Governor, one Don Jacinto de Lara, had just arrived. Being new to America and its ways, he started out himself to try the question, and with fifty soldiers, taking Buenaventura as his guide, went to the missions. As might have been expected, on the journey Buenaventura disappeared, this time alone. `Cette fuite lui donna beaucoup à penser,' says Charlevoix. But having gone so far, the Governor determined to try the question thoroughly.

Father Diaz Taño, one of the best and hardest-working missionaries who ever entered Paraguay, besought the Governor to satisfy himself and search their territory for gold and silver, and requested him to call upon the Bishop for confirmation of the statements he had made. This he did, and then, accompanied by his soldiers, began his search. He gave out that the first man to find a mine should be at once promoted to be captain and have a large reward. After several days' march, and having found no mines, letters were brought him from the Governor of Paraguay and from the Bishop. The first informed him that he had heard rumours of mines, but nothing certain. The second declined to specify the mines, which thus were destined to remain for ever, so to speak, *in partibus*. But he gave advice, and good advice is better than any mine, whether of silver or of gold. He told the Governor to start by turning out the Jesuits, and he would find the profits of their expulsion just as valuable as mines.

Whether this also made the Governor pensive I do not know, but, luckily, the Jesuits, who were concerned in exposing the imposture, had come on Buenaventura, and brought him ironed to the Governor. He, after having tried to make him confess his imposture without success, condemned him to be hung. The Jesuits, with their accustomed humanity (or ingenuity), begged for his life. This was accorded to them, and once again Buenaventura received a good sound whipping for his pains.

Thus ended the journey of Don Jacinto, without profit to himself, except so far as the experience gained. No doubt he saw and marked the Jesuit towns, the churches built of massive timber or of stone, and the contented air of Indians and priests, which always struck all travellers in those times. He saw the countless herds of cattle, the cultivated fields; enjoyed, no doubt for the first time since arriving in South America, the sense of perfect safety, at that time to be experienced alone in Misiones. But in despite of his exposure of the imposture, the rumour as to the existence of the mines never died out, and lingers even to-day, in spite of geological research in Paraguay.

Whilst this was going on in Misiones, in the remote and recently-converted district of the Itatines, in the north of Paraguay, the example set by the Bishop had borne its fruit. The Indians became unmanageable. One of the chiefs broke into open rebellion, and wounded a Jesuit father called Arenas at the very altar-steps. Soon the general corruption of manners became almost universal throughout the district. This, I fancy, must be taken to mean that the Indians reverted to polygamy, for the Jesuits always had trouble in this matter, being unable to persuade the Indians of the advantage of monogamy.

But most fortuitously, just as the general corruption gained all hearts, a tiger rushed into the town, and, after killing fourteen people and some horses, disappeared again into the woods.

The Jesuits, ever ready to take advantage of events like these, called on the Indians to see in the visitation of the tiger the wrath of Heaven, and to leave their wicked ways.

The Indians, always as willing to submit as to revolt, submitted, and the good fathers `prirent le parti de faire un coup d'autorité, qui leur réussit,' as Charlevoix relates.

They decoyed the chief, his nephew, and son, into another district, where they seized and shipped them off two hundred leagues to a remote reduction across the Uruguay. The Spaniards used to say of Ferdinand VII., when he had committed any great barbarity, `He is quite a King' (`Es mucho Rey'), and the Indians of the Itatines esteemed the Jesuits for their `coup d'autorité' in the same manner as the Spaniards their King.

His usual luck attended Cardenas in his exile in Corrientes. This town formed part of the diocese of Buenos Ayres, which happened to be vacant at the time. He therefore took upon himself to act just as he had acted in Paraguay — appointed officers of justice, held ordinations, and instituted a campaign against the Jesuits of the town.

Whilst he was thus occupied in his favourite pastime of usurping other people's functions, two citations were sent him to appear before the High Court of Charcas. He disregarded them, and sent a statement of his case by the hands of his nephew to the Bishop of Tucuman. In the letter he set forth all his complaints against the Governor of Paraguay, calling him a violator of the Church, a heretic, and generally applying to him all those terms in which a thwarted churchman usually exhales his rage. Mixed up with this was a detailed accusation of the Jesuits, to whose account he laid all his misfortunes whilst in Paraguay. Lastly, he called upon the Bishop of Tucuman to summon a provincial council to condemn the monstrous heresies which he attributed to the Jesuits, reminding him that the Council of Trent had recommended the holding of frequent provincial councils, and stating his opinion that, unless a council were called at once, the Bishop would incur a mortal sin.

The answer Cardenas received from Tucuman was most ironically couched in the best style that his long-suffering friend was able to command. After addressing Cardenas as `your illustrious lordship', he proceeded to demolish all his statements in such a manner as to argue that he had had much practice with refractory priests in his own diocese. He told him that the Jesuits were the only Order in Paraguay that really worked amongst the Indians. He reminded him that from that Order the `second Paul', *i.e.*, St. Francis Xavier, had himself issued. He asked him whether, as a churchman, he thought the yearly sum of twelve thousand crowns given by the King out of the treasury of Buenos Ayres towards the Jesuits' work was better saved, or that the thousands of Indians whom the Jesuits had converted should be lost to God. And as to heresy, he said he was no judge, leaving such matters to the Pope; but that no one accused the Jesuits of corruption in their morals, or of any of the greater crimes to which the great fragility of human nature renders us liable. He reminded him the Jesuits had made no accusation on their part, but always spoke of him with moderation and respect. And as to a provincial council, he said that it was impossible, for the following good cause: The Bishop of Misque[135] was too infirm to travel; the Bishop of La Paz was lately dead, and the see still vacant; the Bishop of Buenos Ayres only just arrived, and too much occupied to leave his diocese. Therefore, the only Bishops available were himself and Cardenas, and that they never would agree.

`Moreover,' he remarked, `what is it that your illustrious lordship wishes me to do?

`To advise a Bishop?

`God has only given me the charge of my own sheep. Your lordship knows as well as I do how a Bishop should comport himself.'

He finished with a quotation, saying that a Bishop's state was not to lie `in splendore vestium, sed morum; non ad iram, sed ut omnimodum patientium.'

What Cardenas replied is not set down in any history which has come under my observation, but what he must have thought is easy to divine.

The Governor of Paraguay, not content with having put his case before the Supreme Court of Charcas, sent also to the Council General of the Indies in Seville, detailing all the vagaries of the Bishop. The Jesuits also empowered an officer to represent them there.

During these preparations, and whilst everyone was off his guard, the Guaycurús endeavoured to surprise the capital, and would have done so had not some regiments of Guaranís arrived in time from the mission territory. This should have been an object-lesson to those who always tried to show the Jesuits in the light of enemies to the authority of the King of Spain. Nothing, however, proved of the least avail, and though on several occasions the Spanish power in Paraguay was only saved by the exertions of the Jesuits and their Indians, the calumnies of Cardenas had taken too deep root to be dispelled.

Meanwhile, in Corrientes, Cardenas schemed night and day to return to Paraguay. In his own city of La Plata naturally he had some friends, and these did all they could to get him reinstated. In spite of all their efforts, an order came from Charcas for him to leave the city under pain of banishment.[136] Anyone but Cardenas would have been disconcerted; he, though, pretended, as in the order he was still styled Bishop of Paraguay, that before leaving for Charcas, to present himself before the court, he had to go to Asuncion to name a Vicar-General, and towards the end of 1646 he embarked upon the river for Paraguay.

The Governor was on the alert, and sent a vessel with orders to turn him back, which order was carried out in spite of his remonstrances, and he returned to Corrientes in a miserable state.

Then came another citation to appear at Charcas, and an intimation that he was appointed Bishop of Popayán. As Popayán (in New Granada) was at least three thousand miles from Asuncion, his joy at the appointment must have been extreme.

His fortunes now seemed desperate; as he said himself in a letter to the King, `at an advanced age he could not undertake so great a journey'; and on every side his enemies seemed to have got the upper hand.

In 1648 a change came over everything. Don Gregorio Hinestrosa was removed from Paraguay, and a new Governor, Don Diego Escobar de Osorio, appointed in his place. Immediately the news reached Cardenas he set out for Paraguay. Arriving at Asuncion, his friends all met him and took him in procession to the Cathedral. His first thought was to renew his persecution of the Jesuits. Most unfortunately for them, Don Juan de Palafox, Bishop of Puebla de los Angeles in Mexico, who had himself in Mexico had many quarrels with the Jesuits, wrote begging Cardenas and all the Bishops of South America to join against them.

This Palafox was afterwards beatified, and even in his lifetime enjoyed the reputation of a saint, so that his letter greatly strengthened Cardenas. Notwithstanding this, Palafox in subsequent works of his during the time that he was Bishop of Osma (in Spain) said many things in praise of the work done by the Jesuits in Paraguay.

The new Governor, himself a member of the Supreme Court of Charcas, had never been before in Paraguay, and therefore resolved to treat the Bishop (as Don Gregorio had done) with every respect due to his station. The Bishop wanted nothing better, and saw at once he had another fool to deal with. Therefore he made no secret of his intention of not complying with the citation of the court at Charcas, and set himself at once to preach against the Jesuits, and stir up popular resentment against them. Unluckily, proof was wanting of the crimes he alleged they had committed, so he resorted to the device of getting a petition signed by all and sundry, asking for the expulsion of the Order from Paraguay. Like all petitions, it was largely signed by women and by children and by those who had never thought before about the matter, but liked the opportunity to write their names after the names of others, as sheep go through a gap or members give their votes (out of mere sympathy) in the high court of Parliament.

This device having taken too much time, blank documents were passed about for all to write upon whatever they imagined to the disadvantage of the Jesuits. By an untoward chance, a bundle of these, sent to the agent of the Bishop in Spain, was taken on the voyage by an English corsair. The worthy pirate (no doubt a Protestant) was, if we can believe the Jesuits, extremely scandalized at the bad faith of those who used such means of wreaking their malevolence.

So all seemed once again to smile upon Don Bernardino, who no doubt resumed his flagellations, his midnight services, and his saying of two Masses, and once again became the idol of the people of Asuncion.

But in the north, in the wild district of Caaguayu, hard by the mountains of Mbaracayá, close to the great *yerbales*,[137] the Jesuits had formed two towns amongst the Indians. These two towns were destined to be the outposts of the country against the incursions of the wild Indians from the Chaco.

The Bishop prevailed upon the Governor to let him turn out the Jesuits and replace them by priests of another Order. This being done, the Indians all deserted, leaving the district quite uninhabited.

The court at Charcas, hearing of this folly, sent an order to the Governor to send the Jesuits back. A year was passed in ceaseless searching of the woods and deserts for the Indians, but only half of the population could ever be persuaded to return, and Father Mansilla, the ex-missionary, died of the hardships that he underwent.

From that date down to the time of Dr. Francia (*circa* 1812-35), the district remained a desert. Francia used it as a penal settlement, and to-day, save for a few wild, wandering Indians, known as Caaguas, and a sparse population of *yerba*-gatherers, it still remains almost unpopulated.

Meanwhile, the general indignation against the Jesuits seemed to infect all classes of the population. Certainly, the citizens of Asuncion had good and sufficient causes of complaint against the Jesuits. On several occasions the efforts of the Jesuits and their Indians alone had saved the capital from the wild Indians, and benefits are hard to bear, if only from their rarity.

Popular hatred, to the full as idiotic as is popular applause, fell chiefly upon Father Diaz Taño — he who had saved ten thousand Indians for the King of Spain in his celebrated retreat before the Mamelucos down the Paraná — and he was frequently insulted in the streets. Father Antonio Manquiano, a quiet and learned man, was almost murdered in open day by a furious fanatic, who fell upon him with the openly expressed intent `to eat his heart'.

This was the moment Cardenas pitched on to declare the entire Order of the Jesuits excommunicated. As he had been a year away from the scene of his former exploits, people were not so used to excommunications, and therefore took them seriously.

At this eventful juncture the Governor, Don Diego, died so suddenly that suspicions of his having been poisoned were aroused. Scarce was he dead than all the population assembled at the palace to elect an interim successor. This was a most important thing, as to communicate with Spain took, at the very shortest time, about eight months. By acclamation the choice fell on the Bishop, who thus found himself head of the spiritual and the temporal power at once.

The election was absolutely illegal, as the Spanish law provided that, if a Governor of Paraguay should chance to die, the nomination of an interim successor should rest first with the Viceroy of Peru, and failing him with the High Court of Charcas.

Cardenas based his election on the pretended edict of the Emperor Charles V., but, if he had a copy of the edict, never produced it. As usual, 'good men daring not, and wise men caring not', but only fools and schemers taking part in the election, no serious opposition to his usurpation was encountered.

Cardenas never doubted for a moment that the function of a Governor was to govern, and he began at once to do so with a will.

Xarque, a Spanish writer, gives the following curious description of how he set about to get the people on his side to expel the Jesuits:[138]

Preaching one day in the Cathedral, after the consecration he turned towards the people, and, showing the holy wafer, said, 'Do you believe, my brethren, that Jesus Christ is here?' All, being true believers, answered as one man that such was their belief. In the same way as at a scientific lecture, when the lecturer holds up some substance, and says, 'You all know well that calcium tungstate or barium hydrocyanide has this or the other property,' the hearers nod assent like sheep, being afraid to contradict so glib a statement from so eminent a man.

Then said Cardenas, 'Believe as firmly that I have an order from the King to expel the Jesuits.' The people all believed, and Cardenas forgot to tell them that by the expulsion of the Jesuits twenty thousand Indians would pass into his power, whom he could then distribute amongst his friends as slaves, as he proposed to divide the Indians of the missions amongst the Paraguayan notables to win them to his side.

Being at the head of everything in Asuncion, Cardenas no longer hesitated, but ordered an officer, Don Juan de Vallejo Villasanti, with a troop of soldiers to march to the college of the Jesuits. This he did, and finding the gates all barred, he burst them open, and, entering the college, signified to the rector an order from the Governor (duly countersigned by the Bishop) to leave the city with all his priests, and to evacuate all the missions on the Paraná. The rector answered that the Jesuits had a permission from Philip II., renewed by his successors, to found a college, and Father Taño exhibited the documents. Villasanti, who had but little love for documents, snatched the parchments from his hand, and the soldiers forced the Jesuits in a body to the port like sheep. There they were tied and thrown into canoes almost without provisions, and sent off down the river to Corrientes, the certain haven of the party in Paraguay which has got the worst of an election or a revolution, and wishes to gain time.

Arrived in Corrientes, Don Manuel Cabral, a pious officer, received them in his house, and, curiously enough, the population welcomed the Jesuits with enthusiasm, and pressed them earnestly to build a college in the town.

Their college at Asuncion was treated like a town taken by storm: pulpit and font, confessionals and doors, all were torn down and burnt, and, with a view of justifying what was done, the Bishop's partisans spread a report that, as the Jesuits were heretics, their temple was unclean.

The population, more artistic in its instincts than the Bishop, refused to allow the altar, which had been brought from Spain, to be destroyed. Besides the altar, there were also statues of San Ignacio and San Francisco Xavier. These the Bishop wished to turn into St. Peter and St. Paul. With this design he gave them to an Indian carpenter to work upon. The poor man did his best, but only managed to turn out two monstrous blocks, which looked like nothing human.

A statue of the Blessed Virgin which had the eyes turned up to heaven the Bishop wished to alter, and replace the head by another with the eyes turned down to earth, as being more befitting to the statue's sex. The people, less mad or superstitious than the Bishop, refused to allow it, and the image, too, was placed in the Cathedral.

In 1649 the expulsion of an Order so powerful as were the Jesuits caused some commotion through the world at large. Miracles happened opportunely to strengthen waning faith. A fire placed round their church, though it destroyed, refused to blacken; and ropes fixed to the tower of the church, although attached to windlasses, refused to pull it down, so that the tower and church, though gutted, still remained almost intact, and, on the Jesuits' return, were easily repaired, and served as a monument of victory.

Uneasy lies the head that wears a mitre, as poor Cardenas found out. His popularity suffered some decrease by the lack of treasure found in the Jesuits' college, for he had always dangled millions in prospective before the people's eyes to engage them on his side, and, most unluckily, he had no millions to bestow. So, to make all things right, he sent Fray Diego Villalon[139] to Madrid to represent his interests.

The Jesuits upon their side were not inactive. By virtue of a brief of Gregory XIII. they had the privilege of appointing an official called a judge conservator in cases where their honour or their possessions were attacked. Therefore Father Alfonso de Ojeda was sent to Charcas to arrange about the case. At Charcas they found that Cardenas had been before them, and had instituted proceedings against their Order in the High Court. Father Pedro Nolasco, Superior of the Order of Mercy, was appointed judge conservator.

He at once summoned the Bishop to appear before him, and arranged to try the case and hear the evidence.

Cardenas having refused to appear, sentence went by default against him. The High Court, being convinced that the pretended edict of the Emperor Charles V. did not exist, appointed Don Andres Garabito de Leon to be interim Captain-General of Paraguay, and gave him power, if necessary, to restore order by force of arms. The court then issued a decree summoning Cardenas to appear at once at Charcas and give his reasons why he had had himself made Governor and had expulsed the Jesuits from Paraguay. It then communicated with the Marquis of Mancera, Viceroy of Peru, who quite concurred in its decision as to Cardenas.

Apparently upon the principle which prevails amongst Mohammedans of always appointing, first an officer, and then a caliph to that officer to do the work, the High Court of Charcas also appointed a commander to proceed to Paraguay, pending the time that Don Andres should feel inclined to start himself. As the caliph's name was Sebastian de Leon, it is not improbable that he was a relation of the first-appointed man.

Don Sebastian de Leon seems to have been in Paraguay already, for both Charlevoix and Xarque agree that he and his brothers, after the expulsion of the Jesuits by Cardenas, had retired to an estate some distance from Asuncion. At the estate the news of his appointment reached him, and must have placed him in a most difficult position as to what to do.

On several occasions in the various rebellions which occurred in South America during the Spanish rule, men were appointed to quell rebellions, pacify countries, and restore order, and all without an army or any forces being placed at their command. This was the case with the celebrated La Gasca, who was sent from Spain to put down the rebellion of Gonzalo Pizarro, and succeeded in so doing, though he left Spain without a single soldier in his train. In this connection it is to be remembered that none of the rebellions in Spanish America from the days of Charles I. (*i.e.*, the Emperor Charles V.) to those of Charles III. were for the object of separation from the metropolis, but merely risings against Governors sent out from Spain. It seems that both in Peru and Paraguay the very name of the imperial power was able to draw hundreds of men to the standard of whatever officer held a commission from Madrid, such as that held by Garabito de Leon or by La Gasca on the Paraná.

At first Don Sebastian did not show himself in Asuncion, but sent out messengers on every side to summon soldiers, requisition horses, and collect provisions. He also sent to Corrientes to tell the Jesuits he was ready to reinstate them in their possessions.

Don Bernardino meanwhile was preparing for the great adventure of his life. He seems to have believed most firmly that no power on earth had any right to remove him from the governorship of Paraguay. In a letter which he addressed to Don Juan Romero de la Cruz[140] he says he is on the point of distinguishing himself by heroic exploits and great victories; that he had on his side justice and force (a most uncommon combination); that the entire capital was favourable to him; and that he was resolved neither to readmit the Jesuits nor to recognise Don Sebastian de Leon as Governor.

Asuncion was once again convulsed, and all was preparation for the holy war. The Bishop had given out that angels were to help him, and this so reassured his soldiers that they provided themselves with cords to bind the Indians in the army of Don Sebastian Leon, thinking they would fall an easy prey to them. This matter of the cords explains, perhaps, why the population of Asuncion was almost unanimous in favour of the Bishop.

In the army of Don Sebastian, as well as the militia of the province, marched three thousand Indians from the Jesuit reductions on the Paraná. The Spaniards of the capital were all determined not to kill any of them, but keep them alive for slaves, and hence the cords with which they armed themselves.

The sacred generalissimo led out his army from Asuncion in person, celebrating Mass himself, and then heading his troops like many another Spanish ecclesiastic has done before and after him, and continued doing even to the latest Carlist war.

The armies met not far from Luqué, in a little plain known as the Campo Grande. An open plain with sandy soil, which gave the horses a good footing, with several little stagnant pools in the centre where the wounded men could drink and wash their wounds, with a most convenient forest on all sides for the deserters and the cowards to hide in, made a good battlefield. The village of Luqué, grouped round its church, and with a little plaza in the middle in which sat Paraguayan women selling mandioca, chipa,[141] and rapadura,[142] with sacks of maize and of mani,[143] stood on the summit of a little hill. Upon the plain the earth is red, and looks as if a battle had been fought upon it and much blood spilt. In all directions run little paths, worn deep by the feet of mules and horses, and in which the rider has to lift his feet as if he were going through a stream. To Asuncion there leads one of the deep-sunk roads planted with orange and paraiso[144] trees, constructed thus (as Barco de la Centenera tells us in his `Argentina') so as to be defensible against the Indians after the country was first conquered by the Spaniards.

On the Bishop's side hardly a soldier but thought himself an emissary of God, or doubted of the victory for a moment in his heart. Angels themselves had promised victory to their leader, who, to make all things safe, had issued a proclamation punishing surrender with the pain of death; so they stood quietly in array of battle waiting to be attacked.

Upon his side, Don Sebastian Leon, seeing the attitude of the enemy, immediately ordered an advance, and charged himself, with all his cavalry, upon the Bishop's men. They, with the firmness that fanatics so often show, stood firmly in their ranks, thinking themselves invulnerable. Their valour proved but momentary, for at the second charge they broke their ranks and fled. Flight turned to rout, and Don Sebastian having commanded that they should not be pursued, they still fled on, no man pursuing them.

The Governor then entered the capital without resistance. On the plaza he stopped, and having gathered up the wounded without respect of party, he sent them to the hospital. Then, having seen to the safety of the town, he rode to the Cathedral to give thanks to God for having preserved him from the dangers of the fight. Dressed in his robes and seated on his throne was Cardenas. Don Sebastian entered the church, dismounted, and kissed his hand respectfully, like a true Spaniard, and asked him ceremoniously to deign to give him the baton of the civil power. Cardenas answered not a word, but handed him the baton, and then retired, accompanied by all his priests.

The victory did not terminate the work of Don Sebastian. After a reasonable interval, and before witnesses, he cited the Bishop to appear before the court of Charcas. The Bishop promised to obey, thinking he had another Don Gregorio Hinostrosa to deal with, but quite determined never to comply, acting according to the custom of Governors in South America, who, when an order reached them from Madrid, either absurd or quite impossible to execute, solemnly answered, 'I obey, but I do not comply,'[145] saving by the phrase the honour of their sovereigns and themselves. Upon their side the Jesuits pressed the judge conservator, Father Nolasco, to issue his sentence, and free them from the charges under which they lay. This he did, and gave as his opinion they were quite innocent of all that Cardenas had laid to their account.

As in a palace,[146] things go slow in Spain, and it was not till 1654 that a royal decision confirmed the judgment of Nolasco, and freed the Jesuits from all the charges raised against them.

Order restored, Cardenas deprived of his usurped authority, and the Jesuits reinstated, the temporary commission of Sebastian Leon was at an end. Therefore he retired again to plant his mandioca under his own guayaba-tree. Yet feeling ran so high that he was hardly safe from the vengeance of the partisans of Cardenas, so that he found himself once more obliged to summon the militia of the province, and lead them to a perfunctory campaign against the Payaguás. These Indians the earlier historians of the conquest, Barco de la Centenera and Rui Diaz de Guzman, describe as river-pirates, almost living in canoes, and dashing out on any passing Spanish vessel that they thought weak enough. The Jesuits Montoya and Dobrizhoffer tell us that they went naked, painted in many colours, with a hawk's or parrot's wing passed through the cartilage of their left ear, and that they were, of all the Indians of Paraguay, the most indomitable. A few, when I knew Paraguay some twenty years ago, hung round Asuncion, squalid and miserable, passing their time in fishing in canoes, and as attached to their own mode of life as when the first discoverers called them `sweet-water pirates' and the `most pestilent of all the Indians on the river Paraguay.' The Payaguás chastised, Don Sebastian, upon one pretext or another, did not disband his troops, keeping them always by him, and thus making the position of the Bishop quite untenable, till by degrees his followers fell away and left him almost deserted and his party all dissolved. Seeing the game was up, the Bishop, after having named one Don Adrian Cornejo as his suffragan, took his departure (1650) for Charcas to appear before the court. For eight tumultuous years he had kept his bishopric in a perpetual turmoil, having been the evil genius of the land.

What sort of man he really was is hard to-day to judge, for Xarque, Villalon, Charlevoix, and Dean Funes,[147] who chronicle his doings, were all, on one side or the other, partisans. The Jesuits condemn him as a spoliator, the Franciscans hold him up as one who fought throughout his life for the honour of the founder of their rule. Tracts, books, and pamphlets for and against him have been written in numbers, and in the history of the times in Paraguay his name bulks large. One thing is certain — that the Indians loved and revered him, and followed him up to the end. Even in Charcas, where he lived for years upon a pension of two thousand crowns allowed him by the King whilst his case dragged its weary course to Rome, Madrid, back to Peru, and then to Rome again, the Indians, when he appeared in public, greeted him with flowers. He may have been a saint: so many men are saints, and the world knows them not. He may have been a schemer; but he made nothing by his schemes except the barren honour of his consecration to the see of Paraguay. A preacher certainly he was, able and willing to draw crowds, after the fashion of all those who have the gift of words.

Headstrong and obstinate, through a long life he hated vigorously, thinking all those who differed from him were accursed of God. A strenuous member of the Church militant on earth, he was at least a personality, and those who read the history of his time must reckon with, and take sides for or against, him after the fashion of the men with whom he passed his life, who to a man revered him as a saint, or looked upon him as a devil sent to plague mankind.

Arrived in Charcas, he soon fell on evil times, although at first he made some partisans. Still looking back to Paraguay, he passed his time in drawing out petitions to the King; then, one by one, all his friends fell from him, except some faithful Indians, who considered him a saint. His dreams of saintship were not fulfilled, for his name never figured in the calendar. Years did not tame nor yet did hope ever completely leave him; for in old books I find him always protesting, ever complaining, and still striving, till, in 1665, Philip IV. in pity made him Bishop of Santa Cruz. A sentence from the registers of the Consistory at Rome informs us that, as Bishop of La Paz, in his own province of the Charcas, he left off troubling, and rested from his agitated life.

Chapter VI

Description of the mission territory and towns founded by
the Jesuits — Their endeavours to attract the Indians —
Religious feasts and processions — Agricultural and
commercial organizations

With the death of Cardenas the most dangerous enemy the Jesuits ever had
in Paraguay had disappeared. They worsted him, and drove him from his see;
but the movement set on foot by him and the calumnies he levelled at their
Order still remained and flourished, and in the end prevailed against them
and drove them from the land. A calumny is hard to kill; mankind in general
cherish it; they never let it die, and, if it languishes, resuscitate it under
another form; they hold to it in evil and in good repute, so that, once fairly
rooted, it goes on growing like a forest-tree throughout the centuries.
Therefore, the charges against the Jesuits in Paraguay, which Cardenas first
started, are with us still, and warp our judgment as to the doings of the Order
in the missions of the Paraná and Uruguay even until to-day.

But neither calumny nor the raids of the Paulistas, nor yet the jealousy of the
Spanish settlers in Paraguay, deterred the Jesuits from the prosecution of
their task. The missions gradually extended, till they ranged from Santa Maria
la Mayor, in Paraguay, to San Miguel, in what is now Brazil; and from Jesus,
upon the Paraná, to Yapeyu, upon the Uruguay. Most of the country, with
the exception of the missions of Jesus and Trinidad, upon the Paraná, which
to-day, at least, are only clearings in the primeval forest, is composed of open
rolling plains, with wood upon the banks of all the streams. Covered as it was
and is with fine, short grass, it formed excellent cattle-breeding country, and
hence the great industry of the Indians was to look after stock. The country
being so favourable for cattle, they multiplied immoderately, so that in the
various establishments (*estancias*), according to the inventories published by
Brabo, their numbers were immense.[148]

These open rolling plains, called by the natives *campos quebrantados*, are
generally studded thickly with stunted palms called yatais,[149] but not so
thickly as to spoil the grass which covers them in spring and early summer,
and even in winter they remain good feeding ground. Thick clumps of hard-
wood trees[150] break up the prairie here and there into peninsulas and
islands, and in the hollows and rocky valleys bushy palmetto rises above a
horse's knees. In general the soil is of a rich bright red, which, gleaming
through the trees, gives a peculiarly warm colour to the land. All the French
Jesuit writers refer to it as `la terre rouge des missions'. The Jesuits used it
and another earth of a yellow shade for painting their churches and their
houses in the mission territory. Its composition is rather sandy, though after

rain it makes thick mud, and renders travelling most laborious. The flowers and shrubs of the territory are quite as interesting and still more varied than are the trees. Many of the Jesuits were botanists, and the works of Fathers Montenegro,[151] Sigismund Asperger and Lozano are most curious, and give descriptions and lists of many of the plants unclassified even to-day. The celebrated Bonpland, so long detained by Dr. Francia in Paraguay, unfortunately never published anything; but modern writers[152] have done much, though still the flora of the whole country is but most imperfectly known, and much remains to do before it is all classified. The *Croton succirubrus* (from which a resin known as `sangre-de-drago' is extracted), the sumaha (bombax — the fruit of which yields a fine vegetable silk), the erythroxylon or coca of Paraguay, the incienso or incense-tree of the Jesuits, are some of the most remarkable of the myriad shrubs. But if the shrubs are myriad, the flowers are past the power of man to count. Lianas, with their yellow and red and purple clusters of blossoms, like enormous bunches of grapes, hang from the forest-trees. In the open glades upon the ñandubays,[153] the algarrobos, and the espinillos, hang various Orchidaceæ,[154] called by the natives `flores del aire', covering the trees with their aerial roots, their hanging blossoms, and their foliage of tender green. The Labiatæ, Compositæ, Daturæ, Umbelliferæ, Convolvulaceæ, and many other species, cover the ground in spring or run up trees and bushes after the fashion of our honeysuckle and the traveller's joy.

The lakes and backwaters of rivers are covered with myriads of water-lilies (all lumped together by the natives as `camalote'), whilst in the woodland pools the Victoria Regis carpets the water with its giant leaves. In every wood the orange and the lemon with the sweet lime have become wild, and form great thickets. Each farm and *rancho* has its orange-grove, beneath the shade of which I have so often camped, that the scent of orange-blossom always brings back to me the dense primeval woods, the silent plains, the quiet Indians, and the unnavigated waterways, in which the alligators basked. Except the Sierra de Mbaracayu,[155] on the north-east, throughout the mission territory there are no mountains of considerable height; and through the middle of the country run the rivers Paraná and Uruguay, the latter forming the boundary on the south-east. The rolling plains and woods alternate with great marshes called *esteros*, which in some districts, as of that of Ñeembucu, cover large tracts of land, forming in winter an almost impenetrable morass, and in the spring and early summer excellent feeding-ground for sheep. Throughout the territory the climate is healthy, except towards the woody northern hills. With this rich territory and the false reports of mines, which even unsuccessful exploration could not dispel, it is but natural that the Jesuits were hated far and wide. It must have been annoying to a society composed, as were the greater portion of the Spanish settlements in Paraguay, of adventurers, who treated the Indians as brute beasts,[156] to see a preserve of Indians separated from their territory by no great barrier of Nature, and still beyond their power.[157] Bonpland, in speaking of the country, says: 'The whole of the land exceeds description; at every step one meets with things useful and new in natural history.' Such also was the opinion of the French travellers Demersay and D'Orbigny; of Colonel du Graty, whose interesting work ('La République du Paraguay', Brussels, 1862) is one of the best on the country; the recent French explorer Bourgade la Dardye, and of all those who have ever visited the missions of Paraguay.[158]

In this rich territory the Jesuits, when, after infinite trouble, they had united a sufficient[159] quantity of Indians, formed them into townships, almost all of which were built upon one plan. In Paraguay itself only some three or four remain; but they remain so well preserved that, by the help of contemporary accounts, it is easy to reconstruct almost exactly what the missions must have been like during the Jesuits' rule.[160]

Built round a square, the church and store-houses filled one end, and the dwellings of the Indians, formed of sun-dried bricks or wattled canes in three long pent-houses, completed the three sides. In general, the houses were of enormous length, after the fashion of a St. Simonian phalanstery, or of a 'miners' row' in Lanarkshire. Each family had its own apartments, which were but separated from the apartments of the next by a lath-and-plaster wall, called in Spanish *tabique*; but one veranda and one roof served for a hundred or more families. The space in the middle of the square was carpeted with the finest grass, kept short by being pastured close by sheep. The churches, sometimes built of stone, and sometimes of the hard woods with which the country abounds, were beyond all description splendid, taking into consideration the remoteness of the Jesuit towns from the outside world. Frequently — as, for instance, in the mission of Los Apostoles — the churches had three aisles, and were adorned with lofty towers, rich altars,[161] super-altars, and statuary, brought at great expense from Italy and Spain. Though the churches were often built of stone, it was not usual for the houses of the Indians to be so built; but in situations where stone was plentiful, as at the mission of San Borja, the houses of the Jesuits were of masonry, with verandas held up by columns, and with staircases with balustrades of sculptured stone.[162] The ordinary ground-plan of the priest's house was that of the Spanish Moorish dwelling, so like in all its details to a Roman house at Pompeii or at Herculaneum. Built round a square courtyard, with a fountain in the middle, the Jesuits' house formed but a portion of a sort of inner town, which was surrounded by a wall, in which a gate, closed by a porter's lodge, communicated with the outside world. Within the wall was situated the church (although it had an entrance to the plaza), the rooms of the inferior priest, a garden, a guest-chamber, stables, and a store-house, in which were kept the arms belonging to the town, the corn, flour, and wool, and the provisions necessary for life in a remote and often dangerous place. In every case the houses were of one story; the furniture was modest, and in general home-made; in every room hung images and pious pictures, the latter often painted by the Indians themselves. In the smaller missions two Jesuits managed all the Indians.[163]

The greatest difficulty which the Jesuits had to face was the natural indolence of their neophytes. Quite unaccustomed as they were to regular work of any kind, the ordinary European system, as practised in the Spanish settlements, promptly reduced them to despair, and often killed them off in hundreds. Therefore the Jesuits instituted the semi-communal system of agriculture and of public works with which their name will be associated for ever in America.[164]

The celebrated Dr. Francia, dictator of Paraguay, used to refer to the Jesuits as `cunning rogues',[165] and, as he certainly himself was versed in every phase of cunningness, perhaps his estimate — to some extent, at least — was just. A rogue in politics is but a man who disagrees with you; but, still, it wanted no little knowledge of mankind to present a daily task to men, unversed in any kind of labour, as of the nature of a pleasure in itself. The difficulty was enormous, as the Indians seemed never to have come under the primeval curse, but passed their lives in wandering about, occasionally cultivating just sufficient for their needs. Whether a missionary, Jesuit, or Jansenist, Protestant, Catholic, or Mohammedan, does well in forcing his own mode of life and faith on those who live a happier, freer life than any his instructor can hold out to them is a moot point. Only the future can resolve the question, and judge of what we do to-day — no doubt with good intentions, but with the ignorance born of our self-conceit. Much of the misery of the world has been brought about with good intentions; but of the Jesuits, at least, it can be said that what they did in Paraguay did not spread death and extinction to the tribes with whom they dealt.[166] So to the task of agriculture the Jesuits marshalled their neophytes to the sound of music, and in procession to the fields, with a saint borne high aloft, the community each day at sunrise took its way. Along the paths, at stated intervals, were shrines of saints, and before each of them they prayed, and between each shrine sang hymns.[167] As the procession advanced, it became gradually smaller as groups of Indians dropped off to work the various fields, and finally the priest and acolyte with the musicians returned alone.[168] At mid-day, before eating, they all united and sang hymns, and then, after their meal and siesta, returned to work till sundown, when the procession again re-formed, and the labourers, singing, returned to their abodes. A pleasing and Arcadian style of tillage, and different from the system of the `swinked' labourer in more northern climes. But even then the hymnal day was not concluded; for after a brief rest they all repaired to church to sing the 'rosary', and then to sup and bed. On rainy days they worked at other industries in the same half-Arcadian, half-communistic manner, only they sang their hymns in church instead of in the fields. The system was so different to that under which the Indians endured their lives in the *encomiendas* and the *mitas* of the Spanish settlements, that the fact alone is sufficient to account for much of the contemporary hatred which the Jesuits incurred.

Imagine a semi-communistic settlement set close to the borders of Rhodesia, in which thousands of Kaffirs passed a life analogous to that passed by the Indians of the missions — cared for and fed by the community, looked after in every smallest particular of their lives — and what a flood of calumny would be let loose upon the unfortunate devisers of the scheme! Firstly, to withdraw thousands of 'natives' from the labour market would be a crime against all progress, and then to treat them kindly would be heresy, and to seclude them from the contamination of the scum of Europe in the settlements would be termed unnatural; for we know that native races derive most benefit from free competition with the least fitted of our population to instruct. But besides agriculture the enormous cattle-farms[169] of the mission territory gave occupation to many of the neophytes. The life on cattle-farms gave less scope for supervision, and we may suppose that the herders and the cattlemen were more like Gauchos; but Gauchos under religious discipline, half-centaurs in the field, sitting a plunging half-wild colt as if they were part of him, and when on foot at home submissive to the Jesuits, constant in church, but not so fierce and bloodthirsty as their descendants soon became after the withdrawal of the mission rule.

As well as agriculture and *estancia* life, the Jesuits had introduced amongst the Indians most of the arts and trades of Europe. By the inventories taken by Bucareli, Viceroy of Buenos Ayres, at the expulsion of the Order, we find that they wove cotton largely; sometimes they made as much as eight thousand five hundred yards of cloth in a single town in the space of two or three months.[170] And, in addition to weaving, they had tanneries, carpenters' shops, tailors, hat-makers, coopers, cordage-makers, boat-builders, cartwrights, joiners, and almost every industry useful and necessary to life. They also made arms and powder, musical instruments, and had silversmiths, musicians, painters, turners, and printers to work their printing-presses: for many books were printed at the missions,[171] and they produced manuscripts as finely executed as those made by the monks in European monasteries.

All the *estancias*, the agricultural lands and workshops were, so to speak, the property of the community; that is to say, the community worked them in common, was fed and maintained by their productions, the whole under the direction of the two Jesuits who lived in every town. A portion called *tupinambal* in Guaraní was set aside especially for the maintenance of orphans and of widows. The cattle and the horses, with the exception of 'los caballos del santo', destined for show at feasts, were also used in common. The surplus of the capital was reserved to purchase necessary commodities from Buenos Ayres and from Spain.[172] Each family received from the common stock sufficient for its maintenance during good conduct, for the Jesuits held in its entirety the Pauline dictum that if a man will not work, then neither shall he eat. But as they held it, so they practised it themselves, for their lives were most laborious — teaching and preaching, and acting as overseers to the Indians in their labours continually, from the first moment of their arrival at the missions till their death. Thus, if the mayor of the township complained of any man for remissness at his work, he received no rations till he had improved.

To inculcate habits of providence amongst the Indians, always inclined to consume whatever was given to them and go fasting afterwards, they issued the provisions but once a week, and when they killed their oxen forced the Indians to 'jerk'[173] a certain quantity of beef to last throughout the week. Vegetables each family was obliged to plant both in their gardens and in the common fields; and all that were not actually consumed were dealt out to the workers in the common workshops or preserved for sale.

Certain of the Indians owned their own cows and horses, and had gardens in which they worked; but all the product was obliged to be disposed of to the Jesuits for the common good, and in exchange for them they gave knives, scissors, cloth, and looking-glasses, and other articles made in the outside world. Clothes were served out to every Indian, and consisted for the men of trousers, coarse *ponchos*, straw hats or caps, and shirts; but neither men nor women ever wore shoes, and the sole costume of the latter was the Guaraní *tipoi*,[174] a long and sleeveless shift cut rather high, and with coarse embroidery round the shoulders, and made of a rough cotton cloth. For ornaments they had glass beads and rosaries of brass or silver, with silver rings, and necklaces of glass or horn, from which hung crucifixes. Thus food and clothing cost the Jesuits[175] (or the community) but little, and a rude plenty was the order of the land. The greatest luxury of the Indians was *maté*, and to produce it they worked in the *yerbales* in the same way in which they worked their fields — in bands and with processions, to the sound of hymns and headed by a priest.

This, then, was the system by means of which the Jesuits succeeded, without employing force of any kind, which in their case would have been quite impossible, lost as they were amongst the crowd of Indians, in making the Guaranís endure the yoke of toil. The semi-communal character of their rule accounts for the hostility of Liberals who, like Azara, saw in competition the best road to progress, but who, like him, in their consuming thirst for progress lost sight of happiness.

In addition to the means described, the Jesuits had recourse to frequent religious feasts, for which the calendar gave them full scope, so that the life in a Jesuit mission was much diversified and rendered pleasant to the Indians, who have a rooted love of show. Each mission had, of course, its patron saint,[176] and on his day nobody worked, whilst all was joyfulness and simple mirth. At break of day a discharge of rockets and of firearms and peals upon the bells announced the joyful morn. Then the whole population flocked to church to listen to an early mass. Those who could find no room inside the church stood in long lines outside the door, which remained open during the ceremony. Mass over, each one ran to prepare himself for his part in the function, the Jesuits having taken care, by multiplying offices and employments, to leave no man without a direct share in all the others did.[177] The humblest and the highest had their part, and the heaviest burden, no doubt, fell upon the two Jesuits,[178] who were answerable for all. The foremost duty was to get the procession ready for the march, and saddle `los caballos del santo'[179] to serve as escort, mounted by Indians in rich dresses, kept specially for feasts.

The inventory of the town of Los Apostoles[180] enables us to reconstruct, with some attempt at accuracy, how the procession was formed and how it took its way. All the militia of the town were in attendance, mounted on their best horses, and armed with lances (*chuzos*), lazo, bolas, and a few with guns. The officers of the Indians rode at their head, dressed out in gorgeous clothes, and troops of dancers, at stated intervals, performed a sort of Pyrrhic dance between the squadrons of the cavalry.[181] In the front of all rode on a white horse the Alferez Real,[182] dressed in a doublet of blue velvet richly laced with gold, a waistcoat of brocade, and with short velvet breeches gartered with silver lace; upon his feet shoes decked with silver buckles, and the whole scheme completed by a gold-laced hat. In his right hand he held the royal standard fastened to a long cane which ended in a silver knob. A sword was by his side, which, as he only could have worn it on such occasions, and as the `horses of the saint' were not unlikely as ticklish as most horses of the prairies of Entre Rios and Corrientes are wont to be, must have embarrassed him considerably. Behind him came the Corregidor, arrayed in yellow satin, with a silk waistcoat and gold buttons, breeches of yellow velvet, and a hat equal in magnificence to that worn by his bold compeer. The two Alcaldes, less violently dressed, wore straw-coloured silk suits, with satin waistcoats of the same colour, and hats turned up with gold. Other officials, as the Commissario, Maestre de Campo, and the Sargento Mayor, were quite as gaily dressed in scarlet coats, with crimson damask waistcoats trimmed with silver lace,[183] red breeches, and black hats adorned with heavy lace.

In the bright Paraguayan sunshine, with the primeval forest for a background, or in some mission in the midst of a vast plain beside the Paraná, they must have looked as gorgeous as a flight of parrots from the neighbouring woods, and have made a Turneresque effect, ambling along, a blaze of colours, quite as self-satisfied in their finery as if 'the rainbow had been entail settled on them and their heirs male.' Quite probably their broad, flat noses, and their long, lank hair, their faces fixed immovably, as if they were carved in ñandubay, contrasted strangely with their finery. But there were none to judge — no one to make remarks; most likely all was conscience and tender heart, and not their bitterest enemy has laid the charge of humour to the Jesuits' account.

As in the inventories of the thirty towns I find no mention either of stockings or of shoes for Indians, with the exception of the low shoes and buckles worn by the Alferez Real, it seems the gorgeous costumes ended at the knee, and that these popinjays rode barefoot, with, perhaps, large iron Gaucho spurs fastened by strips of mare-hide round their ankles, and hanging down below their naked feet. But, not content with the procession of the elders in parrot guise, there was a parody of parodies in the *cabildo infantil*, the band composed of children, who, with the self-same titles as their elders, and in the self-same clothes adjusted to their size, rode close upon their heels. Lastly, as Charlevoix tells us, came 'des lions et des tigres, mais bien enchaínes afin qu'ils ne troublerent point la fête,' and so the whole procession took its way towards the church.

The church, all hung with velvet and brocade, was all ablaze with lights, and fumes of incense (no doubt necessary) almost obscured the nave. Upon the right and left hand of the choir (which, as is usual in Spain, was in the middle of the church) the younger Indians were seated all in rows, the boys and girls being separated, as was the custom in all the missions of the Jesuits, who, no doubt, were convinced of the advisability of the saying that 'entre santa y santo, pared de cal y canto.'[184] The Indians who had some office, and who wore the clothes[185] I have described, were seated or knelt in rows, and at the outside stood the people of the town dressed in white cotton, their simple clothes, no doubt, forming an effective background to their more parti-coloured brethren kneeling in the front. Throughout the church the men and women were separated, and if a rumour of an incursion of Paulistas was in the air, the Indians carried arms even in the sacred buildings and at the solemn feasts. Mass was celebrated with a full band, the oboe, fagot, lute, harp, cornet, clarinet, violin, viola, and all other kinds of music, figuring in the inventories of the thirty towns. Indeed, in two of the inventories[186] an opera called 'Santiago' is mentioned, which had special costumes and properties to put it on the stage. Mass over, the procession was reconstituted outside the church, and after parading once more through the town broke up, and the Indians devoted the night to feasting, and not infrequently danced till break of day.

Such were the outward arts with which the Jesuits sought to attach the simple people, to whom they stood in the position not only of pastors and masters both in one, but also as protectors from the Paulistas on one side, and on the other from the Spaniards of the settlements, who, with their *encomiendas* and their European system of free competition between man and man, were perhaps unknowingly the direst enemies of the whole Indian race. There is, as it would seem, implanted in the minds of almost all primitive peoples, such as the Guaranís, a solidarity, a clinging kinship, which if once broken down by competition, unrestrained after our modern fashion, inevitably leads to their decay. Hence the keen hatred to the Chinese in California and in Australia. Naturally, those whom we hate, and in a measure fear, we also vilify, and this has given rise to all those accusations of Oriental vice (as if the vice of any Oriental, however much depraved, was comparable to that of citizens of Paris or of London), of barbarism, and the like, so freely levelled against the unfortunate Chinese.

In Paraguay nothing is more remarkable in a market in the country than the way in which the people will not undersell each other, even refusing to part with goods a fraction lower than the price which they consider fair.[187] It may be that the Jesuits would have done better to endeavour to equip their neophytes more fully, so as to take their place in the battle of the world. It may be that the simple, happy lives they led were too opposed to the general scheme of outside human life to find acceptance or a place in our cosmogony. But one thing I am sure of — that the innocent delight of the poor Indian Alferez Real, mounted upon his horse, dressed in his motley, barefooted, and overshadowed by his gold-laced hat, was as entire as if he had eaten of all the fruits of all the trees of knowledge of his time, and so perhaps the Jesuits were wise.

Strangely enough — but, then, how strangely all extremes meet in humanity! — the Jesuits alone (at least, in Paraguay) seem to have apprehended, as the Arabs certainly have done from immemorial time, that the first duty of a man is to enjoy his life. Art, science, literature, ambition — all the frivolities with which men occupy themselves — have their due place; but life is first, and in some strange, mysterious way the Jesuits felt it, though, no doubt, they would have been the first to deny it with a thousand oaths. But in a Jesuit mission all was not feasting or processioning, for with such neighbours as the Mamelucos they had to keep themselves prepared.[188] As for their better government in home affairs each mission had its police, with officers[189] chosen by the Jesuits amongst the Indians, so for exterior defence they had militia, and in it the *caciques*[190] of the different tribes held principal command. Most likely over them, or at their elbows, were set priests who before entering the Company of Jesus had been soldiers: for there were many such amongst the Jesuits. As their own founder once had been a soldier, so the Company was popular amongst those soldiers who from some cause or other had changed their swords to crucifixes, and taken service in the ranks of Christ.[191] As it was most important, both for defence and policy, to keep the *caciques* content, they were distinguished by better treatment than the others in many different ways. Their food was more abundant, and a guard of Indians was on perpetual duty round the houses where they lived; these they employed as servants and as messengers to summon distant companies of Indians to the field. Their method of organization must have been like that of the Boers or of the Arabs; for every Indian belonged to a company, which now and then was brought together for evolutions in the field or for a period of training, after the fashion of our militia or the German Landwehr. Perhaps this system of an armed militia, always ready for the field, was what, above all other reasons, enabled their detractors to represent the Jesuits as feared and unpopular. Why, it was asked, does this community of priests maintain an army in its territories? No one remembered that if such were not the case the missions could not have existed for a year without a force to defend their borders from the Paulistas. Everyone forgot that Fathers Montoya and Del Taño had obtained special permission from the King for the Indians of the missions to bear arms; and, as no human being is grateful for anything but contumelious treatment, the Spanish settlers conveniently forgot how many times a Jesuit army had saved their territories. The body of three thousand Guaranís sent at the expense of the Company to assist the Spaniards against the Portuguese at the attack upon the Colonia del Sacramento[192] on the river Plate, in 1678, was quite forgotten, together with the innumerable contingents sent by the Jesuits at the demand of Spanish governors against the Chaco Indians, the Payaguás, and even against the distant Calchaquis, in what is now the province of Jujuy. Even when an English pirate, called in the Spanish histories Roque Barloque (explained by some to be plain Richard Barlow), appeared off Buenos Ayres, the undaunted neophytes shrank not a moment from going to the assistance of their co-religionists against the 'Lutheran dog'.[193] Lastly, all Spanish governors and writers, both contemporaneous and at the end of the eighteenth century, seem to forget that if the Jesuits had an army of neophytes within their territory the fact was known and approved of at the court of Spain.[194] But it appears that Calvin had many coadjutors in his policy of 'Jesuitas aut necandi aut calumniis opponendi sunt.'[195] When a Jesuit army took the field, driving before it sufficient cattle to subsist upon, and with its *caballada* of spare horses upon its flank, it must have resembled many a Gaucho army I have seen in Entre Rios five-and-twenty years ago. The only difference seems to have been that the Gauchos of yesterday did not use bows and arrows, although they might have done so with as much benefit to themselves, and no more danger to their enemies, than was occasioned by the rusty, ill-conditioned guns they used to bear. The Indians were armed with bows, and in their expeditions each Indian carried one hundred and fifty arrows tipped with iron. Others had firearms, but all bore bolas on their saddles, and carried lazos and long lances,[196] which, like the Pampa Indians, they used in mounting their horses, placing one hand upon the mane, and vaulting into the saddles with the other leaning on the lance. The infantry were armed with lances and a few guns; they also carried bolas, but they trusted most to slings, for which they carried bags of hide, with a provision of smooth round stones, and used them dexterously. On several occasions their rude militia gave proofs of stubborn valour, and, as they fought under the Jesuits' eyes, no doubt acquitted themselves as men would who looked upon their priests almost in the light of gods. But agriculture and cattle-breeding were not all the resources of the missions; for the Jesuits engaged in commerce largely, both with the outer world and by the intricate and curious barter system which they had set on foot for the mutual convenience of the different mission towns. In many of the inventories printed by Brabo, one comes across the entry 'Deudas', showing a sort of account current between the towns for various articles. Thus, they exchanged cattle for cotton, sugar for rice, wheat for pig-iron or tools from Europe; as no account of interest ever appears in any inventory as between town and town, it seems the Jesuits anticipated Socialism — at least, so far as that they bought and sold for use, and not for gain. Although between the towns of their own territory all was arranged for mutual convenience, yet in their dealings with the outside world the Jesuits adhered to what are known as 'business principles'. These principles, if I mistake not, have been deified by politicians with their 'Buy in the cheapest, sell in the dearest' tag, and therefore even the sternest Protestant or Jansenist (if such there still exist) can have no stone to throw at the Company of Jesus for its participation in that system which has made the whole world glad.

Cotton and linen cloth, tobacco, hides, woods of the various hard-wood forests of the country, and, above all, *yerba-maté*, were their chief articles of export to the outside world. Their nearest market was in Buenos Ayres, and to that port they sent their *yerba* in boats made at their own yards, of which they had several, but notably at Yapeyú upon the Uruguay. The money that was made was sent to the Superior of the missions, who had the disposition of the way in which it was dispensed, either for use at home or to be sent to Europe for necessary goods. As well as *yerba-maté*, they sent great quantities of hides. The inventories of the towns taken at the expulsion state that the number of green hides[197] exported annually was fifty thousand, together with six thousand cured; in addition they sold from three to four arrobas[198] of horse-hair, and wood to the value of twenty-five to thirty thousand dollars every year. The total export of their *yerba* ranged between eighty and one hundred thousand arrobas, which at the lowest price could not have been sold at a profit under seven dollars an arroba,[199] so that the income[200] of the thirty towns must have been relatively large.[201] Two or three hundred barrels of honey[202] and some three or four thousand arrobas of tobacco made up the sum total of their exports, though, had they needed money, it might have been increased in such a country, and with so many willing labourers, almost indefinitely.

Thus it will be seen that the missions were organized both agriculturally and commercially so as to be almost self-supporting, and that of the mere necessaries of life they had sufficient for exportation, no small achievement when we consider how averse from labour were the Indians with whom they had to deal. But that nothing should be wanting that a civilized community could possibly desire, they had their prisons, with good store of chains, fetters, whips, and all the other instruments with which the moral code is generally enforced. The most usual punishment was whipping;[203] and the crimes most frequent were drunkenness, neglect of work, and bigamy, which latter lapse from virtue the Jesuits chastised severely, not thinking, being celibates themselves, that not unlikely it was apt to turn into its own punishment without the aid of stripes.

Chapter VII

Causes of the Jesuits' unpopularity — Description of the
lives and habits of the priests — Testimony in favour of the
missions — Their opposition to slavery — Their system of
administration

Much has been written of the interior government of the missions by the
Jesuits, but chiefly by strong partisans, for and against, on either side, whose
only object was to make out a case to fit the prejudices of those for whom
they wrote. Upon the Jesuit side the Abbé Muratori[204] describes a paradise.
A very Carlo Dolce amongst writers, with him all in the missions is so cloying
sweet that one's soul sickens, and one longs in his 'Happy Christianity' to
find a drop of gall. But for five hundred pages nothing is amiss; the men of
Belial persecute the Jesuit saints, who always (after the fashion of their Order
and mankind) turn both cheeks to the smiter, and, if their purse is taken,
hasten to give up their cloaks. The Indians are all love and gratitude. No need
in the Abbé's pages for the twelve pair of fetters, which Brabo most unkindly
has set down amongst his inventories. Never a single *lapsus* from the moral
rule the Jesuits imposed — no drunkenness, and bigamy so seldom met with
that it would seem that Joseph Andrews had been a swaggerer judged by the
standard of these moral Guaranís. Then comes Ibañez,[205] the ex-Jesuit, on
the other side. In a twinkling of an eye the scene is changed. For, quite in
Hogarth's vein, he paints the missions as a perpetual march to Finchley, and
tells us that the Indians were savages, and quite unchanged in all their
primitive propensities under the Jesuit rule. And for the Jesuits themselves
he has a few home-truths administered with vinegar, after the fashion of the
renegade the whole world over, who sees nothing good in the society that
has turned him out. He roundly says the Jesuits were loafers, accuses them
of keeping the Indians ignorant for their own purposes, and paints them
quite as black as the Abbé Muratori painted them rose colour, and with as
little art. So that, as usually happens in the writings of all polemists, no matter
upon which side they may write, but little information, and that distorted to
an incredible degree, is all that they afford.

In general, curious as it may appear, the bitterest opponents of the Jesuits
were Catholics, and Protestants have often written as apologists. Buffon,
Raynal, and Montesquieu, with Voltaire, Robertson, and Southey, have
written favourably of the internal government of the missions and the effect
which it produced. No other names of equal authority can be quoted on the
other side; but yet the fact remains that the Jesuits in Paraguay were exposed
to constant calumny from the first day they went there till the last member
of the Order left the land.

It is my object first to try to show what the conditions of their government really were, and then to try and clear up what was the cause of unpopularity, and why so many and such persistent calumnies were laid to their account. Stretching right up and down the banks of both the Paraná and Uruguay, the missions extended from Nuestra Senora de Fé[206] (or Santa Maria), in Paraguay, to San Miguel, in what is now the Brazilian province of Rio Grande do Sul; and from the mission of Corpus, on the east bank of the Paraná, to Yapeyú, upon the Uruguay. The official capital was placed at Candelaria, on the east bank of the Paraná. In that town the Superior of the missions had his official residence, and from thence he ruled the whole territory, having not only the ecclesiastical but the temporal power, the latter, from the position in which he was placed, so many hundred miles from any Spanish Governor, having by degrees gradually come into his hands. The little town of La Candelaria was, when I knew it, in a most neglected state. The buildings of the Jesuits, with the exception of the church, were all in ruins. The streets were sandy and deserted, the foot-walk separated from them by a line of hard-wood posts, which, as tradition said, were left there by the Jesuits; but the hard woods of Paraguay are almost as imperishable as iron.

A *balsa* — that is, a flying bridge worked by a cable — plied fitfully across the Paraná to Ytapua, also a little ex-Jesuit town upon the other side. Each shop had a sign outside, as was the case in England a hundred years ago. Indians supplied the place with vegetables, floating down in canoes piled up with fruit, with flowers, with sweet potatoes, and returning home empty, or for their cargo three or four tin pails, a looking-glass, or other of the marvels which Europe sends as a sample of her manufactures to little frontier towns. All was as quiet, or perhaps much quieter than in the time when the Superior of the Jesuits was in residence, and if it had been necessary, during the hot hours of noon, Godivas by the dozen might have ridden down the streets, had they been able to find horses quiet enough to ride, certain that no one in the town would lose his after-breakfast nap to look at them.

In every mission two chosen Jesuits lived. The elder, selected for his experience of the country and knowledge of the tongue from amongst those who had been rectors of colleges or provincials of the Order, was vested with the civil power, and was responsible direct to the Superior. The second, generally styled companion (el Compañero), acted as his lieutenant, and had full charge of all things spiritual; so that they were a check on one another, and their duties did not clash.

In difficulties the Superior transmitted orders, like a general in the field, by mounted messengers, who frequently rode over a hundred miles a day, relays of horses always being kept ready for emergencies every three leagues upon the road.

From La Candelaria roads branched off to every portion of the territory, most of them fit for carts, and all superior to those tracks which were the only thoroughfares but twenty years ago. Roads ran to Corrientes, to Asuncion, others from Yapeyú to the Salto Grande, on the Paraná. Upon the Upper Uruguay were about eighty posts, all guarded, and with horses ready to equip the messengers. But there were also roads in the district of the Upper Paraná, which I myself remember as a wilderness, uncrossed, uncrossable, where tigers roamed about and Indians shot at the rare traveller with poisoned arrows out of a blow-pipe, whilst they remained unseen in the recesses of the woods. In the districts of the Upper Uruguay and Paraná, besides the roads and relays of post-horses, they had a fleet both of canoes and boats in which they carried *yerba*[207] and the other products of the land. Thus, with their fleet of boats and of canoes, their highroads branching out on every side, and their relays of post-horses at intervals, most probably no State of America at the time had such interior means of communication with the seat of government. The Incas and the Aztecs certainly had posts who carried messages and brought up fish from the coast with great rapidity; but all the Spanish colonies contemporaneous with the Jesuits' settlements in Paraguay had fallen into a state of lethargy and of interior decay. The roads the Incas used in Peru were falling fast into disuse, and it took several weeks to send a letter from Buenos Ayres to the Pacific coast.

The system of interior government in the missions was in appearance democratic — that is to say, there were officials, as mayors[208] and councillors; but most of them were named by the Jesuits, and all of them, even although elected, owed their election entirely to their priests. This sort of thought-suggested representation was the most fitting for the Indians at the time,[209] and those who look into the workings of a County Council of to-day cannot but think at times that the majority of the councillors would have been better chosen had the electorate had the benefit of some controlling hand, though from what quarter it is difficult to see. The problem which most writers on the Jesuits have quite misunderstood, is how two Jesuits were able to keep a mission of several thousand Indians in order, and to rule supreme without armed forces, or any means of making their power felt or of enforcing obedience to their decrees. Undoubtedly, the dangerous position in which the Indians stood, exposed on one side to the Paulistas, and on the other to the Spanish settlers, both of whom wished to take them as their slaves, placed power in the Jesuits' hands: for the Indians clearly perceived that the Jesuits alone stood between them and instant slavery. Most controversialists who have opposed the Jesuits assert that the Indians of the missions were, in reality, half slaves. Nothing is further from the truth, if one consults the contemporary records, and remembers the small number of the Jesuits. The work the Indians did was inconsiderable, and under such conditions as to deprive it of much of the toilsomeness which is incident to any kind of work. The very essence of a slave's estate is being obliged to work without remuneration for another man. Nothing was farther from the Indians than such a state of things. Their work was done for the community, and though the Jesuits, without doubt, had the full disposition of all the money earned in commerce,[210] and of the distribution of the goods, neither the money nor the goods were used for self-aggrandisement, but were laid out for the benefit of the community at large. The total population of the thirty towns is variously estimated from one hundred and forty to one hundred and eighty thousand,[211] and, curiously enough, it remained almost at the same figure during the whole period of the Jesuit rule. This fact has been adduced against the Jesuits, and it has been said that they could not have been good rulers, or the population must have increased; but those who say so forget that the Indians of Paraguay were never in great numbers, and that most writers on the wild tribes, as Dobrizhoffer[212] and Azara, remark their tendency never to increase.

All this relatively large population of Indians was ruled, as has been seen, by a quite inconsiderable number of priests, who, not disposing of any European force, and being almost always on bad terms with the Spanish settlers in Paraguay on account of the firm stand they made against the enslaving of the Indians, had no means of coercion at their command. Hence the Indians must have been contented with their rule, for if they had not been so the Jesuits possessed no power to stop them from returning to their savage life. Azara,[213] although in the main an opponent of the Jesuits, in the same way that a `good Liberal' of to-day would oppose anything of a Socialistic tendency, yet has this most significant passage in their favour. After enumerating the amount of taxes paid by the missions to the Crown, he says `en faisant le bilan tout se trouvait égal, et s'il y avait quelque excédant, il était en faveur des Jésuites ou des peoplades.'[214] Seldom enough does such a result take place when the balance is struck to-day in any country between the rulers and their `taxables'. Following their system of perfect isolation from the world to its logical sequence, the Jesuits surrounded all the territories of their different towns with walls and ditches, and at the gates planted a guard to prevent egress or ingress between the missions and the outer world.[215] Much capital has been made out of this, as it is attempted to be shown that the Indians were thereby treated as prisoners in their own territories. Nothing, however, has been said of the fact that, if the ditches, palisades, and guard-houses kept in the Indians, they also had the effect of keeping the Spaniards out. When men who looked upon the Indians as without reason, and captured them for slaves when it was possible, began to talk of liberty, it looks as if the `sacred name of liberty' was used but as a stalking-horse — as greasy Testaments are used to swear upon in police-courts, when the witness, with his tongue in his cheek, raises his eyes to heaven, and then with fervency imprints a kiss upon his thumb.

It will be seen that the communism of the missions was of a limited character, and, though the land was cultivated by the labour of the community, that the products were administered by the Jesuits alone. Though it has been stated by many polemical writers, such as Ibañez and Azara, and more recently by Washburne, who was American Minister in Paraguay during the war with Brazil and the Argentine Republic (1866-70), that the Jesuits had amassed great wealth in Paraguay, no proof has ever been advanced for such a charge. Certainly Cardenas made the same statement, but it was never in his power to bring any confirmation of what he said. This power alone was in the hands of Bucareli (1767), the Viceroy of Buenos Ayres, under whose auspices the expulsion of the Jesuits was carried out. By several extracts from Brabo's inventories, and by the statement of the receivers sent by Bucareli, I hope to show that there was no great wealth at any time in the mission territory, and that the income was expended in the territory itself. It may be that the expenditure on churches was excessive, and also that the money laid out on religious ceremonies was not productive; but the Jesuits, strange as it may appear, did not conduct the missions after the fashion of a business concern, but rather as the rulers of some Utopia — those foolish beings who think happiness is preferable to wealth.

Nothing can give a better idea of the way of life of a Jesuit priest and of his daily labours than the curious letter of Nicolas Ñeenguiru, originally written in Guaraní, but of which a translation is extant in the National Spanish Archives in Simancas:[216]

`The manner of living of the father is to shut all the doors, and remain alone with his servant and his cook (who are Indians of a considerable age), and these only wait on him; but by day only, and at twelve o'clock, they go out, and an old man has care of the porter's lodge, and it is he who shuts the gate when the father is asleep, or when he goes out to see his cultivated ground, and even then they go alone, except it be with an old Indian, who guides them and attends to the (father's) horse; and after that he goes to Mass, and in the evening to the Rosary of the Blessed Virgin, calling us together by the sound of the bell, and before that he calls the boys and girls with a small bell, and after that the good father begins to teach them doctrine and how to cross themselves. In the same way, on every feast day, he preaches to us the Word of God, in the same way the Holy Sacrament of Penitence and of the Communion; in these things does the good Father employ himself, and every night the porter's lodge is closed, and the key taken to the Father's room, which is only opened in the morning in order that the sacristan and the cooks may enter. . . .

`The Fathers every morning say Mass for us, and after Mass they go to their rooms, and then they take some hot water and *yerba* (*maté*), and nothing more; after that he comes to the door of his apartment, and then all those who heard Mass come to kiss his hand, and after that he goes out to see if the Indians are diligent at their tasks, and afterwards they go to their room to read the divine service for the day in his book, and to pray that God may prosper him in all his affairs. At eleven o'clock they go to eat a little, not to eat much, for he only has five dishes, and only drinks wine once, not filling a little glass; and spirits they never drink, and there is no wine in our town, except that which is brought from Candelaria, according to that which the Superior sends, and they bring it from somewhere near Buenos Aires. . . . After he has finished eating, to rest a little he goes into the church; afterwards — yes, he retires to rest a little, and whilst he is resting those who work in the father's house go out, and those who do any kind of indoor work, and also the sacristan and the cook: all these go out, and as long as the bell does not ring the doors are shut, and only an old man guards the gate, and when they ring the bell again he opens the doors so that those who work indoors may go inside, and the father takes his breviary and goes nowhere. In the evening they ring the bell so that the children may come home, and the father comes in to teach them Christian doctrine.'

Perhaps the foregoing simple description, written by an Indian in Guaraní, and translated by someone who has preserved in Spanish all the curious inversions of the Guaraní, presents as good a picture of the daily life of a mission priest in Paraguay as any that has ever been given to the public by writers much more ambitious than myself or Ñeenguiru. Nicolas Ñeenguiru, the writer of the letter, afterwards figured in the war against the Portuguese, and several of his letters are preserved in the archives of Simancas, though none so interesting and simple as that I have transcribed.

Dobrizhoffer, in his history of the Abipones, says of him that he was a simple Indian, whom often he had seen put in the stocks for petty faults; at any rate, he seems to have been one of those Indians whom the Jesuits had at least favourably impressed by the system they employed. After the manner in which he wrote, hundreds of Indians must have thought, or else the missions, placed as they were, surrounded on all sides by enemies, could not have endured a single day. What was it, then, which raised the Jesuits up so many and so powerful enemies in Paraguay, when in the districts of the Moxos[217] and the Chiquitos where their power was to the full as great, amongst the Indians, they never had a quarrel with the Spaniards till the day they were expelled? Many and various causes contributed to all they underwent, but most undoubtedly two reasons must have brought about their fall.

Since the time of Cardenas, the report that the Jesuits had rich mines, which they worked on the sly, had been persistently on the increase. Although disproved a thousand times, it still remained; even to-day, in spite of `science' and its wonderful discoveries, there are many in Paraguay who cherish dreams of discovering Jesuit mines. Humanity loves to deceive itself, although there are plenty ready to deceive it; and if men can both forge for themselves fables and at the same time damage their neighbours in so doing, their pleasure is intense. I take it that many really believed the stories of the mines, being unable to credit that anyone would live far from the world, surrounded but by Indians, for any other reason than to be rich. But let a country have rich minerals, even if they exist but in imagination, and it becomes a crime against humanity to shut it up. So that it would appear one of the reasons which induced hatred against the Jesuits was the idea that they had enormous mineral wealth, which either they did not work or else worked in secret for the benefit of their society.

The other reason was the question of slavery. Once get it well into your head that you and yours are `reasoning men'[218] (*gente de razon*), and that all coloured people are irrational, and slavery follows as a natural sequence; for `reasoning men' have wit to make a gun, and on the gun all reason takes it stand. From the first instant of their arrival in America, the Jesuits had maintained a firm front against the enslavement of the Indians. They may have had their faults in Europe, and in the larger centres of population in America; but where they came in contact with the Indians, theirs was the sole voice raised upon their side.

In 1593 Padre Juan Romero, sent from Peru as Superior to Paraguay, on his arrival gave up an estate (with Indians in *encomienda*) which his predecessors had enjoyed, alleging that he did not wish to give the example of making profit out of the unpaid labour of the Indians,[219] and that without their work the estate was valueless.

On many occasions, notably in the time of Cardenas, the Jesuits openly withstood all slavery, and amongst the concessions that Ruiz Montoya obtained from the King of Spain was one declaring all the Indians to be free.[220] If more examples of the hatred that their attitude on slavery called forth were wanting, it is to be remembered that in 1640, when Montoya and Taño returned from Spain, and affixed the edict of the Pope on the church doors in Piritinanga, threatening with excommunication all slave-holders, a cry of robbery went forth, and the Jesuits were banished from the town. But in this matter of slavery there is no saying what view any one given man will take upon it when he finds himself in such a country as America was during the time the Jesuits were in Paraguay. Don Felix de Azara, a liberal and a philosopher, a man of science, and who has left us perhaps the best description both of Paraguay and of the River Plate, written in the eighteenth century, yet was a partisan of slavery.[221] In a most curious passage for a Liberal philosopher, he says:[222] `The Court ordered Don Francisco, Judge of the High Court of Charcas, to go to Peru in the character of visitor. The first measure which he took, in 1612, was to order that in future no one should go to the Indians' houses with the pretext of reducing them (*i.e.*, to civilization), and that no *encomiendas* (fiefs) should be given of the kind we have explained — that is to say, with personal service (of the Indians). I cannot understand on what he could have founded a measure so politically absurd; but as that judge favoured the *ideas of the Jesuits*, it is suspected that they dictated his conduct.'

What stronger testimony (coming from such a man) could possibly be found, both that the Jesuits were opposed to the enslaving of the Indians and that their opposition rendered them unpopular? In the same way, no doubt, some modern, unwise philosopher, writing in Brussels, would uphold the slavery and massacres in Belgian Africa as evidences of a wise policy, because the end condones the means, and in the future, when progress has had time to fructify, there will be workhouses dotted all up and down the Congo, and every 'native' will be forced to supply himself, at but a trifle above the cost in Belgium, with a sufficiency of comfortable and thoroughly well-seasoned wooden shoes.

So it appears that the aforesaid were the two chief reasons which made the Jesuits unpopular with the Spanish settlers in Paraguay. But in addition it should be remembered that there were in that country members of almost all the other religious Orders, and that, as nearly every one of them had quarrelled with the Jesuits in Europe, or at the best were jealous of their power, the enmities begun in Europe were transmitted to the New World, and constantly fanned by reports of the quarrels which went on between the various Orders all through Europe, and especially in Rome.

But if it were the case that the Jesuits excited feelings of hatred in their neighbours, yet they certainly had the gift of attaching to themselves the Indians' hearts. No institution, condemned with contumely and thrust out of a country where it had worked for long, its supposed crimes kept secret, and its members all condemned unheard, could have preserved its popularity amongst the descendants of the men with whom it worked, after more than one hundred years have passed, had this not been the case.

I care not in the least for theories, for this or that dogma of politicians or theologists, but take my stand on what I heard myself during my visits to the now ruined Jesuit missions in Paraguay. Horsemen say horses can go in any shape, and, wonderful as it may seem, men can be happy under conditions which no writer on political economy would recognise as fit for human beings. Not once but many times have aged Indians told me of what their fathers used to say about the Jesuits, and they themselves always spoke of them with respect and kindness, and endeavoured to keep up to the best of their ability all the traditions of the Church ceremonies and hours of prayer which the Jesuits had instilled.

That the interior system of their government was perfect, or such as would be suitable for men called `civilized' to-day, is not the case. That it was not only suitable, but perhaps the best that under all the circumstances could have been devised for Indian tribes two hundred years ago, and then but just emerged from semi-nomadism, is, I think, clear, when one remembers in what a state of misery and despair the Indians of the *encomiendas*[223] and the *mitas* passed their lives. That semi-communism, with a controlling hand in administrative affairs, produced many superior men, or such as rise to the top in modern times, I do not think; but, then, who are the men, and by the exercise of what kind of virtues do they rise in the societies of modern times? The Jesuits' aim was to make the great bulk of the Indians under their control contented, and that they gained their end the complaints against them by the surrounding population of slave-holders and hunters after slaves go far to prove.

Leaving upon one side their system of administration, and discounting their unalterable perseverance, there were two things on which the Jesuits appealed to the Indians; and those two things, by the very nature of their knowledge of mankind, they knew appealed as much to Indians as to any other race of men. Firstly (and in this writers opposed to them, as Brabo[224] and Azara,[225] both agree), they instilled into the Indians that the land on which they lived, with missions, churches, herds, flocks, and the rest, was their own property. And in the second place they told them they were free, and that they had the King of Spain's own edict in confirmation of their freedom, so that they never could be slaves. Neither of these two propositions commends itself to many writers on the Jesuits in Paraguay, but for all that it seems to me that in themselves they were sufficient to account for the firm hold the Jesuits had on their neophytes.

The freedom which the Indians enjoyed under the Jesuit rule might not have seemed excessive to modern minds and those attuned to the mild rule of the Europeans of to-day in Africa. Such as it was, it seemed sufficient to the Guaranís, and even, in a limited degree, placed them above the Indians of the Spanish settlements, who for the most part passed their lives in slavery.

Chapter VIII

Don José de Antequera — Appoints himself Governor of
Asuncion — Unsettled state of affairs in the town — He is
commanded to relinquish his illegal power — He refuses,
and resorts to arms — After some success he is defeated
and condemned to be executed — He is shot on his way to
the scaffold — Renewed hatred against the Jesuits — Their
labours among the Indians of the Chaco

From the departure of Cardenas in 1650, to about 1720, was the halcyon
period of the Jesuit missions in Paraguay. During that time things went on in
the missions after the fashion I have attempted to describe. The people
passed their time in their semi-communistic labour, sweetened by constant
prayer; their pastors may or may not have done all that was possible to
instruct them in the science of the time; but, still, the Indian population did
not decrease, as it was observed to do from year to year in other countries of
America and in the Spanish settlements in Paraguay.[226] During this period
the Jesuits had made repeated efforts, but without much real success, to
establish missions amongst the wild equestrian tribes in the Gran Chaco
upon the western bank of the river Paraguay. Nothing, apparently, pointed
to the events which, beginning in the year 1721, finally led to their expulsion,
or, at least, furnished additional reasons to King Charles III. to include the
Jesuits in Paraguay in the general expulsion of their order from the
dominions of the Spanish crown.

In that year (1721) Don José de Antequera was appointed to succeed the
Governor of Paraguay, Don Diego de los Reyes Balmaceda, when his term
of office had expired. The situation was, as often happened in the Spanish
colonies, complicated by an inquiry into the conduct of the Governor
(Balmaceda), in progress at the High Court of Charcas, which court, as in the
case of Cardenas, acted most cautiously, both on account of its position, so
far from Paraguay, and on account of the inordinate procrastination of
everything connected with the Spanish law. If Balmaceda were condemned,
then Antequera would step into his shoes at once. If, on the other hand, he
were acquitted, Antequera would have to wait until the legal time of office
had run its course. So far all was in order, but the High Court, either in doubt
of its own wisdom or of its power to pronounce judgment definitely, had
issued a decree suspending Balmaceda from his functions, but without either
condemning or acquitting him. This, too, they did after having taken more
than three years to sift the evidence and summon witnesses, who either had
to cross the country on a mule at the imminent risk of death by famine or by
Indians, or, having descended the river Plate to Buenos Ayres (which journey
often took a month), wait for a ship to take them round Cape Horn to Lima,

and from thence travel to Charcas on muleback, following one of the Incas' roads.

Don José de Antequera y Castro was born at Lima, and being, as Father Charlevoix[227] says, an able, eloquent, but vain and most ambitious man, endowed with plenty of imagination, some talent, and but little ballast, was not content to wait till time should place him in his governorship. So, hearing that a judge inquisitor was to be sent to Paraguay to inquire into the case, and having graduated himself and held the position of procurator fiscal in the Charcas, he solicited the post, and by some error was appointed.

No sooner was the appointment signed than straight he posted off to Paraguay. As he had studied in the college of the Jesuits at La Plata, his first visit was to the reductions of the Jesuits. The missionaries received him well, and sent a troop of Indians to escort him to the boundary of their territories, never suspecting what Antequera was about to do. Having heard that the Governor, Balmaceda, was at a distant port upon the Paraná, Antequera hastened to Asuncion. Arrived there, the same madness of authority seems to have come on him which came fifty or sixty years before his time on Cardenas. Finding no special seat reserved for him in the Cathedral, he publicly reproved the dean, to the great scandal of the worshippers. This seems not to have lost him the respect of the citizens of Asuncion, who were accustomed to all kinds of vagaries, both of their rulers and their spiritual guides. No sort of violence to laws and customs seems ever to affect a people unless the violence is done to benefit them, when instantly they rise against the breaker of the law, however heavily it may bear upon themselves.

But the devoted citizens of Asuncion were so accustomed to perpetual turmoil that, as Dean Funes[228] says, `they only stopped when it was absolutely necessary for them to breathe.' Even the overpraised citizens of Athens at the time of Pericles, who must have been in all their ways so like the Athenians of to-day, were not more instant in the Agora or diligent in writing patriots' names on oyster-shells than the noisy mob of half-breed patriots who in the sandy streets of Asuncion were ever agitating, always assembling, and doing everything within their power to show the world the perfect picture of a democratic State. Strange that such turbulent and patriotic people should have been ancestors of those whom I, after the termination of the war with Buenos Ayres and Brazil in 1870, knew as lethargic and downtrodden, as if the great dictator, Dr. Francia, whom the country people, speaking in bated breath, called `El Difunto', had still oppressed the land. Into the turbulent hotbed of Asuncion fell Antequera, one of those Creoles of Peru who, born with talent and well educated, seemed, either from the circumstances of their birth or the surroundings amongst which they passed their youth, to differ as entirely from the Spaniards as if they had been Indians and not Creoles of white blood. Like

Cardenas, Antequera was endowed with eloquence; but, unlike Cardenas, he set no store on eloquence upon its own account, but only used it for his own advancement in the world. Finding the Governor absent from Asuncion and lying under a decree suspending him from all his functions, it seems at once to have occurred to Antequera to seize his place. On this account, having ingratiated himself with some of those opposed to Balmaceda, he raised an army, and sent to seize him; but the Governor, having notice of the plot, escaped to Corrientes, and Antequera instantly assumed his post. This was too much for the Viceroy of Peru, who, though he had befriended Antequera in the past, had some respect for law. Immediately he issued a decree replacing Balmaceda in the governorship, and ordering Antequera to give him back the power he had usurped. This Antequera had no thought of doing, and he embarked on a career of violence which induced some to believe he intended to proclaim himself an independent king. Whether this was or was not the case, a state of things arose in Paraguay more pandemonic even than in the good old times of Cardenas. The Jesuits, not having seen their way to sustain the cause of their ex-pupil, were expelled once more (1725), and as before took ship for Corrientes amongst the tears of the people, their historians say,[229] and as Ibañez and those who have written against them affirm as strongly, amongst universal joy. Certain it is that in Asuncion they played a different part from that played by them in the mission territory, and no doubt mixed, as did the other Orders of religion, in the intrigues which never seemed to cease in the restless capital of Paraguay.

Not being content with the expulsion of the Jesuits, Antequera defeated several generals sent against him by the Viceroy of Peru, and by a *coup de main* took prisoner the ex-Governor Balmaceda, having surprised him in his house in Corrientes, and carried him back to Asuncion under a close guard. The usual reign of terror then began, and everything fell into confusion, till at last the King (Philip V.) in 1726 commanded that the Jesuits should be reinstated in their college in Asuncion, and that the missions should be taken from the jurisdiction of the Governors of Paraguay and placed under the control of the Governor of the River Plate, as had been previously done in the case of the other Jesuit missions beyond the Uruguay. But Spain was far away, and on one pretext or another so much delay occurred that it was not till March 18, 1728, that the Jesuits were reinstated in the college in Asuncion, which they were now fated to hold but for a little space. At last the Viceroy of Peru, the Marquess of Castel Fuerte, sent Don Bruno de Zavala with a sufficient army and six thousand Indians from the missions against the usurper Antequera, who fled for refuge to the Franciscan convent in Cordoba, where he remained, till, finding his position quite untenable, he fled to Charcas, where he was arrested, and sent to Lima to await his trial. Four years he waited in perfect liberty, going and coming about the town as it best pleased him, whilst the High Court heard evidence, wrote to Madrid, received instructions from the King, and generally displayed the incapacity which in all ages has been the chief distinctive features of every court of law.

In 1731 an order came from Madrid to execute him, and without loss of time he was placed on a horse draped all in black, and, preceded by a herald and guarded by a troop of guards, taken out to the public square to be beheaded. But the good people of the capital, who, in the fashion of the world, would not most probably have stirred a step to save a saint, were mightily concerned to see a rogue receive his due deserts. The streets were filled with thousands crying out `Pardon!' stones flew, and the affair looked so threatening that the Viceroy had to get on horseback and ride amongst the crowd to calm the tumult. The people met him with a shower of stones, and he, fearing the prisoner would escape, called on his guards to fire upon him. Four balls pierced Antequera, who fell dying from his horse into the arms of two accompanying priests. Thus the most turbulent of all the Governors of Paraguay ceased troubling, and the executioner, after having cut off his head, exhibited it to the people from the scaffold, with the usual moral aphorism as to the traitor's fate.

The triumph of the Jesuits in Asuncion was but momentary, following the general rule of triumphs, which take their way along the street with trumpets and with drums amid the acclamations of the crowd, and then, the pageant over, the chief actors fall back again into the struggles and the commonplace of ordinary life.

Between the years 1728 and 1730 the people of Asuncion had been more eager in pursuit of liberty[230] than was their usual wont. The citizens were divided into camps, and daily fought amongst the sandy streets and shady orange-bordered lanes which radiate from almost every quarter of the town. The rival bands of madmen were styled respectively the `Communeros' and the `Contrabandos', and to the first Antequera throughout his residence in Lima gave all the assistance in his power. Neither of the two seems to have had the most elementary idea of real patriotism, or any wish for anything beyond the momentary triumph of the miserable party to which each belonged. One doctrine they held in common — a hatred of the Jesuits, and of the influence they exercised against the enslaving of the Indians, which was the aim of `Contrabandos' and of `Communeros' alike. One of the rival chieftains of the factions having fled for refuge to the missions, the people of Asuncion assembled troops to take him from his sanctuary by force. Arrived upon the frontier of the Jesuit territory, they found themselves opposed by an army of the Indians, who looked so formidable that the troops retired to Asuncion, and the leaders, foiled in the field, and not having force to attack the Jesuits in their own territory, set vigorously to inflame the minds of the people against them.

They worked with such success that when, in 1732, the news of Antequera's death reached Paraguay, the people, inflamed with the idea that he was sacrificed to the hatred of the Jesuits, rose and expelled them once again. The constant expulsions of the Jesuits from Asuncion, the turmoils in the State, and the fact that every now and then the Indians had to take arms to defend their territory, acted most mischievously on the reductions, both in Paraguay and in those between the Paraná and Uruguay. Whole tribes of Indians, recently converted, went back to the woods; land was left quite untilled, and on the outskirts of the mission territory the warlike tribes of Indians, still unsubdued, raided the cattle, killed the neophytes, and carried off their wives as slaves. But still, in spite of all, the Indians clung to their priests — as they said, from affection for the religious care they had bestowed, but quite as possibly from the instinctive knowledge that, between the raiding Portuguese and the maddening patriots in Asuncion, their only safeguard against slavery lay in the Jesuits. Most fortunately for Paraguay at the time (1734), Don Bruno de Zavala, perhaps the most energetic of the Spaniards in the King's service in America, was Viceroy in the River Plate. Having received orders to quiet the dissensions in Asuncion, in spite of being nearly seventy years of age, and having lost an arm in the Italian wars, he marched at once, taking but forty soldiers in his train, as, war being imminent with Portugal, it was not safe to deplete the slender forces in the River Plate. Arrived in Paraguay, he entered the Jesuit missions at the Reduction of San Ignacio Guazu,[231] and, having appealed to the provincial of the Order for his aid, speedily found himself at the head of a large army of the Indians. After some skirmishes he was in a position to enter Asuncion and force the people to receive him as their Governor. By one of those revulsions so frequent in a crowd of reasonable men, the people begged him to invite the Jesuits to return. They did so (1735), and were received in state, the Governor, the Bishop, and the chief clergy and officials of the place attending Mass in the Cathedral with lighted candles in their hands. His duty over, Don Bruno de Zavala set off for Chile, where he had been appointed Governor, and on his journey, at the town of Santa Fe, died suddenly, exhausted with the battles, marchings and countermarchings, rebellions, Indian incursions, the turbulence of the people in the towns, and the other cares which formed the daily duties of a Spanish officer in South America at the middle of the eighteenth century.[232] The next ten years were on the whole peaceful and profitable for the Indians of the missions and for the Jesuits. The Indians followed quietly their Arcadian lives, except when now and then a contingent of them was required to assist in any of the wars, which at that time were ceaseless throughout the eastern part of South America. The Jesuits pushed out their spiritual frontiers, advancing on the north amongst the Tobatines of the woods, and on the west endeavouring to spread their colonies amongst the Chiriguanas and other of the Chaco tribes.

From the conquest of Peru, when those Indians who had been but recently brought under the empire of the Incas retreated into the Chaco, it had been the refuge of the fiercest and most indomitable tribes. The Spanish colonists, the ardour of the first conquest spent, had settled down mainly to agricultural pursuits. Few had efficient firearms, and on the whole, though turbulent amongst themselves, they had become unwarlike.[233] The very name of the wild Indians (Los Indios Bravos) spread terror up and down the frontiers. This terror, which I remember still prevalent both in Mexico and on the pampas of the Argentine Republic, not more than five-and-twenty years ago, was keener upon the confines of the Chaco than anywhere in South America, except, perhaps, in Chile, upon the frontiers of Araucania.

The Tobas, Mataguayos, Lules, Aguilotas, Abipones, and the rest, together with the warlike nations of the Vilelas and the Guaycurús, had from the first rejected Christianity. Attempts had several times been made to establish settlements amongst them, but the ferocity of all the tribes, their nomad habits — for many of them passed their lives on horseback — and the peculiar nature of their country, a vast domain of swamp, pierced by great rivers quite unknown to the Spanish settlers, had hitherto combined to render every effort vain. But, notwithstanding this, the Jesuits laboured incessantly, and not without success, amongst the wildest of the Chaco tribes. The gentle and eccentric Father Martin Dobrizhoffer passed many years amongst the Abipones, of whom he wrote his charming book. He enumerates many tribes, of whom he says[234] 'these are for the most converted by us, and settled in towns.'

Nothing, perhaps, displays the Jesuits at their best, more than their efforts in the Chaco. The enormous territory was sparsely peopled by about seventy tribes,[235] whereof there were fifteen or sixteen of considerable size. Hardly two tribes spoke dialects by which they could communicate with one another, and almost every one of them lived in a state of warfare, not only with the Spaniards, but with the neighbouring tribes. The inventories preserved by Brabo[236] show us the town of Paisanes in the Chaco, with its rough wooden houses, and the Jesuits' habitation in the middle of the place, stockaded, and without doors, and with but narrow openings in the wall, through which the missionaries crept. The inside of the house contained five or six rough rooms, almost unfurnished, but for a few religious books and a plentiful supply of guns.[237] Their beds were of unvarnished wood, with curtains of rough cotton spun by the Indians. Sometimes they had a sofa of leather slung between four stakes, a rack for medicine bottles, and for the wine for Mass. Lastly, one priest, in the settlement amongst the Toquitistines, had among his books copies of Cervantes and Quevedo; one hopes he read them half smiling, half with a tear in his eye, for your true humour is akin to tears. Perhaps, reading 'Don Quixote' or 'El Gran Tacaño', the poor priest forgot his troubles, and, wandering with Sancho in La Manchan oak-woods or through Castilian uplands, thought he was in Spain.[238]

Throughout the territory of the Gran Chaco there were but seven reductions established by the Jesuits. These were San José de Bilelas, with its little town Petacas; San Juan Bautista de los Iristines, with its townlet of the same name; San Esteban de los Lules, with the town of Miraflores; Nuestra Señora del Buen Consejo de los Omarapas, capital Ortega; Nuestra Señora de Pilar de los Paisanes, with Macapillo as its centre; Nuestra Señora del Rosario de los Tobas, with its chief place called San Lucas; and, lastly, the establishment amongst the Abipones, known as La Concepcion. In all these missions the Jesuits lived in constant peril of their lives. In reading their old chronicles one finds the records of their obscure and half-forgotten martyrdoms, their sufferings, and the brief record of their deaths by an arrow or a club. In 1711 Father Cavallero, with all his following, was slain by the savage Pinzocas. In 1717 Father Romero, having, as a Jesuit writer says, `nothing but moral force behind him,'[239] was slain with twelve companions of the Guaranís of Paraguay. In 1718 Fathers Arco and Blende, Sylva and Maceo, received their dusted-over martyrs' crowns.

Right up the western bank of the river Paraguay, in the old maps, the crosses mark the sites where Jesuits were slain. That they all died to further crafty schemes, or for some hidden purpose of a Machiavelian nature, even a Dominican will scarcely urge. That they did good — more or less good than Protestant fanatics of the same kidney might have achieved — it were invidious to inquire. That which is certain is that they were single-hearted men, faithful unto the end to what they thought was right, faithful even to the shedding of their own blood, which is, one may believe, the way in which the scriptural injunction should be rightly read.

In the dim future, when some shadow of common-sense dawns on the world, and when men recognise that it is better to let others follow their destiny as it best pleases them, without the officious interference of their fellows, it may be that they will say all missionaries of whatsoever sect or congregation should have stayed at home, and not gone gadding to the desert places of the earth seeking to remedy the errors of their God by their exertions; but whilst the ideal still remains of sacrifice (which may, for all I know, be useless in itself, or even harmful), they must perforce allow the Jesuits in Paraguay high rank, or else be stultified.

But in the Chaco the Jesuits found conditions most different from those prevailing in their missions between the Uruguay and Paraná. Instead of open plains, vast swamps; instead of docile semi-Arcadians like the Guaranís, who almost worshipped them, fierce nomad horsemen, broken into a hundred little tribes, always at war, and caring little for religion of any sort or kind.

Again, there seems in the Chaco to have been no means of amassing any kind of wealth, as all the territory was quite uncultivated and in a virgin state; but, still, the settlements had existed long enough for cattle to increase.[240] Lastly, the incursions of the barbarous tribes were a constant menace both to the Jesuits and their neophytes. Yet in their indefatigable way the Jesuits made considerable progress amongst the Chaco tribes, as both the curious 'History of the Abipones' by Father Dobrizhoffer and the inventories preserved by Brabo prove.[241]

Besides their seven establishments in the Gran Chaco, they had three establishments in the north of Paraguay in the great woods which fringe the central mountain range of the country, known as the Cordillera de M'baracayu. These missions, called San Joaquin del Taruma, San Estanislao, and Belen, were quite apart from all the other missions of the Guaranís, far distant from the Chaco, and removed by an enormous distance from those of the Order in the Moxos and amongst the Chiquitos, forming, as it were, an oasis in the recesses of the Tarumensian woods. These three reductions, founded respectively in 1747,[242] 1747, and 1760, were, as their dates indicate, the swansong of the Jesuits in Paraguay. Founded as they were far from the Spanish settlements, they were quite removed from the intrigues and interferences of the Spanish settlers, which were the curse of the other missions on the Paraná. The Tobatines Indians[243] were of a different class to the Guaranís, though possibly of the same stock originally. Not having come in contact until recent years with the Spaniards, and having had two fierce and prolonged wars with the nearest settlements, they had remained more in their primitive condition than any of the Indians with whom the Jesuits had come in contact in Paraguay. During the short period of Jesuit rule amongst them (1746-1767) things seem to have gone on in a half-Arcadian way. In San Joaquin, Dobrizhoffer, as he says himself, devoted eight years of unregretted labour to the Indians. Most certainly he was one of the Jesuits who understood the Indians best, and his descriptions of them and their life are among the most delightful which have been preserved. He tells of the romantic but fruitless search during eighteen months throughout the forests of the Taruma by Fathers Yegros, Escandon, Villagarcia, and Rodriguez, for the Itatines who had left the reduction of Nuestra Señora de Santa Fe, and had hidden in the woods.

Then, commenting upon the strangeness of all affairs sublunary, he relates that accident at length effected what labour could not do. In 1746 Father Sebastian de Yegros, after a search of forty days, came on the Indians — as it were, directed by Providence, or, as we now say, accident. He built a town for them, and, as Dobrizhoffer says, 'assembled them in Christian polity.' To the new-founded village cattle of every kind were sent, with clothes — useful, of course, to those who had never worn them — axes, and furniture, and lastly a few music masters,[244] without whose help those who build cities spend their toil in vain.

To the new town (in which the simple-hearted priest remained eight years), in 1753, came Don Carlos Morphi, an Irishman, and Governor of Paraguay; and, having stayed five days with Dobrizhoffer, departed, marvelling at the accuracy with which the new-made Christians (*Cristianos nuevos*) managed their double-basses, their flageolets, their violins, and, in general, all their instruments, whether of music or of war.

Modestly, but with prolixity, as befits a virtuous, God-fearing man, the simple Jesuit relates a special instance of the way in which he was enabled to work both for his own glory and for the profit of the Lord. Not far from San Estanislao was situate the forest of M'baevera, in which grew quantities of trees from which the *yerba-maté* (Paraguayan tea) was made. To reach it was a work of pain and trouble, for through the woods a track called a *picada* had to be cut; the rivers were deep, bridgeless, and had to have branches strewed along the track to give a footing to the struggling mules.[245]

An expedition having been sent under a certain Spaniard called Villalba to collect *yerba*, came suddenly upon a deserted Indian hut. As they had started quite unarmed, except with knives and axes to cut down the boughs, a panic seized them, and, instead of collecting any leaves,[246] they hurried back to San Estanislao. No sooner did Dobrizhoffer hear the news than he set out to find the Indians, with a few neophytes, upon his own account. Having travelled the 'mournful solitudes' for eighteen days, they came upon no sign of Indians, and returned footsore and hungry, 'the improvement of our patience being our sole recompense.'

He himself walked all the way, and 'often barefoot', suffering 'what neither I can describe nor yet my reader credit.' The missionary calling has undergone considerable change since 1750. Hardships which the greater faith or stronger constitutions of the missionaries of the last century rendered endurable are now largely fallen out of fashion, and your missionary seldom walks barefoot, even in a wood, because to do so would give offence, and bring discredit on the society for which he works.

Though unsuccessful in his search that year, Dobrizhoffer, not daunted by his barefoot marching, set out again upon the Gospel trail next spring. After another journey of some twenty days, during the whole course of which it rained incessantly, he came on a community of seemingly quite happy sylvans, whom he proceeded to convert. In the first hut he met with there were eight doors, and in it dwelt some sixty Indians — a palm-built, grass-thatched phalanstery, with hammocks slung from the rude beams, in which 'these heathen' used to sleep. Each separate family had its own fire, on the hearth of which stood mugs and gourds and pots of rudely-fashioned earthenware. Naked and not ashamed 'these savages', and the men wore upon their heads high crowns of parrot feathers. For arms they carried bows and arrows, and the first man Dobrizhoffer saw was holding a dead pheasant in one hand, and in the other a short bow. In the woods around the phalanstery was an 'amazing' quantity of maize, of fruits of divers sorts, and of tobacco. From the hives which the wild bees make in hollow trees, they collected honey in large quantities, which served them (at least so Dobrizhoffer says) for meat and drink alike.

Their name for the god they worshipped was Tupá, but 'of that God and his commandments they care to know but little.' This sounds ambiguous, and would appear at first sight as if the confidence betwixt the creators and their God had been but slight. Perhaps the ambiguity may be set down to the translator[247] who turned the Latin in which the memoirs first were formed into the vulgar tongue.

A thing remarkable enough when one considers how prone mankind is to act differently was that, although the Itatines knew an evil spirit under the name of Aná, yet they paid little adoration to him, apparently content to know as little of him and his laws as they did of their God.

Those hapless, harmless folk, as innocent of God and devil, right and wrong, and all the other things which by all rights they should have known, as they are said to be implanted in the mind of man, no matter what his state, seem to have lived quite happily in their involuntary sin.[248] But Dobrizhoffer, in his simple faith and zeal for what he thought was right, wept bitter tears when he thought upon their unregenerate state.

A sycophantic Guaraní from the reductions then took up his parable, and said: 'God save ye, brothers; we are come to visit you as friends. This father-priest is God's own minister, and comes to visit you, and pray for your estate.' An aged Indian interrupted him, saying he did not want a father-priest, and that St. Thomas in the past had prayed sufficiently, as fruits of every sort abounded in the land. The Indian, in his unsophisticated way, seems to have thought the presence of a priest acted but as manure on the ground where he abode; but the Jesuit, almost as simple-minded as himself, took it in kindliness, and journeyed with the Indian to a large village about three days away. Arrived there, all the inhabitants of the place sat in a circle round the missionary. They appeared (he says) in so much modesty and silence 'that I seemed to behold statues, and not live Indians.' To awaken their attention he played upon the viol d'amore, and, having thus captured their ears, began to preach to them. The good priest probably believed all that he said, for, after dwelling on the perils of the road, he said: 'My friends, my errand is to make you happy.' It did not seem to him that their free life in woods, in which abounded maize, fruits, and tobacco, with game of every kind, could possibly have induced content. Content, as Christians know, comes but with faith, and a true knowledge of the dogma is above liberty. Kindly, but muddle-headedly, he deplored their lot, their want of clothes, their want of interest in their God, their lack of knowledge of that God's commands. Then, coming to the point, he spoke of hell, and told the astonished Indians that it was quite impossible for them to avoid its flames, unless, taught by a priest, they came to know God's law. He then briefly (as he says) explained the mysteries of our faith. They listened rapt, except that `the boys laughed a little' when he spoke of hell.[249] Nothing more painful than to see a child laughing unconscious of its peril in the traffic of a crowded street, and we may well believe that the kind-hearted Dobrizhoffer shuddered at the laughter of these children when he reflected that had he taken the wrong path, crossing the marshes or in the woods, the laughers had been damned. Much more he said to them after exhausting hell, and, to `add weight' to his oration, presented each of them with scissors, knives, glass beads, axes, small looking-glasses, and fishing-hooks, for he knew well that sermons which end in `give me' have but a small effect.

He says himself quite frankly, `I seemed to have borne down all before me because I had mingled my oration with a copious largess.'[250] Glass beads and looking-glasses have from the time when the first Christian missionary preached to the Indians been potent factors in conversion, and still to-day do yeoman service in the great work of bringing souls to God.

Seated around the fire `smoking tobacco through a reed', and pondering perchance over the mysteries of the new expounded faith, the *cacique* of the Itatines took up his parable.

`I have' (said he) `conceived an affection for the father-priest, and hope to enjoy his company throughout my life. My daughter is the prettiest girl in the whole world, and I am now resolved to give her to the father-priest, that he may always stay with me, and with my family, here in the woods.'

The Indians from the missions broke into laughter, after the fashion of all those who, knowing but a little, think that they are wise. The *cacique*, who knew nothing, was astounded that any man, no matter what his calling, could live without a wife, and asked the Jesuit if the strange thing was true. His doubts being satisfied, they fell discoursing on the nature of the Deity, a subject not easy of exhaustion, and difficult to treat of through the medium of an interpreter. `We know' (the *cacique* said) `that there is someone who dwells in heaven.' This vagueness put the missionary upon his mettle, and he set out at once to expatiate upon the attributes of God. They seemed to please the *cacique*, who inquired, `What is it that displeases, then, the dweller in the skies?'

Lies, calumnies, adulteries, thefts, all were enumerated, and received the Indian's assent; but the injunction not to kill provoked a bystander to ask if it was not permitted to a man to slay those who attacked his life. He added, `I have endeavoured so to do since the first day I carried arms.'

`Fanatical casuist' is a stout argument in the mouth of a man nurtured upon Suarez and Molina, but no doubt it did good service, and Dobrizhoffer uses it when speaking of the chief. But Dobrizhoffer did better work than mere theological disputation, for he prevailed upon eighteen of the Indians to accompany him to the settlement of San Joaquin; and after having `for some months tried the constancy' of a youth called Arapotiyu, he admitted him to the sacrament of baptism, and `not long afterwards united him in marriage according to the Christian rites.' It is evident that baptism should precede marriage; but it is an open question as to the duration of the interval between the two ceremonies, and we may be permitted to wonder whether, after all, both might not be advantageously dispensed at the same time. In the case of Arapotiyu the system worked satisfactorily, for he `surpassed in every kind of virtue, and might have been taken for an old disciple of Christianity.' Even `old Christians' occasionally, despite their more laborious induction into the rites and customs of their faith, have fallen from grace, perhaps from the undue prolongation of the term between the ceremonies.

In the case of another youth (one Gato) things did not go so smoothly, for though he, too, by his conduct obtained both baptism and Christian wedlock, Dobrizhoffer adds without comment, `not many months after he died of a slow disease.'[251] The slow disease was not improbably the nostalgia of the woods, from which the efforts of the good missionary had so successfully withdrawn him.

The labours of the Jesuits in the three isolated missions in the north of Paraguay[252] seem to have been as successful as those in the Chaco were unfortunate. In dealing with the wild equestrian tribes of the Gran Chaco, the system of the Jesuits was not so likely to achieve success as amongst the peaceful Guaranís. That of the Spanish settlers was entirely ineffectual, and has remained so down to the present day, when still the shattered remnants of the Lules, Lenguas, Mocobios, and the rest, roam on their horses or in their canoes about the Chaco and its rivers, having received no other benefits from contact with the European races but gunpowder and gin.

Chapter IX

The Spanish and Portuguese attempt to force new laws on the Indians — The Indians revolt against them — The hopeless struggle goes on for eight years — Ruin of the missions

The missions in the Chaco and the Taruma, all founded between 1700 and 1760, the last (Belen) but seven years before the expulsion of the Jesuits from America, go far towards disproving the allegations of some writers,[253] that the apostolic energy of the first foundations had decayed, and that the Jesuits were merely living on the good name of the first founders in the beginning of the past century. But let the zeal of any class of men be what it may, if they oppose themselves to slavery and at the same time are reported to have lands in which is gold, and resolutely exclude adventurers from them, their doom is sealed. Both crimes were set down to the Jesuits. Writing in 1784, or twenty years after the expulsion of his order, Dobrizhoffer refers to the Indians of the reductions as 'being in subjection[254] only to the Catholic King and the royal Governors, not in dreaded slavery amongst private Spaniards as the other Indians;' and Montoya, Lozano, and Del Techo, writing in earlier times, all confirm the statement, which is also doubly confirmed by the various royal edicts on the subject.[255] The reports of gold-mines, too, had never ceased, although they had been repeatedly disproved, and those, together with the stand for freedom for the Indians, led to the events which finally brought about the expulsion of the Order from the territories where they had worked so long.

In 1740, Gomez de Andrade, Governor for the King of Portugal in Rio de Janeiro, being one of those who was convinced that the reason why the Jesuits guarded their territories so religiously was that they had mines, bethought him of a plan. His plan, like most of those conceived on the fantastic reasons which are called 'of State', took no account of sentiment, and therefore, as mankind are and will ever be a thousand times more influenced by sentiment than by hard reasoning, was from the first bound of itself to fail.

The colony of Sacramento upon the river Plate had for a hundred years been the source of conflict between the Spaniards and the Portuguese.[256] Situated as it was almost in front of Buenos Ayres, it served as a depot for smugglers; and, moreover, being fortified, menaced the navigation both of the Paraná and Paraguay. Slavers from England, Holland, and the German ports crowded the harbour. Arms of all kinds were stored there, and were distributed to all adventurers who meditated assaults against the crown of Spain. Twice or three times it had been taken and restored, the Indians of the missions always rendering most efficient help. At the time of which I write (1740) it had passed again by treaty under the dominion of the Portuguese, but still remained a standing menace to the Spaniards. Gomez Andrade advised the court of Lisbon to exchange it against the seven reductions[257] of the Uruguay, and thus at once to secure a country rich in gold and to adjust the frontier at the river Uruguay. Nothing appears so simple to a statesman as to exchange one piece of territory for another. A parchment signed after some international negotiations, and the whole thing is done. If, though, as happened in this case, one of the territories contains a population such as that which inhabited the seven towns upon the Uruguay, and which has conquered the country in which it lives from virgin forest, and defended it against all comers, it sometimes happens that the unreasonable inhabitants, by clinging to their homes, defeat the statesmen's plans. Yet statesmen, once embarked in any plan, do not stick at such trifles as the affection of a people for its home, but quietly pursue their path, knowing that that which is conceived by ministers of State must in the end be beneficial to mankind. Without this patriotic abnegation of their feelings, no statesmen would be worthy of the name. Indifference to the feelings of others is perhaps the greatest proof a public man can give of his attachment to the State. After negotiations, lasting many years, in 1750 a treaty was signed between Portugal and Spain agreeing that the former should give up the Colonia del Sacramento to the Spaniards in exchange for the seven Jesuit towns upon the Uruguay, and that both nations should furnish a commission to fix the frontiers of the two nations on the Uruguay.[258] On February 15, 1750, the Spanish court sent to the Jesuits of the seven towns to prepare their Indians to leave their homes and march into the forests, and there found new towns.

At that date François Retz was General of the Jesuits, and on him devolved the duty of communicating the orders of the courts of Spain and Portugal to the Jesuits in the missions of the Uruguay. Father Bernard Neyderdorffer was the man on whom the Provincial of Paraguay (Father Barreda) imposed the task of communicating to the Indians the wishes of the two courts. Though he had lived already thirty-five years in the missions, and knew the Indians well, and was respected by them as a father, he seems at first to have shrunk from such a task. When the news was brought to the towns upon the Uruguay, none of the Indians at first would credit it. The *caciques* (chiefs) of the seven towns declared that they would rather die than leave their native place. Nothing was heard but lamentations and expressions of hatred of the Portuguese, mingled with denunciations of the Jesuits themselves, who the poor Indians not unnaturally believed were in league with Spain to sell them to the Portuguese. But in a little the clamours turned to action, and, not content with refusing to obey the edict of the two courts, the Indians broke into revolt. Two most important narratives of this revolt exist, one by Father

Cardiel and one by Father Ennis, both of whom were witnesses of the events. After considerable negotiations, which lasted till 1753,[259] the united troops of Portugal and Spain advanced into the mission territory to arrange the occupation of the ceded towns. The commissioners of the two nations were, for Spain, the Marques de Valdelirios, and for Portugal General Gomez Freyre de Andrade, and both of them appear to have come to America already prejudiced against the Jesuits. On March 24, 1753, Andrade wrote to Valdelirios, almost before he could have heard anything definite about the mission territory, to which they both were strangers, telling him that opposition was to be expected, and that the Jesuits were urging the Indians to revolt.[260] The opposition that the two commissioners so confidently hoped to find,[261] and which contemporary writers have set forth in its true colours as but the revolt of ignorant Indians rendered desperate by being arbitrarily dispossessed of lands which they themselves had settled and held for almost a hundred years, was fraught with serious consequences, not only to the Jesuits in Paraguay, but to the Order throughout the world at large. For years their enemies had said the Jesuits were endeavouring to set up in the missions a State quite independent of the Spanish crown. By their own conduct the Jesuits to some extent had given colour to the report, for by excluding (in the interest of the Indians) all Spaniards from the mission territories, it looked as if they were at work at something which they wished to keep a secret, as no one at that time deemed it a serious plea to enter into any line of conduct for the good of Indians, whom in general the Spanish settlers looked upon as beasts. That it was the best policy they could have possibly pursued under the circumstances is proved abundantly by the code of instructions laid down by Don Francisco Bucareli, the Viceroy of Buenos Ayres, under whose auspices the expulsion of the Jesuits in 1760 was carried out. In that code occurs the following article:[262] `You will not allow any strangers, of whatever estate, quality, or condition they may be, to reside in the town (that is, of the missions), even if they be artisans,[263] and much less that they deal or take contracts in them either for themselves or for others, and you shall take especial care that the Laws of the Indies be executed, and specially those which are contained in Article 27 of Book IX.;[264] and also if any Portuguese deserters or other persons of whatever conditions should come to the towns, you will instantly conduct them to this city, taking every precaution to prevent their escape.'

Still, though their policy was pursued, it did not stop the opponents of the Jesuits from denouncing that very policy, both at the cession of the seven towns and at the expulsion of the Order from America. The commissioners, after innumerable delays, having found themselves in 1753 at Santa Tecla, a village near the Uruguay, it becomes necessary to cast a glance at what the Jesuits themselves were doing, and how they tried to do their duty as they saw it both to their Sovereign, their Order, and the Indians over whom they ruled. It seems as if, whilst the superiors of the Order recognised at once the futility of striving against Portugal and Spain, some of the inferior members secretly set on the Indians to armed resistance to the impolitic decree. The council of the province (Paraguay)[265] assembled at the Jesuit college in Cordoba, composed of Fathers Masala, Horos, Caballero, Lopez, and Lozano, sent a memorial[266] both to the Viceroy of Peru and to the High Court of Charcas. In the memorial they first set forth their loyalty, and then exposed the deceit to which the ministers of Spain and Portugal had been subjected by their advisers in America. They pointed out most justly that the treaty was damaging to both the countries concerned,[267] and that in regard to the Indians of the seven towns peculiarly unjust. Both at Charcas and at Lima their memorial (though diffuse) was favourably received, and a copy remitted to the King and Council at Madrid. Ibañez, in his 'Republica Jesuitica', qualifies the action of the Jesuits in this matter as a 'great crime'. Dean Funes only sees duplicity of language, but seems to excuse it in the circumstances in which the Jesuits were placed. Certainly, after efforts extending over almost two hundred years, it was hard on them to see seven of their most flourishing missions arbitrarily broken up, the Indians driven from their homes, and their territory occupied by those very Portuguese who for a hundred years had been their persecutors. There was much to say in extenuation, even for 'duplicity of language', when one remembers that the Jesuits alone (no matter how mistaken their views of treatment may seem to modern eyes) stood out against the assumption that the Indians were a mere flock of sheep, who might be driven from their homes on any pretext, or at the exigencies of ministers at courts who lived ten thousand miles away, and were completely ignorant of the local circumstances. Whether the memorial influenced the court of Spain is hard to say; but it is certain that when, in 1752, the Marques de Valdelirios arrived in Buenos Ayres, with him came as a commissioner to fix the boundary between the two nations of the Uruguay Father Luis de Altamirano, accompanied by his secretary, Rafael de Cordoba, both members of the Order, and that the Marquis took up his lodging in the college of the Jesuits. There papers and memorials rained on him: one came from the Bishop of Tucuman, and one from Don Jaime de San Just, the Governor of Paraguay, with many others from people of inferior note, all in the interest of the Company. It appears as if Valdelirios thought that these memorials were inspired, for his first action was to publish to the priests of the seven towns the wishes of his government as to evacuation by the Indians of the territory. This he did through the prefect of the missions, who seems to have acted in good faith in his endeavours to carry out the wishes of the Spanish court. Just at that moment Barreda, the Provincial of Paraguay, arrived in Buenos Ayres, and Valdelirios asked him his opinion as to the measures best calculated to insure the treaty being quietly carried out. Barreda, though all his interests were against the execution of the treaty, seems to have acted in good faith. He gave the sensible advice that, as the treaty had been made entirely without taking into consideration the difficulties of carrying it out, it could not be held a crime to ask the King for some delay.[268] He advised consulting three ex-Governors of Paraguay, who happened to be in Buenos Ayres,[269] and, lastly, that all hurry, or anything likely to excite the Indians, should be avoided; for it was possible that they, relying on their numbers and local knowledge, might be able to give much trouble even to the joint forces of both crowns. He laid before Valdelirios the condition of the reductions, telling him that they were fertile and well cultivated,[270] and that this of itself would incline the Indians against migrating from their lands. Lastly, he said it was the opinion of the most experienced of the priests that the Indians would yield neither to arguments nor reason, for the hatred of the Portuguese had put them quite beside themselves with fury at the idea of giving up their lands. Valdelirios must have found himself not in too comfortable a state. Lodged as he was in the college of the Jesuits, he must have felt that most of the advice which was so freely tendered him was biassed, and to relieve his mind he called a council, at which the Provincial Barreda, Juan Escadon, his secretary, Altamirano, and Rafael de Cordoba appeared. The council recommended prudence, and, as the majority were Jesuits, pushed their prudence even beyond Lowland Scotch or north of Ireland limits, for they proposed to institute a commission which, after three years' investigation, should report at Buenos Ayres on what it had found out. Commissions, royal or otherwise, have always been a trump-card in the hands of governments, since peddling democracy, with show of noses and the like, came in and put an end to those good old methods which are as dear to-day to rulers' hearts as they have ever been since the beginning of the world, and will be whilst election, battle, fitness, talents, wealth, unfitness, or any other cause, gives power into the hands of anyone to rule.

Valdelirios, who was not a fool, saw their design, and instantly despatched Altamirano (1752) to Castillos to meet Freire de Andrade and the Portuguese, and set about drawing the new frontier line at once. Altamirano, though a Jesuit, appears (at first at any rate) to have been anxious that the treaty should be carried out. In 1752 (September 22) he wrote[271] from the reduction of San Borja to P. Mathias Stroner,[272] ordering all the Jesuits to assist in carrying out the evacuation of the seven towns. By his advice Freire de Andrade and Valdelirios met at Castillos, and, after having laid off some twenty leagues of boundary line, returned respectively to the Colonia and to Buenos Ayres.

But in the missions things were in a state bordering on revolution. When the letter from the prefect of the missions reached San Miguel, the Indians assembled outside the church,[273] and having learned the situation of the lands to which they were to move, their fury knew no bounds. They all refused to stir, saying they had inherited their lands from their forefathers and by the grace of God.[274] Their example was at once followed by three more of the towns, and virtually a state of absolute defiance to the orders of the Spanish crown ensued.

Just at this moment Altamirano, the commissary, arrived, and found the state of things most serious.[275] The commissary Altamirano set to work at once to place before the Jesuits of the seven towns the danger they exposed themselves to if they refused to help him to carry out the orders of the crown. Almost immediately on his arrival he wrote[276] to Don José de Caruajal y Lancastre to send more troops, and to the various priests[277] to destroy their powder, and cease to manufacture any more.[278] It is most likely that, if Altamirano had no secret understanding with his brother Jesuits, his letters must have considerably amazed them, and certainly they gave offence to the Indians, who declared he could not be a Jesuit at all. Six hundred Indians, under a chief called Sepe Tyaragu, marched upon Santo Thomé, where Altamirano had taken up his residence, with the avowed purpose of discussing whether he was a Jesuit or not, and, if the latter supposition proved correct, of throwing him into the river Uruguay;[279] but Altamirano did not wait their coming, and returned precipitately to Buenos Ayres. The commission which had set out to mark the limits between the countries,[280] buried in the woods, or marching along the river, was absolutely unaware of what was going on amongst the Indians till they arrived in Santa Tecla on February 26, 1753. The first notice that they had of it was when they found themselves surrounded by a strong force of Indians. One of the commissaries, Don Juan de Echevarria, is known to have left a curious account of the proceedings, from which Dean Funes, Ibañez, and most of the writers on the subject must have copied.[281]

Historians, like lawyers in conveyancing, catch errors one from another, and transmit them as truths or titles to posterity. Certain it is that Echevarria sent for the nearest Jesuit priest to mediate, and he luckily, or unluckily, proved to be that Father Thadeus Ennis, who played so prominent a part in the futile rising which the enemies of the Jesuits have chosen to dignify with the high-sounding title of the `Jesuit War'.

If Father Ennis really thought the Indians could hold head to both the Spaniards and the Portuguese, or if he thought that the rising would draw attention to the injustice of the treaty, is difficult to say. Whether, indeed, he headed it himself, or if he merely accompanied the Indians as their spiritual guide, giving them now and then the benefit of his advice on matters temporal, after the fashion of the ambitious churchman of all time,[282] is now unknown. Whatever his opinions were upon this matter, Father Ennis showed himself almost from the first irreconcilable. He refused to meet the commissioners, and in his place sent a *cacique* (chief) of the Indians, one Sepe Tyaragu, an official of the reduction of San Miguel. This chief, seeing the escort of the commission was but small, 'put on his boots',[283] and took high ground, daring to talk about the rights of man, of the love of country, and said that liberty consisted in being allowed to enjoy his property in peace, sentiments which, though admirable enough in a white man's mouth, for men of colour are but fit for copy-books.

The *cacique* firmly refused to vacate his lands, and said the King of Spain, as he lived far away, could not have understood the bearing of affairs in Paraguay. Such arguments as these, together with the perhaps offensive tone of the *cacique*, had such effect on the commissioners that, after having threatened him with vengeance, which at the time they had no power to carry out, they both withdrew out of the territory.

As Funes[284] well observes, the Spaniards had established themselves in these parts (the River Plate and Paraguay) to obtain a limitless submission from the Indians. Any resistance drove them to fury, and excited them to take revenge. As all the Indians' crime was their unwillingness to quit the lands on which they had been born, it seemed a little hard to slaughter them, even before their petition to the King had been refused. Most probably all had been prepared before, for Valdelirios at once issued an order, which he had the power to do under a sealed letter from the King, to the Governor of Buenos Ayres, Andonaegui, to prepare for war. Active hostilities broke out in 1754, and Father Ennis has preserved a day-by-day account, written in priestly Latin,[285] of what took place. After some skirmishes, which at the first were favourable to the Indians, who took great courage from them,[286] the first encounter of a serious nature occurred on February 24, 1754. Quite naturally, the victory was on the side of the best-armed battalions, and the Indians lost many of their best men, and their largest piece of ordnance.[287]

With varying success the war dragged on for several years, after the style of the Gaucho warfare in the River Plate which was common twenty years ago, or that in Venezuela which obtains to-day. Alternately each party carried off the other's horses, drove each other's cattle, or, if they caught a straggler, tied his hands and cut his throat or lanced him, the party who had lost the man protesting he was 'massacred' — a term in use even to-day when the party to which one's self belongs sustains reverse. For the first two years — for wars in South America till twenty years ago were to the full as interminable as that of Troy — Father Thadeus Ennis kept his journal, faithfully chronicling all that he saw. Occasionally in a perfunctory way he says his mission with the revolted Indians was as a priest and physician to the souls and bodies of his flock; but now and then he sets down the capture of a convoy of some thirty carts, or the cutting off some messenger carrying despatches from the Generals. In this he sees the hand of God (put forth to help his Jesuits[288]), although he now and then complains the Indians were remiss in following up any success they had. After the first encounter, the Indians seem to have employed the immemorial guerilla tactics which so often waste all the strength of an army which has conquered in the field. Father Cardiel[289] describes the Indian army, quoting from the writing of a Spanish officer who served against them, as quite contemptible. Their cannon were but hollow reeds, bound round with hide, which could only be fired two or three times, and carried balls a pound in weight.[290] Some lances and bows and arrows which they had appeared to him more formidable. Most of them carried banners with the painted figure of a saint, under whose ægis they deemed themselves secure from cannon-balls. Their trenches were but shallow ditches, with a few deeper holes to shelter in, but which, as Cardiel observes, served many of them for graves, as they were open to artillery, having been constructed without `an ounce of military art'. The officer adds that no sooner had the Indians heard the cannon than they fled, leaving almost nine hundred on the field and losing one-sixth prisoners.[291] Finally, the officer remarks with disgust that the official chronicler of the affair `lies from first to last'[292] when he declares that the Indians could make any resistance against disciplined troops. With varying fortune the campaign dragged on, until in 1756 the diary of Father Ennis, bad Latinity and all, comes to an abrupt conclusion at the taking of San Lorenzo, where the stout-hearted priest was taken prisoner. His papers fell into unfriendly hands, and were made use of by Ibañez, with the context duly distorted in various passages, and served as one of the most formidable indictments against the Jesuits in the expulsion under Charles III.

Although Thadeus Ennis and other Jesuits accompanied the troops, and no doubt aided much by their advice, the Indians had as a general one Nicolas Ñeenguiru, styled in the Gazettes of the time the King of Paraguay. About this man all kinds of monstrous legends soon sprang up. One little lying book, entitled `Histoire de Nicolas I., Roy du Paraguai et Empereur des Mamalus',[293] which bears upon its title-page `Saint Paul',[294] 1756, especially excels. In that brief work of but one hundred and seventeen pages, printed on yellowish paper, and with one of the finest little vignettes of a basket of fruit and flowers upon its title-page that one could wish to see, a sort of parody of a Spanish picaresque novel in duodecimo is set forth with circumstance.

Nicolas Roubioni is duly born in 1710, in a small `bourgade de l'Andalousie' bearing the name of Taratos. The name carries conviction from the start, and pronounced à la française, with the accent equal upon all the syllables, is quite as Spanish as the most exigent of comic operas could possibly desire. His father, `ancien militaire', left him alone to educate himself as he best liked. Arrived at eighteen years of age he runs away to Seville, and after several adventures in the style of those of Rinconete and Cortadillo, seen through French spectacles, enters the service of a lady bearing the well-known Spanish name of Donna Maria della Cupidità. Under the unnecessary alias of Medelino, and in the capacity of cook, he becomes the lady's lover as in duty bound. `Chassé' from Seville by a jealous brother of his love, he flies for refuge to a `bourgade' (name not chronicled) some seven leagues away. He then becomes a muleteer, and at Medina Sidonia kills a man, and, forced to flee, repairs to Malaga, where he lives peacefully ten years. Finding life dull there, he journeys to Aragon and joins the Jesuits, and from henceforth his future is assured. After an interval he reappears at Huesca, and at once falls in love with `une belle espagnole', Donna Victoria Fortini, whom he courts under the guise of a gentleman of Seville, returning every night to the convent of the Jesuits to change his clothes. So great becomes his effrontery that under the style and title of `Comte de la Emmandés', he publicly marries `sa belle', the Jesuits either consenting, or too astounded at the fact to intervene. Things getting hot in Huesca, he embarks for Buenos Ayres as a missionary, leaving poor Donna de la Victoria `dans une inquiétude mortelle', as she might well have been. Arrived in Buenos Ayres just at the moment of the cession of the seven Jesuit towns, he sees his opportunity, learns Guaraní in the brief space of six or seven weeks, and joins the Indians. They naturally, having been trained to look on every foreigner outside the Order of the Jesuits as an enemy, receive him as their King. Under the title of the `Son of the Sun and Star of Liberty' he rules them, looked on as a God. The brief mendacious chronicle leaves him on the throne, just after having joined the empire of the Mamalucos to that of Paraguay, and promising to give the world more of his history when it comes to hand.

By stories such as those contained in the mendacious little book imprinted at St. Paul, the easy-minded public — then, as now, always more easily impressed with lies than with the truth — was biassed against the Jesuits in Paraguay. Father Dobrizhoffer,[295] who knew `King' Nicolas from his youth up, has left a very different version of his history, in which no Donna della Cupidità or de la Victoria even remotely flourishes. Nicolas Ñeenguiru was born in the township of La Concepcion, of which in after-life he rose to be the mayor. He married an Indian woman, not `une belle Andalouse', and Dobrizhoffer says a friend of his, one Father Zierheim, had him whipped publicly for petty theft when a young man. At the time (1753) when, in company with another Indian, one José, mayor of San Miguel, he headed the Indian revolt, he was a man of middle age, tall, taciturn and grave, and not ill-looking, though marked across the cheek with a disfiguring scar. At no time was he even a lay brother of the Jesuit Order, as by their rules in Paraguay no Indians were ever taken either as lay brothers or as priests. So little was the man feared by the authorities that, once the Indians' resistance was over, Nicolas went to the Spanish camp, was quietly heard, dismissed, and then continued in his office as the mayor of his native place. The legend sprang from a mistake in Guaraní, to which perhaps a little malice gave its artful charm. In Guaraní the word `Rubicha' signifies a chief, whereas `Nfurabicha' means king. The two, pronounced by one but ill acquainted with the language sound identical. Nothing was more likely than that the Indians should call their general their chief; had they thought really of settling upon a king, it is certain that they would have chosen one of the family of some well-known chief, and not an Indian merely appointed mayor by the Jesuits. But be that as it may, General Ñeenguiru, though he has left some interesting letters, which are preserved in the archives of Simancas, showed no capacity for generalship.[296] Throughout the course of the campaign he endeavoured to replace his want of skill by tricks and by intrigues, but of so futile a nature that they were frustrated and rendered useless at once. His first endeavour was to gain time, when he found himself with seventeen hundred men opposed to Andonaegui, Governor of Buenos Ayres, who had an army well equipped with guns, of about two thousand men. Ñeenguiru wrote to Andonaegui, telling him that the Indians were ready to submit, and then, whilst waiting for an answer, set about fortifying the position which he held. Warned by a spy, Andonaegui attacked at once, and drove the Indians from their trenches like a flock of sheep, taking their wooden cannon, lances, and banners, and killing thirteen hundred of them.

A glorious victory, and, as Father Ennis says, `to be expected, and which, had it chanced otherwise, must have covered the Spaniards and the Portuguese with shame.' In fact, a victory of the same kind as those which since that time have been most usual when well-armed European troops have faced half-naked, ill-armed savages, but which, of course, reflect no credit on the victor, or, at best, just as much credit as a butcher rightfully receives when he defeats a calf.

But even after the victory over the Indians of Nicolas Ñeenguiru the troubles of the allies were not quite at an end. The usual dissensions between allies who mutually detest each other soon broke out, and Gomez Freire, the General of the Portuguese, only prevented a collision with the Spaniards by considerable tact. After a short campaign of a few months, the allies entered the rebellious towns and took possession of them all, with the exception of San Lorenzo, which continued to hold out. A month or two served to reduce it, too, and the whole territory of the seven towns submitted to the power of the joint forces of Portugal and Spain. The struggle over, Ñeenguiru was quietly again reinstated mayor of Concepcion, the bruised wooden cannon duly set up as monuments, the dead left on the plains and the *esteros* for the chimangos[297] and the caranchos[298] to gorge upon, and, law's due majesty once more vindicated, the conquerors set about, in 1757, to trace the limits between the territories of the two Christian Kings.

Most of the seven towns were half deserted, the Indians having fled for refuge to the woods,[299] and the commission set to work upon its labours in a desert which it itself had made. Out of the fourteen thousand Indians who had inhabited the seven flourishing towns upon the Uruguay but few remained; yet still the work of pacification and working at the boundary went on slowly, for from 1753 to 1759 nothing of consequence was done. In 1760 Ferdinand VI. died, and his son Charles III. succeeded him, and still the boundary commission worked on hopelessly in Paraguay. The Jesuits, who had worked unceasingly during the last eight years to annul the treaty handing the seven missions over to the Portuguese, at length, in 1761, obtained from Charles III. a treaty annulling all that had been done, and providing that the seven towns should remain part of the dominions of the Spanish crown.

They triumphed; but their triumph added another step towards their ruin, for the jealousy which they evoked by their persistent fight raised up much animosity towards themselves in Spain. How great a share they had in the resistance of the Indians cannot be known with certainty. Papers preserved in the archives of Simancas charge them with stirring up the Indians to resist;[300] but they are chiefly from Valdelirios and others, who, naturally finding resistance, put it down at once to the Jesuits, whom then, as now, it was the fashion to abuse. The Indians themselves seem to have been perplexed, no doubt encouraged by their priests on one hand, and on the other seeing the commissary Altamirano, himself a Jesuit, calling upon them to submit. In a pathetic letter written to the Governor of Buenos Ayres, and dated `en la estancia de San Luis, Feb. 28 de 1756', Primo Ibarrenda, of San Miguel, says:[301] `This our writing I send to you that you may tell us finally what is to be our lot, and that you take a resolution what it is that you shall do. You see how that last year the father commissary[302] came to this our land to bother us to leave it: to leave our towns and all our territories, saying it was the will of our lord the King: besides this you yourself sent us a rigorous letter telling us to burn our towns, destroy the fields, even pull down our church, which is so beautiful (*tan lindo*), and saying also that you would kill us. You also say, and therefore we ask you if it is the truth, for if it is, we will all die before the Holy Sacrament; but spare the church, for it is God's, and even the infidels would not do it any harm.' They go on to say they have always been obedient subjects of the King, and that it is impossible that his wish could be to injure them — in fact, the letter of innocent men, half civilized, and thinking justice, mercy, and right-doing were to be found with Governors and Kings. Had many of the Jesuits chosen to take the field, their knowledge of the country and the vast influence that they had upon the Indians would have made the campaign perilous enough even for the united military power of Portugal and Spain. As it was, the miserable war dragged on for eight long years, and for result ruined seven missions where before the Indians lived happily. Then, when the fields were desolate, the villages deserted, and the Indian population half dispersed, statesmen in Spain and Portugal saw fit to change their minds, to annul the treaty, and to pass a diplomatic sponge over the ruin and the misery they had caused.

Chapter X

Position of the Jesuits in 1761 — Decree for their expulsion
sent from Spain — Bucareli sent to suppress the colleges
and drive out the Jesuits — They submit without resistance
— After two hundred years they are expelled from Paraguay
— The country under the new rule — The system of
government practically unchanged

'No storm is so insidious' (said St. Ignatius) 'as a perfect calm, and no enemy
so dangerous as the absence of all enemies.'

This dangerous state of calm without an apparent enemy in sight was the
position of the Jesuits in Paraguay in 1761. By desperate efforts and intrigues
in Spain they had kept their thirty missions from being mutilated; their
influence amongst the Indians had never been more absolute. The governors
of Buenos Ayres and of Paraguay had tried a fall with them, and the honours
of the struggle were with the Jesuits. They had succeeded in getting put into
force the clauses of the 'Laws of the Indies', which kept Spaniards out of the
Indian settlements. Even those sent against them had been forced to testify
to their utility[303] in Paraguay. But throughout Spain and her enormous
empire in America and in the East perpetual hostility between the Jesuits and
the regular clergy had been going on for years. In every portion of America
the Jesuits were unpopular, the excuse alleged being their wealth and
power;[304] but the real reason was their attitude on slavery. After repeated
grumblings of distant thunder, at length the storm broke, and the decree for
the expulsion of the Jesuits in Spain and her dominions was signed, and the
order sent to Bucareli, Governor of Buenos Ayres, in June of 1767, to put it
into force in Paraguay. The reasons which induced King Charles III. to expel
the Jesuits, mysterious as they were, and locked up a dead secret in the royal
breast,[305] may or may not have been sufficient in Spain, but could in no
respect have held good for Paraguay, where there existed little scope for
court intrigue, and where the Jesuits were far removed from their fellow
Spanish subjects, and occupied entirely with their mission work. Many and
various have been the explanations which historians have set forth for this
decree. Certain it is in Spain this Order had attained to considerable power,
and that in Rome the abler of their Generals occasionally kept the Popes in
mental servitude.

Some have accounted for the act of Charles III. as being but revenge for the
tumult of Aranjuez under the ministry of Esquilace,[306] arguing that the
Jesuits were in fact the authors of it, and that it was but the precursor of a
plot to dethrone the King and place his brother Don Luis upon the throne,
as being not so liberal in his ideas. Others, again, have stated[307] that the

Jesuits set about a calumny that Charles III. was not the Queen's son by her husband, but by a lover whom they said she had. The only reason which seems feasible is that the King was worked on by the fear that the Order had risen to too much power, and that if he did not at once take steps the monarchy would be rendered but a mere appendage of the General of the Jesuits.[308]

Whether it is sound policy of any government to expel a race, or sect, or order from its domains, no matter what the immediate exigencies of the times seem to require, is a moot point. The expulsions of the Jews, Moriscos, and Huguenots, and the dissolution of the monasteries in the times of that true Protestant Henry VIII. of ever pious memory, do not exactly seem to have had the effect upon the countries where they took place that was at first expected by their instigators. Expelled by Charles III., the Jesuits to-day in Spain have re-acquired much of their influence. So that it seems that persecution, to be effectual, must not stop on this side of extermination, and this our Lord Protector Cromwell understood full well.

The Viceroy Bucareli[309] to whom the task of the expulsion of the Order in the viceroyalty of Buenos Ayres and of Paraguay was entrusted, was no ordinary man.[310] Appointed Viceroy of Buenos Ayres after a distinguished career of public service, he found himself, almost without warning, and without any adequate forces at his command, obliged to execute by far the most important and far-reaching task that had ever fallen to the lot of any Spanish Governor in America to carry out. But as his services had not been chiefly in America, he held the idea which at the time was generally received in Europe, that the Jesuits possessed great wealth, had bodies of trained troops, and so would resist all efforts at expulsion to the death.

Full of these visions, says Dean Funes,[311] he considered the order, which was transmitted to him from Spain, as involving serious military risk, and evidently seems to have looked on every Jesuit village as a strong place of arms. July 22, 1767, was the day he chose, keeping his design a secret, and preparing to strike in Corrientes, Cordoba, Monte Video, and Santa Fe, on the same day, or rather night, for the terror of the Jesuits was so great that he designed to expel them all by night.

On July 2 two ships arrived in Buenos Ayres bringing the news that the decree had been put in force in Spain on April 2 with success. As all the crew of both the ships knew what had happened in Spain, concealment of his plan became no longer possible. Thus, had the Jesuits possessed either the wish or the means to make an armed resistance, they had ample time to stand on their defence.

Nothing was further from their minds, though they had complete dominion over a territory as large as France, and which contained a population of over one hundred and fifty thousand souls.[312] For arms, they had as chief defence some 'very long English guns, with rests if they wished to use them, which were not very heavy, and had a tolerable range.'[313] These were the preparations that the Jesuits (who, not in Paraguay alone, but throughout all the American dominions of the Spanish crown, ruled over territories stretching from California to Cape Horn)[314] had made, and they were found alone in the missions of Paraguay, where, by a special permission of the Kings of Spain, arms were allowed for defence against the Portuguese.

Bucareli, who seems to have been a timid but honest and upright man, made his first experiment upon the Jesuits of Buenos Ayres, Cordoba, and Santa Fe. The colleges in all these places were suppressed on the same night, and without the least resistance from their occupants. He who suppresses a religious Order, takes a town or country, or, in fact, puts into operation any of the forces of the law or military power, always expects, no matter how exalted be his motives at the start, to recoup himself from the treasure of the conquered. *Væ victis*, together with the vestments of the church, the plainsong, and the saints, came as a pagan heritage to the new faith, and has been held as canon law since Constantine looked at the sky and thought he saw a cross.

Great must have been the disgust of the Governor to find the spoil so paltry, and not to have the satisfaction even of saying that the Jesuits had hidden all their gold, as, his own measures having been taken secretly, they had no knowledge of what was in the wind. In the college of Cordoba, esteemed to be a mine of wealth, was found only nine thousand dollars,[315] which sum Ferando Fabro, the commissioner sent by Bucareli to take over the effects of the Jesuits at Cordoba, duly chronicles in his report.

But if the college of Cordoba[316] proved a miserable prey, there still remained the Jesuit missions on the Uruguay and Paraná, with all the riches of their fertile territory, and the enormous wealth which every Spaniard firmly believed the Jesuits had acquired. None of the Jesuits, either in Buenos Ayres, Cordoba, Santa Fe, Corrientes, or Monte Video having made the least resistance, but having opened wide their doors to the soldiers, who in all the towns on the same day at two o'clock in the morning came to signify their expulsion to them, it was only natural to think that the same conduct would be observed in Paraguay. But Governors and Governments never seem in the least accessible to common-sense. Almost a year had passed before he plucked up courage for his dangerous task.[317] He set about it with more preparation than either Cortez or Pizarro made for the conquest of Mexico or of Peru. Having embarked for Spain in the frigate *La Esmeralda* one hundred and fifty Jesuits from the towns of Cordoba, Buenos Ayres, Monte Video, and Santa Fe, he prepared to march upon the missions, when a suspicion of resistance caused him to take precautions which the result proved quite ridiculous. He sent two hundred of the best of the militia of Asuncion to occupy the fords upon the Tebicuari,[318] and a body of equal strength to occupy the port of San Miguel. All these measures being taken for his safety, the conqueror embarked upon May 24, taking with him three companies of grenadiers and sixty dragoons. He disembarked at the town of Salto on the Uruguay, and from thence despatched Captain Don Juan Francisco de la Riva Herrera to occupy the towns upon the Paraná. Don Francisco de Zabala was sent to seize six of the towns upon the Uruguay. Bucareli himself, with several hundred men, marched upon Yapeyu,[319] the southernmost of all the mission towns. The Jesuits, however, gave no trouble to any of the troops, and even stopped the Governor from gathering any laurels, however withered, with which to crown his arms.

As he advanced from town to town, the priests, on his arrival at each place, although living in the midst of Indians, some of whom were armed, and many of whom had served the King of Spain in various wars, and all of whom looked on the Jesuits almost as gods, came out and peacefully gave up the keys of all their houses, and submitted quietly to be made prisoners and be carried off in chains from the territories which they and their order had civilized and ruled over almost two hundred years. Seventy-eight Jesuits and their provincials were sent prisoners to Buenos Ayres, and their places all filled up with other priests taken from different Orders, and none of whom had any experience in mission-work. As Dean Funes tartly writes, the miracle that Bucareli wished, but scarcely dared to hope for, had taken place. The Jesuits, in Paraguay, at least, by their conduct in their last public act, most amply vindicated their loyalty to the Spanish crown. Nothing would have been easier, depleted as the viceroyalty was at the time of troops,[320] than to have defied the forces which Bucareli had at his disposal, and to have set up a Jesuit State, which would have taxed the utmost resources of the Spanish crown to overcome. No doubt the very facility with which Bucareli carried out his plans confirmed him in his own mind of their expediency, for men in general are prone to think that right which they accomplish with success. However, be that as it may, he returned in triumph to Buenos Ayres on September 16, having expended in his expedition less than four months. So in a quarter of a year the Jesuits, after more than two hundred years of rule, were all expelled from Paraguay.

They made no fight, nor offered any resistance, letting themselves be taken as a butcher takes a sheep, and that surrounded as they were by a population of upwards of one hundred and fifty thousand souls, cut off by countless leagues from the outside world, defended on three sides by virgin forests and by marshes hardly passable to European troops. One word from the Provincial would have set the missions in a blaze. A word would have brought clouds of horsemen — badly armed, 'tis true, but knowing every foot of marsh and forest, all the deep-beaten tracks which wind in the red earth across the lonely plains, the passes of the rivers, springs, natural fastnesses, and having the varied knowledge of a country which of old made Border horsemen and Northumbrian prickers formidable upon the Scottish marches — into the field.

The dogged Paraguayan Indians, ancestors of the infantry which, under Lopez,[321] died so bravely under the fire of the Brazilian guns, would, in their red cloaks and scanty linen clothes, have marched from *capilla*[322] and from mission against the enemies of the `father-priests'. Seventy-eight Jesuits were marched off to Buenos Ayres, and then shipped off to Europe[323] to join their fellows, who had been brought together by the ministers of the most liberal King who ever filled the Spanish throne from every quarter of the world. Having expelled the Jesuits, Bucareli was bound by the exigencies of his position to calumniate them. Perhaps, as an official, hidebound in his belief in the inalterable right of Governments to commit injustices, he believed all that he wrote. For the welfare of humanity, one could hope he knew all that he wrote was false. What hope is there left for mankind as long as addle-headed, honest men see naught but justice in whatever order they receive? Better a thousand times a rogue who knows he is a rogue than a good, well-intentioned, blundering man quite unaware he is a fool.

But, still, he had to justify himself either upon his own account or for the benefit of that posterity to conciliate which so many public men have paltered with the truth. So his first care was to extract a letter from thirty Indians whom he chose to dignify with the title of the mayors of the thirty towns, first having, as he says himself in a letter to the Conde de Aranda, the minister of Charles III., dressed them in the Spanish fashion, and treated them in such a way that they might know how much their lot had been improved.[324] The letter, written originally in Guaraní,[325] bears upon every line of it the dictation of the Governor. After a fine paragraph of salutations, it goes on to give the King many and repeated thanks (`muchas y repetidas gracias') for having sent his Excellency Captain-General Don Francisco Bucareli, `who has fulfilled, for the love of God and for the love of your Majesty, all the just orders which your Majesty laid to his charge, aiding our poverty, and clothing us like gentlemen.' Most people, even the heathen, like those who help their poverty and clothe them in the garb of gentlemen. It had not occurred to the poor Indians that the fine clothes might turn out liveries. The mayors all sign their Indian names, which seems to give the lie to the accusation that the Jesuits kept them ignorant. The letter, dated Buenos Ayres, March 10, 1768, seems to show that the Indians, be they who they might have been, were not free agents at the time they wrote. The Indians' letter duly despatched, the Governor indited a report, in which he fairly and with circumstance reiterates all the old charges against the Jesuits in Paraguay which the inventive brain of Cardenas had first conceived; but to them he adds several little touches of his own, which show he had some observation and an imaginative mind.

Amongst his numerous letters to Aranda and to the King, one dated Buenos Ayres, October 14, 1768,[326] contains the fullest account of his proceedings in the missions and of his views (or of what he thought to be his views) about the work in which he was engaged. Time was of small account in 1768 either in Paraguay or in Madrid, so Bucareli relates with some prolixity all that he did, with comments, movements of troops, regrettable occurrences — as when his soldiers let themselves be surprised and lost their horses — and now and then scraps of morality and theology, which shows quite plainly that the art of writing maundering despatches is not so new as optimists may have supposed. Quite in the manner of a modern special correspondent, he sets down all that he suffered from the weather; that it rained incessantly, and, marvellous to tell, that after rain the rivers rose, and gave him difficulty to cross. The roads were bad, provisions scarce and dear, and now and then wild Indians `massacred' an outpost of his men, whilst his brave fellows, when God willed it, occasionally `chastised' the infidel, and by the grace of Heaven slew no small number of them. Still, in the monstrous farrago of words, extending to some sixteen pages of close print, he lets us see he was a man of some capacity, but leaves it doubtful whether he really thought he was engaged upon a noble work, or if he wrote ironically, or if his only object was to satisfy his conscience and his King. But making much of little difficulties is but to be expected from a leader of an expedition or from a General in the field. Without it, how could they justify their existence, or prove to the world at large that they were needed, or but more important than a mere ceremony?[327]

When the land troubles were got over, and Bucareli, having arrived at Yapeyu, embarked upon the river, the very winds proved contrary, so that it took him many days to arrive at Candelaria, which port he reached upon August 27, 1768. But before quitting Yapeyu the Governor made a solemn feast, riding himself before his grenadiers, whose caps, he says, caused much amazement, the Indians never having seen such headgear in their lives. The difficulties of his journey over, the Jesuits dispossessed and sent downstream to be remitted home, Bucareli in his letter next deals with questions of religion, about which he shows himself as well informed as all the Spanish conquerors seem to have been in the New World. If for the dogma of the faith he was a bar of iron, for `cold morality', as Scottish preachers of the perfervid type used to refer to it, he was most keen. The Indians' clothes, especially the graceful *tupoi* worn by the women, shocked him exceedingly. It was impossible to touch upon it without an outrage upon modesty.[328] Masculine virtue is a most precarious thing, but little, if at all, more stable than its female counterpart; therefore perhaps the Governor was right not to expose his soldiers to temptation, so he did well, as he informs us, in serving out clothes which obscured their charms, or perhaps hid them quite from view. 'Such tyrannies,'[329] says the modest Governor, 'occasioned many offences against God, and frequent illnesses and epidemics.' The sentence is a little doubtful in its meaning, for if a scantiness of women's dress occasioned illnesses and epidemics amongst the population of a town, Belgravia and Mayfair should surely be the most unhealthy spots on earth; though even there, I verily believe, no more offences against God occur than amongst the Moors, whose women show only their eyes to the shrinking gaze of easily offended men.

As in duty bound, Bucareli kept for the end of his despatch a rehash of all the old charges made against the Jesuits. They kept the Indians in slavery, would never let them learn Spanish, and were themselves inordinately rich. The first two accusations Father José Cardiel, in his 'Declaracion de la Verdad', abundantly disproves.[330] The last the Governor disproves himself; for had he found much treasure he most assuredly would have made haste to send it to the King. What he did find, a reference later to Brabo's inventories will show, and the same source discloses all the wealth the richest Order in the world, according to their enemies, took with them in their involuntary journey back to Spain. All being finished in the missions and the Jesuits expelled, Bucareli found himself obliged to institute some system for the government of the Indian population, which he had deprived both of its spiritual and of its temporal guides.

The Jesuits' government having been so bad, according to his own despatch, the Indians having been kept in such a miserable state, their education having been so neglected, and, above all, their women having been dressed in such light attire that Bucareli could not with modesty even describe their dress, it might have seemed but natural that he should have evolved some system of government differing in all respects from that he had destroyed. So far from that, in his instructions to his interim successor, dated at Candelaria,[331] August 23, 1768, he practically followed slavishly all the policy which the Jesuits had pursued. He ordered Captains Riva Herrera and Bruno de Zavala, to whom the arrangements were committed, to see that the Indians were instructed 'in the true knowledge of our holy faith', a work which the Jesuits, whatever might be their faults, had not neglected to insure. After some platitudes as to the vivifying effects of free and open trade, and an injunction to his captains to take care the Indian girls were decorously and virtuously dressed, he launched into a sermon about honest work, which, as he said, would make the Indians rich, happy, and virtuous, and alone could ever make a kingdom prosper; in fact, he used almost precisely similar language to that to-day used by a European Governor in Africa when about to make a people slaves. On the whole, however, his instructions were wise and liberal, and had they been carried out in the same spirit, and with fidelity, the Indians might have long continued in the same half-Arcadian, half-Christian state in which the Jesuits left them, and to which it seems they could attain, but not go farther without exposure to that vivifying commerce without which nations cannot prosper, but with which the greater portion of their citizens must remain ever slaves.

The instructions given, he left the missions never to return, leaving behind him the reputation of an honest man, having made, as it would appear, no money during his sojourn in their territories. On October 20, 1768, he wrote from Buenos Ayres to Aranda, telling him that his work was done, and asking him as a particular favour to implore the King to give him some employment 'out of America, and particularly not under either the secretaryship or the Council of the Indies.'[332] Thus it appears that either the work in which he had been engaged was uncongenial to him, or he mistrusted the future and the Indians when the Jesuits' sheltering hands had been withdrawn, and thought the King might blame him for what was sure to come. One passage in his letter of instructions shows that the antique, but still current, fashion of going to any length to obtain a country in which are situated even supposititious gold-mines had its influence even with such an honest man as Bucareli was. He specially enjoins upon the officials left in charge 'to find out from what quarter the Indians of those towns extract those pieces of the precious metals which they sometimes bring to their priests.' So that the fable of the false mines started by Cardenas, although a thousand times disproved, still lingered in the minds of those who could not understand what motive except that of growing rich could cause the Jesuits to bury themselves in the recesses of the Paraguayan woods. The release from things American and under the jurisdiction of the Council of the Indies did not come to Bucareli for almost two more years, during which time he struggled manfully with the affairs of the Jesuit missions, repelled the Chaco Indians on one side, and on the other implored for troops to defend the island of Chiloe against the heretic English, who at that time appear to have been meditating the advancement of their empire in the extremest south. One curious letter was reserved for Bucareli to indite before he quitted Buenos Ayres for the last time. On January 15, 1770, he sent a long declaration signed by the celebrated Nicolas Ñeenguirú and other Indians, giving an account of the part played by him in the abortive resistance which he made against the cession of the seven towns. This is the last time that Nicolas, the `King' of Paraguay and `Emperor of the Mamelucos', appears in any document as far as I can find. His name at one time was well known in Paraguay, the River Plate and Spain, and served to father many lies upon; and at the last, the Jesuits gone, he seems to have turned against them, and said all that was required by Bucareli to get up his case. It appears from Bucareli's letter that the family of the Ñeenguirú had been well known in the missions from the time of Cardenas. In 1770[333] we find him shorn of his kingly and imperial dignities, the mayor of Concepcion in Paraguay, tall, taciturn, with long, lank hair, and much respected by his brother Indians, who held his stirrup for him when he got upon his horse. To find him in the humour to give tongue about the Jesuits was a trump-card in Bucareli's hand, for if it could be proved that in 1750 they had resisted the forces of the crown of Spain, the public, always anxious to believe a lie, would naturally applaud the action of the King in their expulsion from his territories. Nicolas, who seems to have been but a poor creature at the best, testified that everything which he had done as General of the Indians was by the order of Fathers Limp and Ennis, and that he was a poor Indian who did but that which he was told. He finished up his testimony with thanks to the good King for having taken him out of the power of the Jesuits, and kept him in his post of mayor at Concepcion. In fact, all was the same to him as long as he was left with his alcalde's staff.[334]

Upon August 14, 1778, Bucareli sailed for Spain, leaving Don Juan José Vertiz as his successor in the viceroyalty of the provinces of the River Plate. The missions were all placed under the care of friars of the begging Orders, chiefly Franciscans, and the system of the Jesuit government was left unchanged. In 1771, writing from San Lorenzo (el Escorial) in Spain, Bucareli, who seemed fated never to escape from the affairs of Paraguay, sends a long constitution for the thirty towns which follows all the Jesuits' rules of government to the last tittle of their policy. Brabo has preserved the document, which runs to forty-seven pages of close print in its entirety. A carefully thought-out and well-conceived digest of a constitution it most certainly is, and yet it follows to the most minute particular the policy the Jesuits laid down.

Dean Funes[335] seemed to see that the flattering of Nicolas Ñeenguiru and the other Indian chiefs was an entire affair of artifice, and that it was but a mere crowning of the victims who were destined to be sacrificed. It may be that the constitution made by Bucareli at the Escorial was similarly but a blind to keep the Indians quiet till the Government had time to exploit them at its ease. Still, Bucareli in all his actions seems to have been an honest man; one of those honest, narrow-minded men who have sown more misery in the world than all the rogues and scoundrels since the flood. Be all that as it may, his constitution in a thousand ways recalled the Jesuits' polity in their days of rule. In a former chapter[336] I have pointed out a curious instance in which this constitution traverses entirely statements made by the Jesuits' enemies that their exclusive policy was for their own ends, and not, as they alleged, for the protection of the Indians. But there are other instances quite as remarkable which show that the Jesuits not only had grasped perfectly what the best course of treatment was for their subjects, but that the official mind of Bucareli, trained as he was, so to speak, in the strictest sect of Pharisees, and prejudiced against the Jesuits in every way, yet discerned clearly as an honest man that the plan they had laid down was the most suitable for future rulers to pursue.

At the time of forming his constitution he had been gone but scarce a year from Buenos Ayres, and yet he writes[337] complaining bitterly of what was happening in the missions of Paraguay. He points out that all his trouble will have been in vain 'if the Governor and his lieutenants are not stimulated to address themselves to the service of God and of the King, with that zeal which everyone should impart to his duty.' Then, after a puff preliminary of the beauty of freedom, human and Divine, he sets forth how the Indians are in future to be ruled. First, as in duty bound, he points out that anything savouring of communism is against the laws of Heaven and of man; that the Indians in their semi-communism were really slaves, the industrious working for the idle, and so forth; that their clothes were scanty; that they were not allowed to freely mix with Spaniards, and were kept a race apart. Then like a prudent statesman having made his apologia 'pro existentia sua', and blown off much virtuous steam, he comes to business, and business, as we know, is the great soberer of theorists, no matter on what side they theorize.

After the article to which I have referred in Chapter IX. comes this most curious paragraph, taken in connection with the inalienable right which, according to himself, the Indians had of free communication with the outer world:[338] 'And because I am informed that many Indians who have been absent in the army of the Portuguese, and have resided for lengthened periods in Rio Pardo, Viamont and other parts, have returned to their towns, you will take care that all these with their families shall be removed to those (towns) either in the interior or distant from those frontiers, as it is not convenient that they should remain on them (the frontiers) or close to them; and thus you will proceed successively with the Indians who return, without leaving one, in order to avoid any chance of communication, which might be most prejudicial.' Surely a satire on his own abuse of the Jesuits for keeping the Indians mewed up from intercourse with the outside world. It may be that he had perceived the Indians were not fit to hold their own; indeed, it is certain he had done so, for on p. 326 he writes, 'It is not convenient to leave them (the Indians) entire liberty,[339] for it would be in the extreme fatal and prejudicial to their interests, because the astuteness and sagacity of the Spaniards would triumph easily over their rusticity.' 'Sagacity' is an ingenious euphuism, and might well be used with good effect in the like circumstances, when occasion serves, to-day. But as no single article of any document set forth by any Government can be straightforward and single in its purpose, and as all laws are made with an eye upon some party presently in power, after the paragraph just quoted, on the next page occurs the following sentence under the head of 'Commerce with the Spaniards is to be free'.[340] 'It is laid down that between the Indians and the Spaniards commerce should be free, in order that mutual dealings should unite them in friendship.' Therefore to the ordinary mind it is impossible to make out what really was intended, and whether commerce was to be free or not. Those little differences apart, the constitution ran entirely upon Jesuit lines. That semi-communism which was so prejudicial during the Jesuits' rule was formally re-organized in chapter iv. of the constitution (p. 343) the instant that their power was placed in other hands. Even the prohibition to the Spaniards to enter the Jesuit towns, and reside there, was formally kept up in chapter iii., with the sole alteration that for three months of the year they might reside amongst the Indians on certain well-defined conditions most prolixly set forth. So that it will be seen that, if the Jesuits did ill, as usual, any ill they did was carefully perpetuated by their successors, and, quite as naturally, all that they strove to do in favour of the Indians was most carefully undone.

Chapter XI

Conclusion

It is the fashion of some to say that history, of whatever nature, can but be written dispassionately at a period sufficiently removed from the events of which it treats to have allowed the heat of passion to evaporate. This is as false as almost every other dictum which men take on trust, forgetting that to have passed into the proverbial stage a saying must have been foolish at the start, in order that it should have got itself commended by the majority of mankind.

The heat of passion never evaporates in regard to events which at the epoch of their acting caused great controversies. From writings of contemporaries the coolest-headed take a bias, in the same way that men unconsciously pass on the microbes of disease to their best friends. Only from inventories and rolls of court, State Papers and the like is it possible to get unbiassed matter, and even then figures, those chief deceivers of mankind, can be well cooked for or against, according to the bias of the man who draws them up. Still, when they are drawn up by enemies, they often quite unwittingly show out the truth. In a letter dated October 30, 1768, Bucareli sends a list to Aranda of the effects of many of the Jesuits taken from Paraguay and sent by him to Spain. The list itself speaks volumes in defence of the Jesuits in Paraguay. Whatever may have been their faults, the Governor himself (or even Charles III.) could not have charged upon the captured priests that they had got together a large stock of property during their mission life.[341] The first upon the list, P. Pedro Zabaleta, took ten shirts, two pillow-cases, two sheets, three pocket-handkerchiefs, two pairs of shoes, two pairs of socks, and a pound and a half of snuff. The others were in general less well set up with shirts,[342] some few had cloaks, and one (P. Sigismundo Griera) a nightcap; but all of them had their snuff, the only relic of their luxurious mission life. Manuel Vergara, their Provincial, testifies in a paper sent with the list that most of the clothes were taken from the common stock, and all the snuff. What sort of treatment they endured upon their passage in the two frigates *San Fernando* and *San Nicolas* is quite unknown, but certainly their luggage could not have been in the way; and for their snuff, no doubt they husbanded it with care during the long two months, which in those days was thought a record run.[343] In the missions which they had so long tended with such care, giving their muddle-headed love to the Indians in their Machiavelian way, all was confusion in the space of six short months. Dean Funes and Don Feliz de Azara[344] are the only two contemporary writers who treat of the expulsion of the Jesuits from Paraguay outside the official world. The Dean, a man of the old school, was kindly and humane, well educated, and, having been brought up in Tucuman amongst an Indian population, looked on the Indians in a kindly way as fellow-creatures, though differing in essential points from races which had been for centuries exposed to civilization and its effects. His description of the Indians has for veracity and observation not often been surpassed. 'Those natives[345] (he says) are of a pale colour, well made, and well set up. Their talent and capacity are capable of much advancement. Though they lack invention in themselves, yet are they excellent in imitation. Idleness seems natural to them, although it may be more the effect of habit than of temperament; their inclination towards acquiring knowledge is decided, and novelty has its full effect upon their minds. Ambitious of command, they acquit themselves with honour in the positions to which they may attain. Eloquence is held amongst them in the first place, and avarice in no respect degrades their minds. An injurious word offends them more than punishments, which they solicit rather than undergo the former outrage. Incontinency in their women they look upon but with indifference, and even husbands are little sensible to acts of infidelity. Conjugal love has but slight influence upon the treatment which they give their wives. Fathers of families care for their sons but little. The serenity of mind of all these Indians in the midst of the greatest troubles is without equal in the world; never a sigh with them takes off the bitterness of suffering.'

No one who knows the Indians but must confess that Dean Funes had made a study of their character deeper than is his own. Azara, on the other hand, was a man of science; his books upon the birds and quadrupeds of Paraguay still hold the field, and are esteemed for curious and minute observation and accuracy as to scientific facts. The man himself was an extremely able writer, a captain in the Spanish navy, and well educated. For twenty years he served in Paraguay and in the River Plate, with credit to himself and profit to the country which he served. Educated as he was in the school of the Encyclopædists, amongst the strictest of the pharisees of Liberalism, to him the very name of Jesuit was anathema. After the fashion of his kind, he seemed unable to distinguish between the scheming Jesuits at European courts and the simple and hard-working missionaries in Paraguay. All were anathema, and therefore all their system was repugnant to him; and though a kindly man, as is set forth abundantly in all his works, he never paused to think that there could be a difference between his ideal free Liberal citizen, voting and exercising all his right of citizenship in a free commonwealth, after the fashion of a dormouse freely exercising his natural functions in the receiver of an air-pump, and a simple Indian of the Paraguayan woods.

Freedom to him, as it has been to many theorists, was an abstract thing, possessing which a man, even though starving, must in its mere possession find true happiness. He never paused to inquire, as even Bucareli did, if the mission Indians could hold their own under free competition with the 'sagacity' of the surrounding Spanish settlers. Therefore he is the authority whom Liberals always quote against the system of the Jesuits. When he inveighs against their semi-communism, the modern Liberal claps his hands, and sees a kindred Daniel come to judgment, as he would do to-day if in Damaraland the Germans set up a Socialistic settlement amongst the negro tribes, and some Liberal economist denounced it with an oath. Azara quite forgets that, as Dean Funes says, the `sentiment of property was very weak amongst the Indians,' and that their minds were `not degraded by the vice of avarice.' Still, Azara was an honest man — a keen observer and impartial, as far as his upbringing and the tenets he had imbibed in youth permitted him to be. Upon the question of the Jesuits he was entirely prejudiced, although few have stood up more stoutly to condemn the faulty system which the Spaniards pursued towards the Indians in both Americas. But on account of his political proclivities Azara is quite silent as to the state into which the missions fell after the Jesuits had been expelled. No doubt he thought that, once their faulty system was removed, the Indians would soon become what he judged civilized, and hold their own with those around them, though of another race and blood.

Funes, upon the contrary, fully exposes all the rapacity and incompetence of the new shepherds left by Bucareli to guard the Jesuits' sheep.

`Ignorant[346] of Guaraní, and without patience to acquire it, confusion reigned in the missions as in a tower of Babel,' and he goes on to say `an imperious tone of order was substituted for the paternal manner (of the Jesuits), and as a deaf man who cannot hear has to be taught by blows, that was the teaching they (the Indians) had to bear.' Shortly, he says, `a wall of hatred and contempt began to rise between the Indians and their masters; and the priests, who by the virtue of their office ought to have been the ministers of peace, being without influence to command . . . and not entirely irreproachable in their ministry . . . added themselves to the discord and dissension which arose.'

Bucareli, as soon as he knew what was going on, advised that all the priests appointed by himself should be replaced by others. This accordingly was done, but it was even then too late: the missions went from bad to worse; of the vast quantities of cattle few were left; the priests followed the example of their prototypes Hofni and Phineas, went about armed, took Indian mistresses, and neglected all religious duties, treating the Indians after the fashion of the Spaniards in the settlements. Thus the Arcadian life, which had subsisted more than two hundred years, in the brief space of two short years was lost.

The vast estancias, in which at the expulsion more than a million head of cattle pastured,[347] were but bare plains, in which the cattle that were left had all run wild or perished from neglect. Wild beasts roamed round the outskirts of the half-deserted towns. A dense low scrub of yatais and of palmettos invaded all the pasture-lands, and in the erstwhile cultivated fields rank weeds sprang up, and choked the crops which in the Jesuits' times had made the mission territories the most productive of the American possessions of the Spanish crown. The churches were unserved, and in the evening air no more the hymns resounded, nor did the long white-robed processions headed by a cross pass to the fields to peaceful labour, marshalled by their priests. The fruit-trees round the missions were either all cut down for firewood or had degenerated, and the plantations of the Ilex Paraguayensis,[348] from which they made their *yerba*, which had been brought from the up-country forests with vast pains, were in decay, and quite uncultivated.

The Indian population had almost disappeared within the space of eight-and-twenty years.[349] The Guaranís collected from the woods with so much effort to the missionary, then guided down the Paraná by the most noble and self-sacrificing of their priests, Ruiz Montoya, and after that redeemed with blood from the fierce Mameluco bands, had shrunk away before the baneful breath of unaccustomed contact with the civilizing whites.

The simple ceremonious, if perhaps futile, mission-life had withered up at the first touch of vivifying competition — that competition which has made the whole world gray, reducing everything and everyone to the most base and commonest denominator.

The self-created goddess Progress was justified by works, and all the land left barren, waiting the time when factories shall pollute its sky, and render miserable the European emigrants, who, flying from their slavery at home, shall have found it waiting for them in their new paradise beyond the seas.

The world, it would appear, is a vast class-room, and its Creator but a professor of political economy, apparently unable to carry out his theories with effect. Therefore, to us, the Western Europeans, he has turned for help, and upon us devolved the task of extirpating all those peoples upon whom he tried his 'prentice hand. On us he laid injunctions to increase at home, and to the happier portions of the world to carry death under the guise of life unsuitable to those into whose lands we spread.

Let those made cruel by the want of sympathy with men that the mere poring over books so often superinduces in the mind protest when judging of the Jesuits in Paraguay against the outrage done to their theories by the scheme the Jesuits pursued.

It has been nobly said[350] `that the extinction of the smallest animal is a far greater loss than if the works of all the Greeks had perished.' How much the greater loss that of a type of man such as the Indians, whom the semi-communistic Jesuit government successfully preserved, sheltering them from the death-dealing breath of our cold northern life and its full, fell effects!

There are those, no doubt, who think that a tree brought from the tropics should be planted out at home, to take its chance of life in the keen winter of the north, in holy competition with the ash and oak; and if it dies, there are still pines enough, with stores of dogwood, thickets of elder, and a wilderness of junipers. They may be right; but, after all, that which has felt the tropic sun is for the tropics, and to grow under the tantalizing sunshine of the north, which lights but does not warm, it must have glass, and shelter from the cold.

But of aforethought to deliberately transplant our fogs and chilling atmosphere, and so to nip and kill plants which crave only the sun to live, that is a crime against humanity; a crime posterity with execration will one day taunt us with, and hold us up to execration, as we to-day in our hypocrisy piously curse the memories of Pizarro and Cortés.

In the eternal warfare between those who think that progress — which to them means tramways and electric light — is preferable to a quiet life of futile happiness of mind there is scant truce, so that my readers have to take their choice whether to side with Funes or Azara in judging of the Jesuits' rule in Paraguay. There is no middle course between the old and new; no halting-place; no chink in which imagination can drive in its nail to stop the wheels of time; therefore, no doubt, the Jesuit commonwealth was doomed to disappear. But for myself, I am glad that five-and-twenty years ago I saw the Indians who still lingered about the ruined mission towns, mumbling their maiméd rites when the Angelus at eventide awoke the echoes of the encroaching woods, whilst screeching crowds of parrots and macaws hovered around the date-palms which in the plaza reared their slender heads, silent memorials of the departed Jesuits' rule.

Indians and Jesuits are gone from Paraguay, the Indians to that Trapalanda which is their appointed place; and for the Jesuits, they are forgotten, except by those who dive into old chronicles, or who write books, proposing something and concluding nothing, or by travellers, who, wandering in the Tarumensian woods, come on a clump of orange-trees run wild amongst the urundéys.

FINIS NON CORONAT OPUS

Notes

About the author:

Robert Bontine Cunninghame Graham (1852-1936)

Born in London. Lived in Argentina, mostly ranching, from 1869 to 1883, when he returned to Scotland. Member of the British House of Commons for North West Lanark (1886-1892). Strong socialist tendencies. Was elected first president of the Scottish Labour Party in 1888, first president of the National Party of Scotland in 1928, and first Honorary President of the Scottish National Party in 1934. Died in Argentina. He was the model for a number of fictional characters in books by his friend, Joseph Conrad, and also by G. B. Shaw.

Notes to the etext:

Corrections made:

Preface:

(p. viii) (first footnote)
It is difficult to tell — it may be merely a smudge — and if not, it is probably an error, but the first "c" in "concilium" seems to have a cedilla.

Chapter I:

(p. 6) (footnote)
[`Commentarios Reales' (en Madrid CI}. I}CCXXIII., en la oficina]

> where "}" marks a character that is the mirror image of
> "C", which was formerly used in Roman Numerals as
> follows: "CI}" = "M" [1,000]; "I}" = "D" [500]; and
> subsequent "}"s multiply by ten, as "I}}}" = 50,000.

changed to:

[`Commentarios Reales' (en Madrid 1723, en la oficina]

> Let us all take this moment to give thanks for Hindu-
> Arabic numerals, Amen.

(p. 19)
[`Descripcion y Historia del Paraguay, `the Guaranís were spread]
  changed to:
[`Descripcion y Historia del Paraguay', `the Guaranís were spread]

(p. 24) (footnote)
[del Sr Provisor Alonso Joseph Gomez de Lara.]
  changed to:
[del Sr. Provisor Alonso Joseph Gomez de Lara.]

(p. 34)
[and his mother Doña Teresa Cabeza de Vaca,]
  changed to:
[and his mother `Doña Teresa Cabeza de Vaca,]

> as the best guess as to where the quoted section begins,
> which is later marked with a closing quote.

Chapter II:

(p. 52) (footnote)
[de la Compagnie de Jésus, vol. iii., cap v., p. 322]
  changed to:
[de la Compagnie de Jésus', vol. iii., cap v., p. 322]

(p. 74)
[militia of the missions could no nothing with their bows and arrows]
  changed to:
[militia of the missions could do nothing with their bows and arrows]

Chapter V:

(p. 129)
[to divine will, which, will, as the Bishop]
  changed to:
[to divine will, which will, as the Bishop]

(p. 131) (footnote)
[[121] Exod. xxxii. 27.]
  updated to:
[[121] Exod. 32:27.]

(p. 138)
[sending to him one Father Lopez, Provincial of the Dominicians.]
  changed to:
[sending to him one Father Lopez, Provincial of the Dominicans.]

Chapter VI:

(p. 181) (footnote)
[`Declaracion de la Verdad, p. 295:]
  changed to:
[`Declaracion de la Verdad', p. 295:]

(p. 184) (footnote)
[la Historia del Paraguay', etc., cap. i., vol. ii.]
  changed to:
[la Historia del Paraguay', etc., cap. i., vol. ii.).]

Chapter IX:

(p. 237)
[After negotiations, lasting many years, in 1758 a treaty was signed]
  changed to:
[After negotiations, lasting many years, in 1750 a treaty was signed]

> 15 January 1750, to be exact.

Chapter X:

(pp. 263-264) (footnote)
[Ibañez rarely spoke he truth, not even when it would]
  changed to:
[Ibañez rarely spoke the truth, not even when it would]

(p. 268) (footnote)
[The war commenced in 1868 and finished in 1870,]
  changed to:
[The war commenced in 1865 and finished in 1870,]

> (the dates generally given for this war, though the opening
> stages arguably occurred late in 1864.)

(p. 275)
[signed by the celebrated Nicolas Ñeengiurú and other Indians,]
  changed to:
[signed by the celebrated Nicolas Ñeenguirú and other Indians,]
  and:
[the family of the Ñeengiurú had been well known]

changed to:

[the family of the Ñeenguirú had been well known]

    (as it appears elsewhere in the text)

(p. 276)

[the flattering of Nicolas Ñeengiuru]
  changed to:

[the flattering of Nicolas Ñeenguiru]

> This wrong spelling is given throughout Chapter X, but
> Chapter X only. Elsewhere, the accents are occasionally
> missing from a name that seems to be the same.

The original Map has been omitted by necessity.

The original Index has been omitted as unnecessary in a searchable text.

This etext was transcribed from the edition published in London in 1901.

The excellent film, "The Mission" (1986), was based on events apparently related to the `Jesuit War' referred to in Chapter IX.

HTML 4.0, the current standard at the time this file was created, does not recognize the breve accent for the letter i, but following the standard for (a breve), I have gone ahead and coded i breve, as there are only two instances, and it may yet become a standard.

The text file for this book was manually entered twice, and then electronically compared, to assure a clean text. Then the HTML file was prepared, with care taken to avoid introducing errors, which has hopefully proved successful. All this was done by Alan Robert Light, presently of North Carolina (July 1998).

Footnotes:

[1] The doctrine of the `Ciencia Media' occurs in the celebrated `Concordia gratiæ et liberi arbitrii', by Luis de Molina (1588). The concilium de Auxiliis was held to determine whether or not *concordia* was possible between freewill and grace. As the Jesuits stuck by Molina and his doctrines in despite of councils and of popes, the common saying arose in Spain: `Pasteles en la pasteleria y ciencia media en la Compañia.'

[2] Dean Funes, `Ensayo de la Historia Civil del Paraguay', etc., Buenos Aires, 1816.

[3] *Idem.* The letter is dated 1771 and the Jesuits were expelled in 1767. As the writer of the letter was on the spot in an official position, and nominated by the very Viceroy who had been the expeller of the Jesuits, his testimony would seem to be as valuable as that of the ablest theorist on government, Catholic or Protestant, who ever wrote.

[4] This, of course, applies to the possessions of all European States in America equally with Spain.

[5] Madrid, 1770.

[6] Though in this respect Charlevoix is not so credulous as Padre Ruiz de Montoya and the older writers, he yet repeats the story of the bird that cleans the alligator's teeth, the magic virtues of the tapir's nails, and many others. See Charlevoix, vol. i., bk. i., p. 27, Paris, 1756.

[The story of the bird that cleans the teeth of alligators is very nearly true — *Pluvianus aegyptius* has a symbiotic relationship with crocodiles in parts of Africa, and similar relationships exist throughout the natural world. — A. L., 1998.]

[7] Dobrizhoffer's book was written in Latin, and printed in Vienna in 1784 under the title of `Historia de Abiponibus', etc. A German translation by Professor Keil was published at Pesth in the same year. The English translation is of the year 1822.

[8] It is to be remembered that the Spanish colonists were as a rule antagonistic to the Jesuits, and that, therefore, Spanish writers do not of necessity hold a brief for the Jesuits in Paraguay. Moreover, the names of Esmid (Smith), Fildo (Fields), Dobrizhoffer, Cataldini and Tomas Bruno (Brown, who is mentioned as being *natural de Yorca*), Filge, Limp, Pifereti, Enis, and Asperger, the quaint medical writer on the virtues of plants found in the mission territory, show how many foreign Jesuits were actually to be found in the reductions of Paraguay. For more information on this matter see the `Coleccion de Documentos relativos á la Expulsion de los Jesuitas de la Republica Argentina y Paraguay', published and collected by Francisco Javier Brabo, Madrid, 1872.

[9] The Inca Garcilaso de la Vega, in his `Commentarios Reales' (en Madrid 1723, en la oficina Real y á costa de Nicholas Rodriguez Franco, Impressor de libros, se hallaran en su casa en la calle de el Poço y en Palacio), derives the word from the Quichua *Chacú* = a surrounding. If he is right, it would then be equivalent to the Gaelic `tinchel'. Taylor, the Water-poet, has left a curious description of one of these tinchels. It was at a tinchel that the rising under the Earl of Mar in the '15 was concocted.

[10] See the curious map contained in the now rare work of P. Pedro Lozano, entitled, `Descripcion Chorographica . . . del Gran Chaco, Gualamba', etc. Also in the interesting collection of old maps published in 1872 at Madrid by Francisco Javier Brabo.

[11] It is, of course, to be taken into consideration that my two journeys in Paraguay were made after the great war which terminated in 1870, after lasting four years; but the writings of Demersay (`Histoire du Paraguay et des Établissements des Jésuites', Paris, 1862), those of Brabo, and of Azara, show the deserted state of the district of Misiones in the period from 1767, the date of the expulsion of the Jesuits, to the middle of the nineteenth century.

[12] *Cocos Australis.*

[13] See the reports of the Marques de Valdelirios and others in the publications of Francisco Javier Brabo, Madrid, 1872, and in the `Ensayo de la Historia Civil de Paraguay, Buenos-Ayres y Tucuman', por Dr. Don Gregorio Funes, Buenos Ayres, 1816.

[14] Bernal Diaz, `Historia de la Conquista de la Nueva España', vol. iv., cap. 207, Madrid, 1796.

[15] Especially noting down the appearance and qualities of `el caballo Motilla', the horse of Gonzalo de Sandoval. Thus does he minutely describe Motilla, `the best horse in Castille or the Indies'. `El mejor caballo, y de mejor carrera, revuelto á una mano y à otra que decian que no se habia visto mejor en Castilla, ni en esa tierra era castaño acastañado, y una estrella en la frente, y un pie izquierdo calzado, que se decia el caballo Motilla; é quando hay ahora diferencia sobre buenos caballos, suclen decir es en bondad tan bueno como Motilla.'

[16] `La Argentina', included in the `Coleccion de Angelis', Buenos Ayres, 1836.

[17] `Historia y Descubrimiento de el Rio de la Plata y Paraguay', Hulderico Schmidel, contained in the collection made by Andres Gonzalez Barcia, and published in 1769 at Madrid under the title of `Historiadores Primitivos de las Indias Occidentales'.

[18] The great Las Casas, who made seven voyages from America to Spain — the last at the age of seventy-two — to protect the Indians, had a strong opinion about `conquerors' and `conquests'. In the dedication of his great treatise on the wrongs of the Indians, he says: `Que no permita (Felipe II.) las atrocidades que los tiranos inventaron, y que prosiguen haciendo con titulo de "conquistas". Los que se jactan de ser "conquistadores" a que descienden de ellos son muchomas orgullosos arrogantes y vanos que los otros Españoles.' Strange that even to-day the same *atrocidades* of *tiranos* are going on in Africa. No doubt the descendants of these `conquerors' will be as arrogant, proud, and vain as the descendants of the *conquistadores* of whom Las Casas writes.

[19] Mendoza left (`Azara Apuntamientos para la Historia Natural de los Quadrupedes del Paraguay', etc.) five mares and seven horses in the year

1535. In 1580 Don Juan de Garay, at the second founding of the city, already found troops of wild horses. The cattle increased to a marvellous extent, and by the end of the century were wild in Patagonia. Sarmiento (`Civilisation et Barbarisme') says that early in this century they were often killed by travellers, who tethered their horses to the carcasses to prevent them from straying at night.

[20] Hulderico Schmidel, `Historia del Descubrimiento de el Rio de la Plata y Paraguay'.

[21] Perhaps the two most important works upon the language are the `Tesoro de la Lengua Guarani', by Ruiz de Montoya, Madrid, 1639 (it is dedicated to the `Soberana Virgen'); and the `Catecismo de la Lengua Guarani', by Diego Diaz de la Guerra, Madrid, Año de 1630. He also wrote a `Bocabulario y Arte de la Lengua Guarani'.

[22] P. Guevara, in his `Historia del Paraguay', relates a curious story which he said was current amongst the Indians. Two brothers, Tupi and Guaraní, lived with their families upon the sea-coast of Brazil. In those days the world was quite unpopulated but by themselves. They quarrelled about a parrot, and Tupi with his family went north, and populated all Brazil; whilst Guaraní went west, and was the ancestor of all the Indians of the race of Guaranís.

[23] Azara, in his `Descripcion y Historia del Paraguay', has a similar passage: `Recibe bien todo Indio silvestre, al estrangero que viene de paz.'

[24] `Por lo comun reparten pedazos de este cuerpo, del qual pedazo cozido en mucha agua hacen unas gachas (*fritters*) y es fiesta muy celebre para ellos que hacen con muchas cerimonias.'

[25] `Histoire du Paraguay et des Établissements des Jésuites', L. Alfred Demersay, Paris, 1864.

[26] `La Argentina', a long poem or rhyming chronicle contained in the collection of `Historiadores Primitivos de Indias', of Gonzales Barcia, Madrid, 1749.

[27] Lozano, in his `Historia del Paraguay', compares it to Greek, but in my opinion fails to establish his case; but, then, so few people know both Greek and Guaraní.

[28] He passed through the whole Chaco, descending the Pilcomayo to its junction with the Paraguay, through territories but little explored even to-day. Perhaps the most complete description of the Chaco is that of P. Lozano, with the following comprehensive title:

`Descripcion chorographica de Terreno Rios, Arboles, y Animales de los dilatadisimas Provincias del Gran Chaco, Gualamba, y de los Ritos y Costumbres de la inumerables naciones barbaros é infideles que le habitan. Con un cabal Relacion Historica de lo que en ellos han obrado para conquistarlas algunos Gobernadores y Ministros Reales, y los Misioneros Jesuitas para reduc irlos à la fe del Verdadero Dios.' Por el Padre Pedro Lozano, de la Compañia de Jesus, Año de 1733. En Cordoba por Joseph Santos Balbas.

This book did not appear in a clandestine manner, for it had: 1. Censura, por C. de Palmas. 2. Licencia de la Religion, por Geronymo de Huróza, Provincial de los Jesuitas de Andalucia. 3. Licencia del Ordinario por el Dr. Don Francisco Miguel Moreno, por mandado del Sr. Provisor Alonso Joseph Gomez de Lara. 4. Aprobacion del Rdo. P. Diego Vasquez. 5. Privelegio de su Majestad por Don Miguel Fernandez Morillo. 6. Fé de Corrector por el Licenciado, Don Manuel Garcia Alesson, Corrector General de su Majestad (who adds in a note, `este libro corresponde à su original'). 7. Sumo de Tassa, as follows: `Tassaron los señores del Consejo este libro à seis maravedis cada pliego.'

Palma, in the first *censura*, says that he had read it several times `con repetida complacencia', and that, though it was `breve en volumen' (it has 484 quarto pages), that it was also short in its concise style, kept closely to the rules of history, and was `muy copiosa en la doctrina'.

[29] This race at one time spread from the Orinoco to the river Plate, and even in the case of its offshoot, the Chiriguanás, crossed to the west bank of the Paraguay. Padre Ruiz Montoya, in his `Conquista Espiritual del Paraguay', cap. i., speaking of the Guaraní race, says: `Domina ambos mares el del sur por todo el Brasil y ciñiendo el Peru con los dos mas grandes rios que conoce el orbe que son el de la Plata, cuya boca en Buenos-Ayres es de ochenta leguas, y el gran Marañon, à el inferior en nada e que pasa bien vecino de la ciudad de Cuzco.'

---

[30] Barco de la Centenera, in `La Argentina', canto v., also refers to `La Casa del Gran Moxo'. It was situated `en una laguna', and was `toda de piedra labrada'.

---

[31] Their numerals are four in number (*peteî, mocoî, mbohap, irând*); after this they are said to count in Spanish in the same way as do the Guaraní-speaking Paraguayans. Much has been written on the Guaraní tongue by many authors, but perhaps the `Gramatica', `Tesoro', and the `Vocabulario' of Padre Antonio Ruiz Montoya, published at Madrid in 1639 and 1640, remain the most important works on the language. Padre Sigismundi has left a curious work in Guaraní on the medicinal plants of Paraguay. Before the war of 1866-70 several MS. copies were said to exist in that country. See Du Gratz's `République du Paraguay', cap. iv., p. 214.

---

[32] See Demersay, `Histoire du Paraguay', p. 324, for names of Guaraní tribes. Alfred Maury also, in his `La Terre et l'Homme Américain', p. 392, speaks of `le rameau brasilio-guaranin, ou Caráibe, qui s'etendait jadis depuis les Petites-Antilles jusqu'au Paraguay.'

---

[33] Few modern `conquerors' in Africa seem to have engaged in personal combat with the natives. Even of Mr. Rhodes it is not set down that he has killed many Matabele with his own hands. Times change, not always for the bettering of things.

---

[34] Santiago, as in duty bound, usually appeared whenever Spaniards were hard pressed. Few writers had the courage of Bernal Diaz, who of a similar appearance said: `But I, sinner that I was, was not worthy to see him; whom I did see and recognise was Francisco de Morla on his chestnut horse' (Bernal Diaz, `Historia de la Conquista de Nueva España', cap. xxxiv., p. 141; Madrid, 1795).

---

[35] Thus it will be seen that the Franciscans were at work in the country long before the arrival of the Jesuits. It may be on this account that they became such bitter enemies of the later comers.

[36] `Comentarios de Alvar Nuñez Cabeza de Vaca'. Published by Don Andres Gonzalez Barcia in his collection of `Early Historians of the Indies' (Madrid, 1749).

[37] It must be allowed, however, that in their writings few of the Spanish *conquistadores* of America bragged much. They mostly gave the credit of all their doings to the God of Battles. The boasting has been reserved for the conquerors of Africa in our own time.

[38] *Asiento* is a contract. The contract which Charles V., at the well-meant but unfortunate instigation of Las Casas, made with the Genoese to supply negroes for America is known as `El Asiento de los Negros'.

[39] In the *capitulacion* made by Alvar Nuñez with the King occurs the celebrated clause, `Que no pasasen procuradores ni abogados a las Indias', *i.e.*, that neither solicitors nor barristers should go to the Indies. It is unfortunate it was not held to stringently, as in Paraguay, at least, the Reptilia were already well represented.

[40] This is perhaps the first account of the levying of the tithe in the New World.

[41] These backwaters are known in Guaraní by the name of *aguapey*.

[42] The vinchuca is a kind of flying bug common in Paraguay. Its shape is triangular, its colour gray, and its odour noxious. It is one of the Hemiptera, and its so-called scientific appellation is *onorhinus gigas*.

[43] R. B. Cunninghame Graham writes elsewhere: "All over South America the jaguar is called a tiger (tigre)." — A. L., 1998.

[44] Azara, in his `Historia del Paraguay', etc., tells us that in 1551 Domingo de Irala at Asuncion bought a fine black horse for five thousand gold crowns. He bound himself to pay for him out of the proceeds of his first conquest.

[45] `Comentarios de Alvar Nuñez Cabeza de Vaca', contained in Barcia's `Historiadores Primitivos de las Indias Occidentales'.

[46] The `patriots' are always those of the prevailing party in a State.

[47]

`(I.H.S.)

`God preserve your Excellency, say we, the Cabildo, and all the Caciques and Indians, men, women and children of San Luis, as your Excellency is our father. The Corregidor, Santiago Pindo and Don Pantaleon Caynari, in their love for us, have written to us of certain birds which they desire we will send them for the King. . . . We are sorry not to have them to send, inasmuch as they live where God made them, in the forests, and fly far away from us, so that we cannot catch them. Withal we are the vassals of God and of the King, and always desirous to fulfil the wishes of his Minister . . . so we pray to God that that best of birds, the Holy Ghost, may descend upon the King. . . . Furthermore, we desire to say that the Spanish custom is not to our liking — for everyone to take care of himself, instead of helping one another in their daily toil.'

This quaint and touching letter was written originally in Guaraní, and is preserved at Buenos Ayres. `That best of birds, the Holy Ghost,' shows faith grounded, at least, on ornithology, and the whole spirit of the simple document is as pathetic as its unconscious philosophy is true.

[48] Guevara, `Historia del Paraguay' (printed in `La Coleccion de Angelis', Buenos Aires, 1836), book vi., p. 108, says of Alvar Nuñez: `Merecia estatua por su rectitud, justicia y Christiandad.' And in another place Guevara says: `La Florida lo cautivó con inhumanidad; La Asuncion lo aprisionó con infamia; pero en una y otro parte fue ejemplar de moderacion . . . recto, prudente y de sano corazon.' Alvar Nuñez died holding the office of `Oidor de la Audiencia de Sevilla', according to P. del Techo (`Historia del Paraguay'); or as a member of the Consejo de Indias, according to Charlevoix.

[49] Acquaviva was General of the Order at this time; he was a man of marked ability and great energy.

[50] Before this date the Jesuits in Paraguay had been under the ecclesiastical jurisdiction of the Bishops of Peru.

[51] Paranapané = the White Paraná, or, according to others, the Paraná without fish.

[52] Reduction (*reduccion*) was the Spanish name for a missionary establishment.

[53] Some of the Spanish writers refer to Filds as Padre Tom Filds. His real name was Fields, and he was a Scotchman.

[54] The Paulistas were the inhabitants of the Portuguese (now Brazilian) town of São Paulo. Azara, who hated the Jesuits (his brother, Don Nicolas de Azara, having been concerned in their expulsion), says that fear of the Paulistas contributed to the success of the Jesuits with the Indians. Dean Funes ('Historia del Paraguay', etc.) says just as reasonably that it was fear of the Spanish settlers.

[55] There was, however, a royal Order (*cedula real*) which applied to all America, which especially prohibited Spaniards from living in the Indian towns, and, moreover, provided that even for purposes of trade no Spaniard should remain for more than three days in an Indian town.

[56] 'Histoire Politique et Philosophique des Indes', vol. i., p. 289 (Genève, 1780).

[57] Cretineau Joly, 'Histoire Religieuse, Politique et Littéraire de la Compagnie de Jésus', vol. iii., cap. v., p. 322 (Paris, 1846).

[58] 'Historia General de los hechos de los Castellanos en las Islas y tierra firme del Mar Oceano', decad. v., lib. iv., cap. xl.

[59] `Historia General de los hechos de los Castellanos en las Islas y tierra firme del Mar Oceano', decad. v., lib. x., cap. lxxx.

[60] `Inventarios de los bienes hallados á la Expulsion de los Jesuitas' (Madrid, 1872).

[61] The Franciscans had already five or six settlements.

[62] The word in Brazil is used to designate a half-breed, but the etymology seems unknown.

[63] `Me he de salvar a pesar de Dios, porque para salvarse el hombre no ha menester mas que creer' (Ruiz Montoya, `Conquista Espiritual'). Montoya adds with a touch of humour quite in Cervantes' vein: `Este, sabe ya por experiencia la falsedad de su doctrina, porque le mataron de tres balazos, sin confesion.'

[64] The Mamelucos sometimes pushed their forays right through Paraguay into the district of the Moxos, and Padre Patricio Fernandez, in his curious `Relacion de los Indios Chiquitos' (Madrid, 1726), relates their adventures in that far-distant district, and the conflicts which the Indians, led by their priests and helped by the Spanish settlers, sustained.

[65] Lahier (Francisci) S. I., `Annæ Paraguarie, Annor. 1635, et duor. sequ.'

[66] `Relazioni della Provincia del Paraguai'.

[67] Brabo.

[68] An *estero* is a tract of country covered by water to the depth of two or three feet. The bottom is usually hard, but it is full of holes and hummocks. High pampa grass and reeds not infrequently obscure the view, and clouds of insects make life miserable. If the tract extends to more than a day's journey, the night passed on a dry hummock, holding one's horse and listening without a fire to the wild beasts, is likely to remain present to one in after-life, especially if alone; the only things that seem to link one to humanity are one's horse and the familiar stars. Perhaps that is why Capella has always seemed to me in some sort my own property.

[69] This curious berry, about the size of a large damson, grows on a little shrub in sandy and rocky soils. It has a thick yellow rind and several large seeds, and the property of being icy cold in the hottest weather — a true traveller's joy. Dr. de Bourgade de la Dardye, in his excellent book on Paraguay (the English edition published in London in 1892), thinks it is either a eugenia or a myrtus.

[70] Charlevoix, vol. i., liv. vii., p. 384.

[71] *Ibid.*, liv. vii., p. 359.

[72] Charlevoix, `Histoire du Paraguay', vol. lvi., p. 285.

[73] `Conquista Espiritual del Paraguay', Ruiz de Montoya, introductory chapter.

[74] This may either mean to the service of God or to the service of the King (Philip III.), for in the time of Montoya `Majesty' was used in addressing both the King of Spain and the King of Heaven.

[75] Yapeyu, or Reyes, was the southernmost of the Jesuit reductions. It was situated upon the Uruguay in what is now the Argentine province of Entre Rios.

[76] `Conquista Espiritual', p. 22.

[77] This time, it is to be hoped, without omissions.

[78] `Dando gracias por agravios negocian los hombres sabios.'

[79] Soon afterwards ruined by the Paulistas.

[80] *Cacique* = chief.

[81] These raids were known as *malocas*.

[82] In Paraguay it was not unusual for foreign Jesuits to hispaniolize their names; thus, Smith became Esmid. But it was more usual to add a Spanish name, as appears to have been the case with P. Vansurk Mansilla. Father Manuel Querini, in his report to the King of Spain in 1750, mentions the names of Boxer, Keiner, and Limp, with many other French, English, and German names, amongst those of priests at the various missions.

[83] Montoya, `Conquista Espiritual'. Also Charlevoix.

[84] It is certain that the Guaranís, like many other Indians, were polygamists, and Xarque, in his `Vida Apostolica del P. Joseph Cataldino', thus explains the matter: `El tener tanto numero de concubinas, no solamente lo ocasiona su natural lascivo, sino tambien, el vicio de la embriaguez, pues teniendo tantas criadas tenian con mas abundancia su cerveza y vino.' Thus Xarque seems to agree with the late Miss Mary Kingsley, who in one of her books (though she says nothing about the `natural lascivo' of the negroes of the West Coast of Africa) seems to attribute the polygamy of the negroes to the difficulty a man experiences, in the countries in which she travelled, in getting his food prepared by one wife.

[85] Charcas is situated in what is now Bolivia, and was extremely inconvenient for all dwellers on the eastern side of the Andes to reach. Whether this was a masterpiece of policy calculated to discourage lawsuits, or whether it was merely due to Spanish incuriousness and maladministration, is a moot point.

[86] The Indians of the missions were not allowed to possess firearms at this period.

[87] `Paraguay', Dr. E. de Bourgade la Dardye; English edition by George Philips junior (London, 1892). The Indians call it Salto de Canandiyú, which, according to Azara, was the name of a *cacique* whom the first Spaniards met there.

[88] `Descripcion y Historia del Paraguay', Madrid, 1847.

[89] `Y es un espantoso despeñadero de agua', etc. (`Descripcion del Paraguay', tomo i., p. 39).

[90] `No dan cuartel'.

[91] At least, I have been unable to discover any other account by an eye-witness.

[92] This city was situated near the great falls of Guayrá, and was destroyed by the Paulistas, as well as the city of Villa Rica, after the Jesuits and their Indians left the province.

[93] `Conquista Espiritual', p. 48.

[94] `Rigoroso examen' (`Conquista Espiritual').

[95] In all the books and pamphlets I have searched about the Jesuits in Paraguay, both friendly and unfriendly to the Order, I have never found a charge of personal unchastity advanced against a Jesuit. In regard to the other religious Orders it is far otherwise.

[96] Azara, `Descripcion e Historia del Paraguay', tomo i., p. 40: `En las inmediaciones del Salto hay proporcion para tomar las medidas geometricas

que se quiera y metiendose por el bosque se puede reconocer lo inferior del Salto, bien que para este es menester desnudare totalmente porque llueve mucho.'

---

[97] Azara records (book i.) the Indian fable that no living thing could exist near the cataract. Though this is of course untrue, yet in most Paraguayan forests near water, game is both scarce and hard to find.

---

[98] `Con buenas prendas de su salud eterna' (`Conquista Espiritual').

---

[99] Fathers Suarez, Contreras, and Espinosa were Montoya's lieutenants in this memorable retreat. It is difficult to give the palm to the energy and courage of the four priests, or to the resignation and faith of the immense multitude of Indians who were saved by them.

---

[100] *Culebra* is the Spanish for a serpent. These fish may have been waterboas, or, again, as seems probable by their digestive powers, some kind of hypothetical fish not yet catalogued.

---

[101] The name of this river seems to have passed through the machine of some medieval typewriter, for it is like no name in any language, and Montoya knew Guaraní well, having written much in that language.

---

[102] Even so late as the year 1777, in which the last treaty of boundaries was signed at San Ildefonso, Portugal was the gainer, though not so greatly as by the former treaties of 1681 and 1750.

---

[103] `Efemerides o Diario de la Guerra de los Guaranies', por P. Tadeo Hennis. This journal has, I think, never been published in its entirety, but portions of it are to be found in the collection of documents, Bulls, despatches, etc., published at Madrid in 1768 under the title of `Causa Jesuitica de Portugal'. The author of this book calls Hennis a German, but his name, Thadeus Ennis (as it is often spelt), and his love of fighting look un-Germanic. Portions of the diary are also to be found in the work of Bernardo Ibañez de Echegarray, entitled `Histoire du Paraguay sous les Jésuites' (Amsterdam, 1780). Either the original or an old manuscript copy

exists in the archives of Simancas, where I have seen, but unfortunately did not examine, it. A portion of the work is also included in the `Coleccion de Angelis' (Buenos Ayres, 1836).

[104] `Histoire d'un Voyage faict en la Terre du Brésil'.

[105] The way of the neophyte even to-day is hard, so many priests of different jarring sects disputing for his soul as hotly as if it were a preference stock which they had private intimation was just about to rise.

[106] This province was sometimes called Guayrá, and sometimes La Provincia de Vera, Vera being the family name of Alvar Nuñez Cabeza de Vaca. Its position, etc., may be determined by reference to the curious volume of maps published at Madrid by Don Francisco Javier Brabo in 1872.

[107] That a mission could be so undefended as to need trenches, that a Jesuit should ask leave to make such elementary defences, even in the face of imminent danger, seems to prove that the Jesuits at least in 1636 had no intention of defying the sovereign power, as was so often alleged against them.

[108] San Joaquin, Santa Teresa, Santa Ana.

[109] `Histoire du Paraguay', liv. ix., p. 446.

[110] This territory is now the Argentine province of Misiones.

[111] This seems to prove the malice of those who set about that the Indians of the missions paid no taxes to the Crown.

[112] Vieyra, the great Portuguese Jesuit, said that all miracles were possible to God, but yet that he had never heard that our Lord had ever cured anyone of folly.

[113] Now a province of the Argentine Republic.

[114] `Historia Paraquariæ', book xii., cap. xii.

[115] La Plata was sometimes called Chuquisaca, and is to-day known as Sucre.

[116] `Histoire du Paraguay', vol. i., book ix., p. 478.

[117] Charlevoix, vol. i., book xi. Dean Funes, in his `Ensayo de la Historia Civil de Paraguay, Buenos Ayres y Tucuman', vol. ii., book iii., p. 10 (Buenos Ayres, 1816), says of him: `Se adquirió muy en breve una reputacion mas brillante que solida.'

[118] But besides putting into execution all his histrionic talents, he had the adroitness to address himself to those feelings of self-interest which he knew were perhaps more powerful than those of admiration and respect for his own saintly proceedings in his new diocese. Crétineau Joly, in his `Histoire de la Compagnie de Jésus', vol. iii., p. 333 (Paris, 1845), tells us that Cardenas `parle aux Espagnols, il s'addresse à leurs interêts, il réveille les vieux levain de discorde . . . et il accuse les missionnaires d'être seuls les apôtres de la liberté des Indiens.'

[119] `Oraculo Manual y Arte de Prudencia' (Amsterdam, en casa de Juan Blau, 1659).

[120] Charlevoix.

[121] Exod. 32:27.

[122] The arroba is about twenty-five pounds weight.

[123] Charlevoix.

[124] Camalote is a species of water-lily which forms a thick covering on stagnant rivers and lakes in Paraguay and in the Argentine Republic.

[125] This was untrue, as the Jesuit missions were not at that time (1644) apportioned into parishes under the authority of the Jesuits, and such tribute as then was customary was all collected by government officials.

[126] This was also untrue, as the tithes were never regulated in Paraguay till 1649.

[127] This accusation was quite untrue, for the edict referred to was not obtained under misapprehension, but after a complete exposition of all the facts. Moreover, it was subsequently renewed on several occasions by the Spanish Kings.

[128] The Venetians did not expel the Jesuits, they left Venetia of their own accord.

[129] Fathers Montoya and Taño went respectively to Rome and to Madrid to lay the sorrows of the Indians before the King and Pope. Having obtained the edict from the King that Cardenas referred to, and a brief from the Pope (Urban VIII.) forbidding slavery, they had the hardihood to appear within the city of San Paulo and affix both edicts to the church door. As was to be expected, the Paulistas immediately expelled them from their territories, and hence the semi-truth of the sixth charge made by Bishop Cardenas.

[130] Funes, `Historia Civil del Paraguay, Buenos-Ayres, y Tucuman'.

[131] The testimony of Funes is as follows: `Á juicio de testigo ocular no es más admirable la sangre fria de sus capellanes' (`Historia Civil del Paraguay', book iii., cap. viii.).

[132] Literally, `taking out the blocks to air'. The effigies are made of hard and heavy wood, and I remember once in Concepcion de Paraguay assisting on a sweltering day to carry a Madonna weighing about five hundredweight.

[133] The proverb says in Paraguay, `No se fia de mula ni mulata'.

[134] `Pagar y apelar'.

[135] Misque is at least fifteen hundred miles from Tucuman.

[136] `Que lo hagan salir de nuestros Reynos y Señorios como ageno y estraño, por importar assi para la quietud de aquellas Provincias, y al servicio de su Majestad.'

[137] A *yerbal* is a forest chiefly composed of the *Ilex Paraguayensis*, from the leaves of which the *yerba maté*, or `Paraguayan tea', is made.

[138] Xarque, book ii., cap. xl., p. 30.

[139] This Villalon has left some curious memoirs in the case which he submitted to the Council of the Indies which sat in Seville.

[140] Charlevoix, book xii., p. 115.

[141] Chipa is a kind of bread made of mandioca flour.

[142] Rapadura is a kind of coarse sugar, generally sold in little pyramid-shaped lumps, done up in a banana leaf. It is strongly flavoured with lye.

[143] Mani is ground-nut. ["Peanut" in American English. — A. L., 1998.]

[144] The paraiso is one of the Paulinias.

[145] `Obedesco, pero no cumplo.'

[146] `Cosas de palacio van despacio.'

[147] Dean Funes, in his `Ensayo de la Historia Civil del Paraguay, Buenos Ayres y Tucuman' (book ii., cap. i., p. 10), says he was `Dotado de un temperamento muy facil de inflamarse, de una imaginacion viva, de una memoria feliz, y de un ingenio no vulgar.'

[148] At the date of the expulsion the number of the cattle was 719,761; oxen, 44,183; horses, 27,204; sheep, 138,827 (`Inventarios de los bienes hallados á la expulsion de los Jesuitas', Francisco Javier Brabo, Madrid, 1872).

[149] *Cocos yatais.*

[150] Urunday (*Astrenium fraxinifolium: Terebinthaceæ*), curapay (*Piptadenia communis: Leguminaceæ*), lapacho (*Tecoma curialis* and *varia: Begoniaceæ*), taruma (*Vitex Taruma: Verbenaceæ*), tatane (*Acacia maleolens: Leguminaceæ*), and cupai (*Copaifera Langsdorfii*). These and many other woods, such as the Palo Santo (*Guaiacum officinalis*), butacæ, and the *Cedrela Braziliensis*, known to the Jesuits as `cedar', and much used by them in their churches, comprise the chief varieties.

[151] `Libro compuesto por el Hermano Pedro de Montenegro de la C. de J., Ano 1711', MS. folio, with pen-and-ink sketches, formerly belonged to the Dukes of Osuna, and was in their library. Padre Sigismundi also wrote a herbal in Guaraní, and a Portuguese Jesuit, Vasconellos, has left a curious book upon the flora of Brazil.

[152] Domingo Parodi, in his `Notas sobre algunas plantas usuales del Paraguay' (Buenos Ayres, 1886), has done much good work.

[153] *Acacia Cavenia.*

[154] *Prosopis dulcis.* The famous `balm of the missions', known by the vulgar name of *curalo todo* (all-heal), was made from the gum of the tree called aguacciba, one of the Terebinthaceæ. It was sold by the Jesuits in Europe. It was so highly esteemed that the inhabitants of the villages near to which the tree was found were specially enjoined to send a certain quantity of the balsam every year to the King's pharmacy in Madrid.

[155] It was from those mountains that the Jesuits procured the seed of the *Ilex Paraguayensis* to plant in their reductions. The leaves beaten into a finish powder furnished the `Paraguayan tea', called *yerba-maté* by the Spaniards and *caa* by the Indians, from which the Jesuits derived a handsome revenue. After the expulsion of the Order all the *yerba* in Paraguay was procured, till a few years ago, from forests in the north of Paraguay, in which the tree grew wild.

[156] It was by the Bull of Paul III. — given at the demand of two monks, Fray Domingo de Betanzos and Fray Domingo de Minaya — that the Indians were first considered as reasoning men (*gente de razon*), and not as unreasonable beings (*gente sin razon*), as Juan Ortiz, Bishop of Santa Marta, wished.

[157] Ibañez (`Histoire du Paraguay sous les Jésuites M.D.CCIXXX.'), a great opponent of the Jesuits, says that European offenders and recalcitrant Indians in the missions were sent as a last resource to the Spanish settlements. This is not astonishing when we remember the curious letter of Don Pedro Faxardo, Bishop of Buenos Ayres (preserved by Charlevoix), written in 1721 to the King of Spain, in which he says he thinks `that not a mortal crime is committed in the missions in a year.' He adds that, `if the Jesuits were so rich, why are their colleges so poor?'

[158] It is to be remembered that, of the thirty Jesuit missions, only eight were in Paraguay; the rest were in what to-day is Brazil and the Argentine provinces of Entre Rios, Corrientes, and Misiones.

[159] Sometimes, when they had been assembled, they all deserted suddenly, as did the Tobatines, who in 1740 suddenly left the reduction of Santa Fé, and for eleven years were lost in the forests, till Father Yegros found them, and, as they would not return, established himself amongst them (Cretineau Joly, 'Histoire de la Compagnie de Jésus', vol. v., cap. ii.).

[160] P. Cardiel, 'Declaracion de la Verdad', p. 282: 'Todos los pueblos estan bien formados con calles á cordel. Las casas de los Indios son en algunos pueblos de piedras cuadradas pero sin cal . . . otras de palos y barro todas cubiertas de teja, y todas tienen soportales ó corredores, unas con pilares de piedras, otras de madera.'

[161] Don Francisco Graell, an officer of dragoons in service during the War of the Seven Towns in 1750, gives the following description of the church of the mission of San Miguel: 'La iglesia es muy capaz, toda de piedra de silleria con tres naves y media naranja. Muy bien pintada y dorada con un portico magnifico y de bellisima arquitectura, bovedas y media naranja son de madera, el altar mayor de talla, sin dorar y le falta el ultimo cuerpo.'

[162] 'Galerias con columnas, barandillas y escaleras de piedra entallada' (Don Francisco Graell). See also P. Cardiel ('Declaracion de la Verdad', p. 247), 'En todos los pueblos hay reloj de sol y de ruedas,' etc. The work of Padre Cardiel was written in 1750 in the missions of Paraguay, but remained unpublished till 1800, when it appeared in Buenos Ayres from the press of Juan A. Alsina, Calle de Mexico 1422. It is, perhaps, after the 'Conquista Espiritual' of Father Ruiz Montoya, the most powerful contemporary justification of the policy of the Jesuits in Paraguay. It is powerfully but simply written, and contains withal that saving grace of humour which has, from the beginning of the world, been a stumbling-block to fools.

[163] The mission of San Miguel had 1,353 families in it, or say 6,635 souls. San Francisco de Borja contained 650 families, or 2,793 souls (Report by Manuel Querini to the King, dated Cordoba de Tucuman, y Agosto 1o, 1750).

[164] In their extensive missions in the provinces of Chiquitos and Moxos they pursued the same system. As they were much more isolated in those provinces than in Paraguay, and consequently much less interfered with, it was there that their peculiar system most flourished. After the expulsion of the Jesuits from America in 1767, the Spaniards in Alta Peru, and subsequently the Bolivians, had the sense to follow the Jesuit plan in its

entirety; whereas Bucareli, the Viceroy of Buenos Ayres, entirely changed the Jesuits' rule in Paraguay. The consequence was that in Bolivia the Indians, instead of dispersing as they did in Paraguay, remained in the missions, and D'Orbigny (`Fragment d'un Voyage au Centre de l'Amérique Méridianale') saw at the missions of Santiago and El Santo Corazon, in the province of Chiquitos, the remains of the Jesuits' polity. There were ten missions in Chiquitos, and fifteen in Moxos. At the present time the Franciscans have some small establishments in Bolivia.

---

[165] `Pillos muy ladinos' (Robertson, `Letters from Paraguay').

---

[166] Ferrer del Rio, in his `Coleccion de los articulos de la Esperanza sobre Carlos III.' (Madrid, 1859), says: `Fuera de las misiones de los Jesuitas particularmente en el Paraguay se consideraban los Indios entre los seres mas infelices del mundo.'

Jorge Juan and Antonio de Ulloa, in their celebrated `Secret Report' (`Noticias Secretas de America'): `La compañia (de Jesus) atiende a sus fines particularmente con los misioneros que llevan de España; pero con todo eso no se olvida de la conversion de los Indios, ni tiene abandonado este asunto pues aunque van poco adelante en el, que es lo que no se esperimenten en las demas religiones.'

---

[167] Many travellers, as Azara, Demersay, Du Graty, and D'Orbigny, have remarked how fond of music was the Guaraní race, and how soon they learned the use of European instruments. D'Orbigny (`Fragment d'un Voyage au Centre de l'Amérique Méridianale'), in his interesting account of the mission of El Santo Corazon, in the district of Chiquitos, says: `Je fus très étonné d'entendre exécuter après les danses indigènes des morceaux de Rossini et ... de Weber ... la grande messe chantée en musique était exécutée d'une manière très remarquable pour des Indiens.'

Vargas Machuca, in his most curious and rare `Milicia y Descripcion de las Indias', says, under the heading of `Musica del Indio': `Usan sus musicas antiguas en sus regocijos, y son muy tristes en la tonada.' To-day the Indians of Paraguay have songs known as *tristes*. The brigadier Don Diego de Alvear, in his `Relacion de Misiones' (Coleccion de Angelis), says that the first to teach the Guaranís European music was a Flemish Jesuit, P. Juan Basco, who had been *maestro de capilla* to the Archduke Albert.

---

[168] See also P. Cardiel, `Declaracion de la Verdad', p. 274: `. . . y esta acabada, se toca á Misa á que entran todos cantando el Bendito, y alabado en su lengua, ó en Castellano, que en las dos lenguas lo saben.'

[169] Dean Funes, in his `Ensayo de la Historia del Paraguay', etc., says that in the *estancia* of Santa Tecla, in the missions of Paraguay, during the time of the Jesuits, there were 50,000 head of cattle.

[170] `Inventarios de los bienes hallados á la expulsion de los Jesuitas', Introduction, xxvii, Francisco Javier Brabo.

[171] The rare and much-sought-after `Manuale ad usum Patrum Societatis Jesu qui in Reductionibus Paraquariæ versantur, ex Rituale Romano ad Toletano decerptum', was printed at the mission of Loreto. It contains prayers in Guaraní as well as in Latin. Here also was printed a curious book of Guaraní sermons by Nicolas Yapuguay, many Guaraní vocabularies, and the `Arte de la Lengua Guaraní' of Ruiz Montoya.

[172] P. Cardiel, `Declaracion de la Verdad', p. 295: `De estos granos comunales se da para sembrar', etc.

[173] This jerked beef is called *charqui* in South America.

[174] The poorer classes in Paraguay all used to wear the *tipoi*. They covered themselves when it was cold with a white cotton sheet wrapped in many folds.

[175] The Jesuits themselves were dressed in homespun clothes, for Matias Angles — quoted in the introduction to the `Declaracion de la Verdad' of Father Cardiel, published at Buenos Ayres in 1900 (the introduction by P. Pablo Hernandez) — says: `El vestuario de los Padres es de lienzo de algodon teñido de negro, hilado y fabricado por las mismas Indias de los pueblos; y si tal qual Padre tiene un capote ó manteo de paña de Castilla se sucede de unos á otros, y dura un siglo entero.'

[176] In the 'Relacion de Misiones' of the Brigadier Don Diego de Alvear, written between 1788 and 1801, and preserved in the 'Coleccion de Angelis', occurs the following curious description of the feast-day of a patron saint of a Jesuit reduction: 'They make a long alley of interwoven canes, which ends in a triumphal arch, which they adorn with branches of palms and other trees with considerable grace and taste (*con bastante gracia y simetria*). Under the arch they hang their images of saints, their clothes, their first-fruits — as corn and sugar-cane, and calabashes full of maize-beer (*chicha*) — their meat and bread, together with animals both alive and dead, such as they can procure (*como los pueden haber con su diligencia*). Then, forming in a ring, they dance and shout, 'Viva el rey! Viva el santo tutelar!'

[177] Many and curious are the names by which the office-bearers went. Thus, in the Mission of el Santo Corazon, in the Chiquitos, I find the following: Corregidor, the Mayor; Teniente, Lieutenant; Alferez, Sub-Lieutenant; Alcalde Primero, Head Alcalde; Alcalde Segundo, Second Alcalde; Commandante, Captain (of the Militia); Justicia Mayor, Chief Justice; Sargento Mayor, Sergeant-Major. Then came fiscales, fiscals; sacristan mayor, head-beadle; capitan de estancia, chief of the cattle farm; capitan de pinturas, carpinteria, herreros, etc. — captain of painters, carpenters, smiths, etc. All the offices were competed for ardently, and those of Corregidor and Alcalde in especial were prized so highly that Indians who were degraded from them for bad conduct or carelessness not infrequently died of grief.

[178] In each reduction there were two priests. In all Paraguay, at the expulsion of the Order in 1767, there were only seventy-eight Jesuits (Dean Funes, 'Ensayo de la Historia del Paraguay', etc., cap. i., vol. ii.).

[179] In the mission of Los Apostoles there were 599 of these 'horses of the saint', according to an inventory preserved by Brabo.

[180] Furnished to Bucareli, Viceroy of Buenos Ayres at the expulsion, and first printed by Brabo ('Inventarios de los bienes hallados á la expulsion de los Jesuitas').

[181] The Jesuits exercised the Indians a great deal in dancing, taking advantage of their love of dancing in their savage state. D'Orbigny and

Demersay ('Fragment d'un Voyage au Centre de l'Amérique Méridianale', and 'Histoire Physique, etc., du Paraguay') found between the years 1830 and 1855 that the Indians of the Moxos and Chiquitos still danced as they had done in the time of the Jesuits.

I have seen them in the then (1873) almost deserted mission of Jesus, buried in the great woods on the shore of the Paraná, dance a strange, half-savage dance outside the ruined church.

---

[182] Cardiel, in his 'Declaracion de la Verdad', p. 239, says: 'Todos los pueblos ponen su castillo en la plaza y en el medio de el colocan el retratro del Rey, y el Indio Alferez Real . . . va al castillo con el Estandarte Real y alli hace su homenage con otros rendimientos anteel Retratro Real,' saying in Guaraní, 'Toicohengatú ñande Mbaru bicha guazú! Toicohengatú ñande Rey marangatú! Toicohengatú ñande Rey Fernando Sesto!' ('Long live our King, the great chief! Long live our good King! Long live our King Ferdinand VI.').

---

[183] 'Chupas de damasco carmesi con encajes de plata.'

---

[184] It may be roughly translated, 'a good stone wall between a male and female saint.'

---

[185] These clothes were the property of the community, and not of the individual Indians.

---

[186] Brabo, xxxv., Introduction to 'Los inventarios de los bienes.'

---

[187] A recent writer in the little journal published on yellow packing-paper in the Socialist colony of Cosme, in Paraguay (*Cosme Monthly*, November, 1898), has a curious passage corroborating what I have so often observed myself. Under the heading of 'A Paraguayan Market', he says: 'The Guaraní clings stubbornly to the Guaraní customs. This is irritating to the European, but who shall say that the Guaraní is not right? . . . European settlement cannot but be fatal to the Guaraní, however profitable it may be to land-owning and mercantile classes. . . . The Paraguayan market is a woman's club . . . they will come thirty or forty miles with a clothful of the white curd-cheese of the country, contentedly journeying on foot along the narrow paths. They will cut a cabbage into sixteenths and eat their cheese themselves

rather than sell it under market price.' Long may they do so, for so long will they be free, and perhaps poor; but, then, in countries such as Paraguay freedom and poverty are identical.

---

[188] As the Gaucho proverb says, `Las armas son necesarias pero "naide" sabe cuando.'

---

[189] Corregidores, alcaldes, regidores, alguaciles, etc.

---

[190] Hereditary or sometimes elected chiefs.

---

[191] I remember seeing on the tombstone of a Spanish sailor his hope of salvation through the intercession of the Lord High Admiral Christ. After the Spanish custom, officers were often generals both by sea and land, so that soldiers were not excluded from the Lord High Admiral's intercession.

---

[192] Dean Funes (`Ensayo de la Historia de Paraguay', etc.) says: `These Indians went under the command of Don Antonio de Vera Moxica; their sergeants were Guaranís and their captains Spaniards. Their *cacique* was Ignacio Amandaá, who commanded in chief under Vera Moxica.' They fought bravely, and returned again and again to the assault of the town after several repulses, manifesting the same dogged courage and indifference to death which their descendants showed in the war against Brazil in 1866-70. In that war bodies of Paraguayans frequently attacked strong positions defended by artillery, and allowed themselves to be shot down to the last man rather than retire. At other times, concealed behind masses of floating herbage, from their canoes they sprang on board Brazilian ironclads, and were all killed in the vain endeavour to capture the vessels. I knew a little pettifogging lawyer, one Izquierdo, who, with ten companions, attempted in a canoe to take the Brazilian flagship (an ironclad); left alone on her deck, after the death of his companions, he sprang into the water under a shower of bullets, and, badly wounded, swam over to the Chaco, the desert side of the river. There for three days he remained, subsisting on wild oranges, and then swam across again on a raft of sticks, in spite of the alligators and many fierce fish which abound in Paraguay. He got well, and, though lame, was, when I knew him, as arrant a little scrivening knave as you could hope to meet in either hemisphere.

On many other occasions the mission Indians performed notable services for the Spanish Government. In 1681, when the French attacked Buenos Ayres, a detachment of two thousand Indians was sent to its assistance. Philip V. himself wrote to the Provincial of Paraguay on this occasion asking him to send troops to the defence of the city.

In 1785 four thousand Guaranís, commanded by Don Baltazar Garcia, were at the second siege of the Colonia del Sacramento. Funes says of them: `A juicio de un testigo ocular, no es menos admirable la sangre fria de sus capellanes.'

[193] `Perro Luterano'. It is astonishing how in Spain the comparatively innocuous Luther has fallen heir to the heritage of hatred that should more properly have belonged to the inhuman and treacherous Calvin.

[194] Philip V. in 1745, after an examination which lasted six years, approved of all the actions of the Jesuits in Paraguay (Cretineau Joly, `Histoire de la Compagnie de Jésus', vol. v., p. 103). So that a curious letter of a Jeronimite friar (one Padre Cevallos), written in 1774, is well within due limits when it says that all the Jesuits did in Paraguay was `todo probado por reales cedulas ó procedia de ordenes expresas.'

[195] One is obliged to allow, in common fairness, that Calvin carried out in his own practice what he advocated — as witness his conduct with Servetus, whom he first calumniated, then entrapped, and lastly murdered in cold blood.

[196] Don Francisco Corr sent the following list of arms to the Viceroy Zabala, of Buenos Ayres (Funes, `Ensayo', etc.): `Armas buenas, 850; lanzas de hierro, 3,850; pedreras (culverins), 10. Las flechas no se cuentan.' He says: `Todos los Indios quando han de salir a compaña llevan 150 flechas de hierro, menos los que llevan armos de fuego. Asi mismo cargan "bolas" que son dos piedras en una cuerda. Los de a pie que no llevan escopetas tienen lanza, flecha, y honda con su provision de piedras en un bolson como de granaderos. Se prestan caballos entre los pueblos.'

[197] Ibañez (`Histoire du Paraguay sous les Jésuites') states the hides sold at about three dollars apiece.

[198] The arroba was twenty-five pounds.

[199] These figures are from Brabo's inventories.

[200] Ibañez states that only eighty-four dollars a year were set apart for the maintenance of each priest.

[201] Dean Funes (`Ensayo de le Historia Civil del Paraguay', etc.) puts it at a million reales, which almost equals £20,800.

Ibañez (`La Republica Jesuitica'), with the noble disregard of consequences so noticeable in most polemical writers, boldly alters this to a million dollars, his object being to prove that the Jesuits exacted exorbitant taxation from the neophytes.

[202] The honey of the missions was celebrated, and the wax made by the small bee called `Opemus', according to Charlevoix (livre v., p. 285), `était d'une blancheur qui n'avait rien de pareil, et ces neophytes ont consacré tout qu'ils en peuvent avoir à bruler devant les images de la Ste. Vierge.'

[203] In the inventory of the mission of San José I find: `Item, doce pares de grillos'; but I am bound to say that in this instance they were for the use of `los Guaicurus infieles prisioneros que estan en dicha mision.'

[204] `Il Cristianesimo Felice nelle Missione dei Padri della Compagnia di Jesu nel Paraguay'.

[205] `L'Histoire du Paraguay sous les Jésuites', Amsterdam, 1700, lxxv.

[206] In all, the missions amounted to thirty; and for their relative situations *vide* the curious map [this map is not yet available in this HTML text], the original of which was published in the work of Padre Pedro Lozano, C. de J., `Descripcion chorographica del terreno, rios, arboles y animales de las dilatadissimas provincias del Gran Chaco, Gualanba', etc. Cordoba, del Tucuman, en el Colegio de la Assumpcion, por Joseph Santos Balbas, 1733.

[207] A letter of a certain Jesuit (name lost, but dated 1715) says that there were at least two thousand canoes in constant use on the Paraná, and almost as many more on the Uruguay (Brabo, `Inventarios', etc.).

[208] Corregidores, regidores, alcaldes, etc.

[209] It is not to be supposed, however, that the Indians were kept in ignorance. P. Cardiel (`Declaracion de la Verdad', p. 222), quoting from the Cedula Real of 1743, says that `in every one of the towns there is a school established to teach reading and writing in Spanish, and that on that account a great number of Indians are to be met who write well.' Cardiel adds, on the same page, `Dos de ellos estan copiando ahora esto que yo escribo, y de mejor letra que la mia.'

[210] Dean Funes (`Ensayo Critico', etc.) puts the income from commerce of the thirty towns at a hundred thousand dollars, and informs us that, after taxation (to the Crown) had been deducted from it, it was applied to the maintenance of the churches and other necessary expenses, and by the end of the year little of it remained.

[211] Don Martin de Barua, in his memorial to the King (1736), complaining of the Jesuits, puts the number of taxable Indians at forty thousand. The Commission appointed to examine into the charges in 1736, which reported in 1745 (a reasonable interval), affirmed that the taxable Indians only numbered 19,116. Each Indian paid an annual poll-tax of one dollar a year to the Crown. In addition to that, every town gave one hundred dollars a year. The salary of the priests was six hundred dollars a year (Azara, `Voyage dans l'Amérique Méridionale').

[212] `Account of the Abipones'. London: John Murray, 1822.

[213] `Voyage dans l'Amérique Méridionale'. Paris: Denton, 1809.

[214] Perámas (`De vita et moribus sex sacerdotum Paraguaycorum, Petrus Joanes Andrea', lxxxiv.) states that it appeared, from papers left after their expulsion, that the income of the Jesuit College of Cordoba just paid the expenses of administration (`era con escasa diferencia igual á los gastos').

In the Archivo General of Buenos Ayres, legajo `Compañia de Jesús', there is a document referred to by P. Hernandez in his introduction to the work of P. Cardiel (`Declaracion de la Verdad'), which states that in the year of the expulsion the income of the thirty towns fell a little short of the expenses.

---

[215] Azara, `Voyage dans l'Amérique Méridionale'; also Funes, `Ensayo Critico de la Historia del Paraguay'; and Padre Guevara, `Historia del Paraguay, Rio de la Plata y Tucuman'.

---

[216] Archivo General de Simancas, Estado, legajo 7,450, folios 21 y 22, 5*a*, Copia de las cartas (sin firma; la siguiente es de Nicolas Neenguirú) que se hallaron en letra Guaraní traducidas por los interpreto nombrados en las sorpresa hecha al pueblo de San Lorenzo por el Coronel D. José Joaquin de Viana, Gobernador de Montevideo, el dia 20 de Mayo de 1756:

`El modo de vivir del Padre es, cerrar bien todas las puertas y quedarse el solo, su Mayordomo, y su muchacho. Son ya Indios de edad, y solo estos asisten solo de dia adentro, y á las doce salen afuera, y un viejo es quien cuida de la Porteria, y es quien Sierra la puerta quando descansa el Padre, ó quando sale el Padre á ver su chacara. Y aun entonces van solos, sino es con un Indio de hedad quien los giua y cuida de el caballo y despues de esto á misa y á la tarde al Rosario de Maria Santisima llamandonos con toque de campana, y antes de esto á los muchachos y muchachittas los llama con una campánilla y despues de eso el bueno de el Padre entra ha enseñarles la Doctrina, y el persinarse de el mismo modo, todos los dias de fiesta nos Predica la palabra de Dios, del mismo modo el Santo Sacramento de la Penitencia y de la Communion, en estas cosas se exercitta el bueno del Padre y todas las noches se sierra la porteria y la llave se lleva al aposento del Padre y solo se vuelve á abrir por la mañana quando entra el Sachristan y los cosineros. . . .

`Los Padres todas las mañanas nos dicen misas, y despues de misa, se van a su aposento y hai cogen un poco de aqua caliente con Yerva y no otra cosa mas; despues de esto sale a la puerta de su aposento y ahai todos los que oyeron misa se arrimen a besarle la mano, y despues de esto sale afuera a ver los Indios si trabajan en los oficios que cada uno tiene, y despues se van a su aposento a resar el oficio divino, en su libro, y para que Dios le ayude en todas sus cosas. A las once de el dia van a comer un poquitto, no á comer mucho solo coge cinco plattitos y solo beve una vez el vino, no llenando un vaso pequeño, y aguardiente nunca lo toman y el vino no lo hai en nuestro pueblo, solo lo traen de la Candelaria segun lo que envia el Padre Superior lo trahen de acia Buenos Aires. . . . Despues que sale de comer y para descansar an poco, y mientras descansa salen fuera los que assisten en la casa del Padre, y los que trabajan dentro en algunas obras y tamvien el Sachristan y el cosinero: todos estos salen fuera y quando no se toca la campana estan serradas las puertas, y solo un viejo es el que cuida de las puertas, y quando vuelvan a tocar la campana, vuelve este a abrirlas para que vuelvan a entrar los que trabajan dentro, y el Padre Coge el Brebiario no a ir a parte ninguna. A la tarde tocan la campanilla paraque se recojan las criatturas, y entre el Padre á ensenarles la doctrina christiana.'

[217] Perhaps the entire isolation of the Jesuits in these two provinces accounts for their absolute quiet; and if this is so, it goes far to prove that they were right to attempt the same isolation in Paraguay. The comparative nearness of the Spanish settlements frustrated their attempts in this instance.

[218] For `reasoning men', and how this monstrous superstition still prevails in Venezuela, see the charming book of S. Perez Triana, `De Bogota al Atlantico', etc., pp. 156-158 (Paris: Impresa Sud Americana). A really interesting book of travels, without cant, and without an eye on the public. Strange to relate, the author seems to have killed nothing during his journey.

[219] Charlevoix, book iv.

[220] `Conquista Espiritual', Ruiz Montoya.

[221] `Voyage dans l'Amérique Méridionale'.

[222] Azara, `Viage al America Meridional', tomo 2, cap 12. `La corte ordenó a Don Francisco de Alfaro oidor de la Audiencia de Charcas pasar al Perú en calidad de visitador. La primera medida que tomó en 1612 fue ordenar que ninguno en lo sucesivo pudiese ir a casa de Indios, con el pretexto de reducirlos, y que no se diesen encomiendas del modo que hemos explicado, es decir con servicio personal. No alcanzo sobre que podia fundarse una medida tan politicamente absurda: pero como este oidor favorecia las *ideas de los Jesuitas*, se sospechó que por aquel tiempo que ellos dictaron su conducta.'

[223] For *mitas* and *encomiendas*, see foregoing chapters.

[224] Brabo, `Inventarios de los bienes hallados a la expulsion de las Jesuitas'.

[225] `Voyage dans l'Amérique Méridionale'.

[226] P. Cardiel (`Declaracion de la Verdad', p. 449), quoting from Xarque (`La Vida Apostolica del Padre Joseph Cataidino', Zaragoça por Juan de Ypa, 1664), says, *re* the diminution of the Indians under the Spanish rule: `Para que se vea cuanta razon tiene el Juez reparese que segun los padrones del siglo pasado (vg. 1600-1700) en la ciudad y jurisdicion de Santiago del Estero habia 80,000 Indios y ahora, apenas hay ochenta. En la jurisdicion de Cordoba de Tucuman, habia 40,000; hoy no hay 40. En la jurisdicion y cercanias de la ciudad de Buenos Ayres, habia 30,000; hoy apenas hay 30.'

[227] Charlevoix, vol. ii., livre xvii.

[228] Funes, `Ensayo de la Historia Civil del Paraguay', etc., vol. ii., cap. v., p. 231.

[229] Del Techo, Lozano, Guevara, Charlevoix, etc., etc.

[230] Liberty is commonly only attained by blood. It is, I think, quite legitimate in playing the liberty game to kill all who disagree with your party, or to banish them. In these degenerate times, lovers of liberty have to stop short at calumny, just as if they were mere tyrants.

[231] *Guazu* = `great' in Guaraní. It is frequent in place-names both in Paraguay and Corrientes.

[232] Dean Funes, vol. ii., cap. xii., p. 372, says of Zavala: `Por caracter era manso, pero usó algunas veces de severidad, porque sabia que para servir bien a los hombres es preciso de cuando en cuando tener valor de desagradarlos. . . . La pobreza en que murio despues de tantos años de mando, es una prueba clasica de que no estaba contagiado con esa commun flaqueza de los que gobieran en America.'

[233] In the long and interesting letter of Jaime Aguilar, the provincial of the Jesuits in Paraguay, to the King of Spain (Philip V., 1737), occurs the following passage:

`Y si alguna vez, que no son muchas, se animan los Españoles a perseguir y castigar los Indios, muchos huyen de la tierra, o se esconden, por no ir a la entrada. . . . Otras (vezes) quando llegan allá, el Enemigo les quitan la Cavallada, dexandolos a pie y se vuelven a casa como pueden.'

This I have seen myself, not thirty years ago, on the frontiers of the Argentine Republic. The popular Argentine poem, `La Vuelta de Martin Fierro', by José Hernandez (Buenos Ayres, 1880), has an illustration showing an expedition against the Indians returning. Some of the men are on foot; others are riding two on the same horse, and officers are animating their men with the flat of their swords.

[234] `Account of the Abipones', p. 125.

[235] Brabo, `Inventarios', p. ix.

[236] Francisco Xavier Brabo, `Inventarios de los bienes hallados á la expulsion de los Jesuitas' (Madrid, 1872).

[237] The lists of cannons, guns, and arms of all kinds in the inventories of the Chaco towns, preserved by Brabo, serve to show not only the dangers to which the Jesuits were exposed, but also how thoroughly the Jesuits understood the fickle nature of those with whom they lived.

[238] Another priest, the list of whose effects Brabo has preserved in his `Inventarios', had a book called `El Alivio de Tristes'. Even a Protestant may be excused for hoping that it merited its title.

[239] Cretineau Joly, tome v., chap. ii., p. 95. Your moral force is excellent in a civilized country; but your modern missionary usually prefers something more in accordance with the spirit of the times.

---

[240] The total number of cattle was 78,171, as against 698,353 in the towns of the Guaranís. See Brabo, `Inventarios de los bienes hallados á la expulsion de los Jesuitas', Appendix, p. 668.

---

[241] `History of the Abipones', from the Latin of Martin Dobrizhoffer, London, 1822.

It is a curious circumstance that in the missions in the Chaco there were negro slaves, though in the Paraguayan missions they were unknown. In the inventory of the town of San Lucas appear the following entries, under the head of `Negros Esclavos':

`Justo, que sirve de capataz en el campo; será de edad de veinte y siete años, mas ó menos segun su aspecto.'

`Item, Pedro, será de diez y seis años y es medio fatuo.'

`Item, José Felix, será de un mes y medio.'

---

[242] Though 1747 was the date of the final founding of these reductions, as early as 1697 about four hundred Indians were discovered in the woods of the Taruma by Fathers Robles and Ximenes, and established in the mission of Nuestra Señora de Fe; but in the year 1721 they all returned to the woods, a famine and an outbreak of the small-pox having frightened them. After being again established in a mission, and again having left it, in 1746, they were established definitely at San Joaquin.

---

[243] Dobrizhoffer calls the Tobatines by the name of Itatines. Charlevoix and others refer to them as Tobatines.

---

[244] `Account of the Abipones', p. 54.

---

[245] In 1873, when I visited the outskirts of this forest, the conditions were similar to those which Dobrizhoffer describes, with the addition that the depopulation of the country, owing to the recent long war, had allowed the tigers to multiply to an extraordinary degree, and my guide and myself, after feeding our horses, had to sleep alternately, the waker holding the two horses hobbled and bridled.

---

[246] The whole operation of collecting and preparing the leaves of the *Ilex Paraguayensis*, to make the *yerba-maté*, was most curious. Bands of men used to sally out for a six-months' expedition, either by land with bullock-waggons, or up one of the rivers in flat-bottomed boats, which were poled along against the rapid current by crews of six to twelve men. Arrived at the *yerbal*, as the forest was called, they built shelters, after the fashion of those in use amongst the larger of the anthropoid apes. Some roamed the woods in search of the proper trees, the boughs of which they cut down with machetes, whilst others remained and built a large shed of canes called a *barbacoa*. On this shed were laid the bundles of boughs brought from the woods, and a large fire was lighted underneath. During forty-eight hours (if I remember rightly) the toasting went on; then, when sufficiently dry, the leaves were stripped from the twigs, and placed on a sort of open space of hard clay, something like a Spanish threshing-floor. On this they were pounded fine, and the powder rammed into raw-hide bags. This concluded the operations, and the *yerba* was then ready for the `higgling of the market'.

---

[247] *Traduttore traditore*, as the proverb says.

---

[248] Charlevoix says, in his `Histoire de la Nouvelle France', speaking of the Indians in general: `L'expérience a fait voir qu'il étoit plus à propos de les laisser dans leur simplicité et dans leur ignorance, que les sauvages peuvent être des bons Chrétiens sans rien prendre de notre politesse et de notre façon de vivre, ou du moins qu'il falloit laisser faire au tems pour les tirer de leur grossièreté, qui ne les empêche pas de vivre dans une grande innocence, d'avoir beaucoup de modestie, et de servir Dieu avec une piété et une ferveur, que les rendent très propres aux plus sublimes opérations de la grâce.' Had more people thought with Charlevoix, and not been too anxious to draw savages incontrovertibly to our `politesse' (*sic*) and `façon', and left more to time (`au tems'), how much misery might have been saved, and how many interesting peoples preserved! For, in spite of the domination of the Anglo-Saxon race, it might have been wise to leave other types, if only to remind us of our superiority.

---

[249] Hell not infrequently seems to have struck the Indians as a joke, for Charlevoix relates that when the first missionaries expatiated on its flames to the Chirignanós, they said, 'If there is fire in hell, we could soon get enough water to put it out.' This answer scandalized the good priest, who could not foresee that the flames of Tophet would be extinguished without the necessity of any other waters than those of indifference.

[250] 'Account of the Abipones', p. 74.

[251] Padre del Techo, in his 'History of Paraguay', says of the wood Indians that 'they died like plants which, grown in the shade, will not bear the sun.'

[252] San Joaquin, San Estanislao, and Belen.

[253] Notably those of Azara.

[254] 'Account of the Abipones', p. 15.

[255] As that of Philip V., from the palace of Buen Retiro, December 28, 1743, and his two letters to the Jesuits of Paraguay. Also the previous edict obtained by Montoya from Philip II., and by the various additions on the same head made from time to time to the code known as 'The Laws of the Indies'.

[256] Since the discovery of America the Spaniards and the Portuguese had been in constant rivalry throughout the south-eastern portion. Their frontier, between what are now Brazil and Argentina, had never been defined. In 1494 King John II. of Castile concluded a treaty signed at Tordesillas with the King of Portugal, placing the dividing-line between the countries two hundred leagues more to the westward than that of the famous Bull of Pope Alexander VI. (May 4, 1493), which placed it at one hundred leagues west of Cape Verd, cutting the world in two from the Arctic to the Antarctic Pole. From the signing of the treaty of Tordesillas trouble began in South America between the Powers, as by that treaty a portion of Brazil came into the power of Portugal.

[257] These were the towns of San Angel, San Nicolas, San Luis, San Lorenzo, San Miguel, San Juan, and San Borja.

[258] According to the 1913 edition of the Catholic Encyclopedia (in the article titled "Reductions of Paraguay") this treaty, signed in secret on 15 January 1750, was a deliberate assault on the Jesuit Order by the Ministers of Spain and Portugal, the latter of whom, Pombal, is said to have been responsible also for the false and libelous `Histoire de Nicolas I., Roy du Paraguai et Empereur des Mamalus' (referred to in this chapter) which was distributed throughout Europe as another attack on the Jesuits. As anyone familiar with the situation could see that the Indians would not be happy about the treaty's requirement to abandon their homes, it was a well-calculated, though detestable, move. — A. L., 1998.

[259] Most of the dates of the events subsequent to the cession of the seven reductions on the Uruguay are taken from `La Causa Jesuitica de Portugal' (Madrid, 1768), written by Ibañez, a great enemy of the Jesuits. In it is also an account of the events in Paraguay between 1750 and 1756, called `Relacion de la Guerra que sustentaron los Jesuitas contra las tropas Españolas y Portuguesas en el Uruguay y Paraná'. No proof has ever been brought forward that the Jesuits as a body ever incited the revolt of the Indians, though undoubtedly Father Tadeo Ennis, a hot-headed priest, stirred up his own particular reduction to resist. It does not seem likely that the Jesuits could have thought it possible to wage a successful war against Spain and Portugal. The dates taken from Ibañez tally with original letters from the Marques de Valdelirios, the Spanish boundary commissioner, and others, which are preserved in the Spanish national archives at Simancas.

[260] *Vide* `Exc. por los cartas que recibi con los avisos, y llegada del P. Altamirano, entiendo acabará de persuadirse a que los Padres de la Campañia son los sublevados, sino los quitan de las aldeas sus Santos Padres (como ellos los llaman) no experimentarán mas que rebeliones insolencias y desprecios. . . .' — Letter quoted by Ibañez (`Causa Jesuitica'), and also preserved at Simancas.

[261] The Marques de Valdelirios, writing to Don José de Carvajal from Monte Video, June 28, 1752 (Simancas, Legajo 7,447), says: `Estoy cierto de que los padres estan ya en la persuasion de que el tratado no se ha de dejar de executar.' This being so, it was evident that the Marquis, at the date of writing, was of opinion that the Jesuits were not going to oppose the execution of the treaty, as he goes on to say: `Y es credible que con este desengaño trabajan seriamente en la mudanza de sus pueblos.'

[262] The instructions were prepared in 1768 by Bucareli for the guidance of Don Juan Joseph de Vertiz, his interim successor in the government of the River Plate, and were delivered to him in 1770 when Bucareli returned to Spain. They are printed by Brabo in his `Coleccion de Documentos relativos á la Expulsion de los Jesuitas', Madrid, 1872, p. 320.

[263] `Oficiales mecanicos'.

[264] This refers to the same subject, and prohibits any Spaniard from settling in an Indian town in any part of America.

[265] Dean Funes, `Ensayo de la Historia Civil del Paraguay', etc., tome iii., p. 45.

[266] Dean Funes says `una difusa memoria'; but, then, even though friendly, churchmen and cats rarely forego a scratch. The proverb has it, `Palabras de santo, uñas de gato'.

[267] Though Ibañez (`Republica Jesuitica', tome i., cap. i.) says: `This treaty caused entire satisfaction to all the world except the English, who feared their commerce would suffer by it (*i.e.*, by the closing of the Colonia del Sacramento as an entry for smuggled goods), and the Jesuits.'

Raynal, also an ex-Jesuit, but a man of far higher character than Ibañez, says (tome iii., lib. 97): `This treaty met censure on both sides, the ministers in Lisbon themselves alleging that it was a false policy to sacrifice the Colonia del Sacramento, the clandestine commerce of which amounted to two millions of dollars a year . . . for possessions whose advantages were uncertain and position remote. The outcries were even stronger in Madrid. There they imagined that the Portuguese would soon rule all along the Uruguay . . . and from thence penetrate up the rivers into Tucuman, Chile, and Potosi.'

[268] Quoting the Pope who advised St. Augustine on his first mission visit to England, to convert the natives to Christianity, to go slowly.

[269] D. Martin de Echaria, Don Rafael de Menedo, and Don Marcos de Lauazabel.

[270] From a letter preserved at Simancas (Legajo 7,447), written by P. Diego Palacios to P. Luiz de Altamirano, dated San Miguel, June 20, 1752, it appears that there were in the territory of the seven towns plantations of *yerba* trees, cotton, and valuable woods.

[271] Archivo de Simancas, Legajo 7,378, folio 17 — a long and curious letter.

[272] `Stroner' may have been `Stoner', in which case he must have been an Englishman. There were few English names amongst the Paraguayan Jesuits, if one except Juan Bruno de Yorca (John Brown of York), Padre Esmid (Smith), the supposititious `Stoner', and the doubtful Taddeo Ennis, who, though said to be a Bohemian, was not impossibly a Milesian.

[273] Dean Funes, `Ensayo de la Historia Civil de Paraguay', etc., book v., p. 52.

[274] They also said, in a memorial presented to the Marquis of Valdelirios by the Provincial Barreda, preserved at Simancas (Legajo 7,447), `That they had voluntarily made themselves vassals of the King of Spain — despues de Christianarnos, nos hizimos voluntariamente vasallos de nuestro Catholico Rey de España para que amparandonos con su poder fomentase nuestra devota Christiandad.' It was not likely, therefore, that they would voluntarily become subject to the Portuguese, their most bitter persecutors.

[275] José Barreda, the Father Provincial of the missions, in a curious letter under date of August 2nd, 1753, tells the Marquis of Valdelirios that he fears not only that the 30,000 Indians resident in the seven towns may rebel, but that they may be joined by the Indians of the other reductions, and that it is possible they may all apostatize and return to the woods. Brabo, in the notes

to his 'Atlas de Cartas Geograficas de los Paises de la America Meridianal' (Madrid, 1872), gives a synopsis of this letter, which formed part of his collection, and contained the greatest quantity of interesting papers on the Jesuits in Paraguay and Bolivia which has ever been brought together. In 1872, after publishing his 'Atlas', his 'Coleccion de Documentos', and his 'Inventarios', he presented his papers (more than 30,000 in number) to the Archivo Historico Nacional of Madrid. There they remain, and form a rich mine for dogged scholars who have not passed their youth on horseback with the lazo in their hands.

---

[276] Archivo de Simancas, Legajo 7,378, folio 146.

---

[277] *Ibid.*: 'Que toda la polvora que tengan los curas y misioneros se queme o se inutilize y pierda hechandola al rio, y que en los pueblos donde se fabrica, cese luego este labor.'

---

[278] In another letter, also preserved at Simancas, and dated at Yapeyu, he complains bitterly of his own suffering on the journey: 'Me moli tanto con el traqueo violento del carreton que no he podido volver sobre mi.' The roads to the missions seem to have been as bad as those which produced the historical exclamation, 'O dura tellus Hispaniæ!' It is certainly the case that Ibañez, in his 'Republica Jesuitica' (Madrid, 1768), gives a very different version of the doings of Altamirano; for he says that Rafael de Cordoba, Altamirano's secretary, 'embarked in a schooner called *La Real* a great quantity of guns and lead for balls, packing them all in boxes, which, he said, were full of objects of a pious nature. . . . This,' says Ibañez, 'was told me by the master of the schooner *José el Ingles*, a man worthy of credence.' This is pleasing to one's national pride, but, still, one seems to want a little better authority even than that of 'Bardolph, the Englishman'.

---

[279] Dean Funes, book v., cap. iii., p. 54.

---

[280] In a most curious letter (preserved at Simancas, Legajo 7,447), the mayor and council of the reduction of San Juan write to Altamirano upbraiding him with being their enemy, and tell him that 'St. Michael sent by God showed their poor grandfathers (*sus pobres abuelos*) where to plant a cross, and afterwards to march due south from the cross and they would find a holy father of the Company.' This, of course, turned out as the saint had foretold,

and after a long day's march they encountered the Jesuit and became Christians.

[281] This account seems to have been lost, and a careful search has not disinterred it from the Maelstrom of Simancas, that prison-house of so many documents, without whose aid so much of Spanish history cannot be written.

[282] His `Efemerides', or Journal, printed and mutilated by Ibañez in his `Republica de Paraguay', gives the best account of the brief `war' which has come down to us; it is supplemented by the `Declaracion de la Verdad' of Father Cardiel, which deals with the misstatements of Ibañez and others against the Jesuits. In regard to his own share in the war, Padre Ennis says: `Atque in exercitas curatorem, spiritualem medicum secum ire postulat.'

[283] `Se puso las botas'.

[284] Dean Funes, `Ensayo de la Historia Civil del Paraguay', Buenos Ayres, etc., book v., cap. iv., p. 58.

[285] Luckily Ibañez (`Republica Jesuitica de Paraguay') has not corrected the many faults of spelling and Latinity into which Padre Ennis fell. Those, though left in from malice, as Ibañez was a bitter enemy of the Jesuits, serve to present the man in his habit as he wrote. However, Ibañez has so much mutilated the text of the journal that occasionally the sense is left obscure.

[286] `Hoc itaque nuncio læti altero ac incensi . . . Sacramento expiationis et pane fortim roborati' (Ennis, `Efemerides').

[287] Cardiel, in his `Declaracion de la Verdad', p. 426, says: `Lo mismo es 28,000 mil Indios que igual numero de muchachos.'

[288] `Nec tamen resipiscebat et Divinam Nemesim quamquam clare experiebatur pro causâ Societatis.'

[289] `Declaracion de la Verdad', p. 404.

---

[290] In fact, they much resembled those `crakys of warre' which, with the `tymmeris for helmys', Barbour, in the `Bruce', takes notice of as the two noteworthy events of a battle that he chronicles:

> `Twa noweltyis that day thai saw,
> That forouth in Scotland had bene nane.
> Tymmeris for helmys war the tane,
> That thaim thoucht thane off gret bewté
> And alsua wondyr for to se.
> The tothyr, crakys war, off wer,
> That thai befor herd neuir er.'
> *The Bruce*, Booke Fourteene, p. 392.

---

[291] This was in an action in the year 1756.

---

[292] `Miente de la cruz a la fecha'.

---

[293] The Mamalucos, or Paulistas, were, of course, the bitterest enemies of everything Paraguayan, so that a King had as well been styled of `Iceland and of Paraguay'.

---

[294] If this assumes to be Sâo Paulo de Piritinanga in Brazil, it is not unlikely one of the few books published there in the eighteenth century, if not the only one. Happy is the city of one book, especially when that work has nothing of a theological character in it, even though it lies from *la cruz á la fecha*.

---

[295] `Account of the Abipones', vol. i., p. 32.

---

[296] The only man the Indians produced who showed any aptitude as a leader was a chief called Sepe Tyaragu. At his death in action in 1756 Nicolas Ñeenguiru succeeded to his post.

---

[298] *Polyborus tharus.* In relation to the word `tharus', which figures as a sort of scientific (or doggerel) cognomen to this bird, Mr. W. H. Hudson once pointed out to me that, like some other `scientific facts', it originated in a mistake. The Pampa Indian name of the bird is `traré'. Molina (Don Juan Ignacio), in his `History of Chile', happened to spell the word `tharé', instead of `traré', and then proceeded to make a dog-Latin form of it. Thus the bird has received its present scientific name.

[299] Cardiel, `Declaracion de la Verdad', p. 430: `. . . llego alli despues de la fuga y desamparo de los pueblos . . . saco a los dos Padres que estaban muy afligidos por la soledad y alboroto.'

[300] In a letter (Archivo de Simancas, Legajo 7,378, folio 128), Valdelirios, writing to the governor of Buenos Ayres, Don José de Caravajal y Lancastre, says: `Inagotables son los recursos de los Padres para que se dilate y no se ratifique el tratado. . . .' But he gives no proof except that they had sent petitions to the King — surely a very constitutional thing for them to do.

[301] The letter was written originally in Guaraní, and a certified translation of it exists at Simancas, Legajo 7,385, folio 13.

[302] Altamirano.

[303] Don Pedro Cevallos, Governor of Buenos Ayres, who was in Paraguay in 1755, sent there to fight the troops of King Nicolas, found, as he himself says, `no King, and no troops, but a few half-armed Indians.' Writing to the King, he says: `Los Jesuitas son utiles en el Paraguay.'

[304] The figures in Chapter VII. serve to show that in Paraguay, at least, they were not exactly millionaires. In Mexico, Palafox, the saintly Bishop of Puebla, had set about all kinds of stories as to their riches, but Geronimo Terenichi, an ecclesiastic sent to Mexico to examine into the question of the Jesuits and their wealth, after a year of residence, expressly says `they were very poor, and laden with debt' (`eran muy pobres y estaban cargados de deudas'): `Coleccion de los articulos de la Esperanza, sobre la Historia del Reinado de Carlos III.', p. 435. Madrid, 1859.

---

[305] They were expressly proclaimed to be `ocultas y reservadas'. Carlos III., in defence of his `occult' and `reserved' reasons, said, `mis razones, solo Dios y yo debemos conocerlas' (`Reinado de Carlos III.', vol. iii., p. 120. Ferrer del Rio, Madrid, 1856). No doubt Carlos III. satisfied his conscience with this dictum, but it is permissible to doubt whether the power alluded to in such a cousin-like manner by the King was equally satisfied.

---

[306] This celebrated tumult, generally known in Spain as `el Motin de Aranjuez', and sometimes as `el Motin de Esquilace', occurred on Palm Sunday, 1766. The ostensible reason was an edict of the King (Charles III.) prohibiting the use of long cloaks and broad-brimmed hats, which had been for long popular in Spain. The tumult assumed such formidable dimensions that the Walloon Guards were unable to quell it, but two friars, Padre Osma and Padre Cueva, in some manner were able to stem the confusion. The King and the court were so much disturbed that they quitted Madrid and went to Aranjuez. There is no proof that the Jesuits had any hand at all in the affair.

---

[307] Ferrer del Rio, in his history of the reign of Charles III.

---

[308] Such, at least, several of his letters to the Pope, Clement XII., would seem to indicate. It is not impossible that the strenuous opposition which the Jesuits gave to the Inquisition may have had something to do with their expulsion. Some of them went great lengths in their attacks. P. Antonio Vieyra, the celebrated Portuguese Jesuit, in his `Relaçaõ Exactissima, Instructiva, Curioza, Verdadeira, Noticioza do Procedimento das Inquiziçois de Portugal' (Em Veneza, 1750), is almost as severe as Protestant writers have been against the Inquisition. Particularly does he inveigh against the prison system of the Holy Office (pp. 3-5, chap. i.). In the last chapter (p. 154), Vieyra calls Saavedra, the founder of the Portuguese Inquisition, a tyrant, and in recounting his deeds calls him *tyranno, cruel, falsario, herege*, and *ladram* (a thief), and finishes by asserting that the tribunal invented by such a man `had its roots in hell', and that `its ministers could not go to heaven'.

---

[309] His full name was Don Francisco de Paula Bucareli y Ursua.

---

[310] Brabo (`Coleccion de Documentos', etc.) says of him, `speaking of the petty jealousies and intrigues which the decree of expulsion evoked: `En medio de tantas contrariedades, crimenes y miserias destaca serena la figura de Bucareli, no solo llevando a cabo con incansable celo su cometido, si no atendiendo a suplir en la organizacion religiosa, intelectual y civil los numerosos vacios que dejaba la falta del absorbente y decisivo influjo jesuitico.'

[311] `Ensayo de la Historia Civil del Paraguay', etc., vol. iii., cap. viii., p. 119.

[312] Funes, `Ensayo de la Historia Civil', etc., vol. iii., cap. viii.

[313] `Tambien en algunos pueblos hay unas escopetas inglesas muy largas con sus horquillas si se quieren usar de ellas no son muy pesadas y tienen buen alcance' (Funes, `Ensayo de la Historia Civil del Paraguay', etc., vol. iii., cap. viii.).

[314] There were in the year 1759 throughout the world 271 Jesuit missions, 1,542 religious houses, 61 cattle farms, 340 residences, 171 seminaries, 1,542 churches, and 22,589 Jesuits, whereof 11,293 were priests. Of the above houses, missions, and churches, the greater portion were in America (Ferrer del Rio, `Historia del Reinado de Carlos III.', Madrid, 1856).

In the River Plate and Paraguay there were about 400 Jesuits, of whom 300 were priests. The other hundred, according to Ibañez (`Republica Jesuitica'), were `mostly poor devils who were in want of food, and came into the Order for a meal.' Ibañez rarely spoke the truth, not even when it would have been expedient to do so; and certainly amongst these `poor devils' could not have been included Asperger, the writer on Indian medicines, and other distinguished men who inhabited the Paraguayan missions as lay brothers.

[315] Dean Funes, `Ensayo de la Historia Civil', etc., vol. iii., book v., cap. ix.

[316] The fine library was dispersed, and many priceless MSS. treating of the discovery and conquest, and of expeditions by the Jesuits amongst tribes of Indians now extinct, were lost. Nothing seems to have been preserved except matter which the dispersers thought might prove incriminating to the Jesuits. It is a well-known principle to judge and condemn a man, and then to search for evidence against him. The books were kept in a place known as La Granja de Santa Catalina, and a man of letters, Dr. Don Antonio Aldao, was charged to catalogue and remit them to the capital. Dean Funes says (book v., cap. ix., p. 156) that he complied with his instructions (`verificóla felizmente y con arreglo a sus instrucciones'), but, anyhow, most of the books were lost. It is a common phrase amongst doctors, `The operation was entirely successful, but the patient unfortunately succumbed.' Amongst the books was the celebrated `Monita Secreta', used by Ibañez in his charges (after the expulsion) against the Jesuits.

---

[317] Dean Funes (`Ensayo de la Historia Civil', vol. iii., cap. viii.) seems to have gauged the feelings of the Governor when he says: `Temblo de susto Bucareli considerando en riesgo una conquista, que debia aumentar su gloria y su fortuna.' `Su fortuna' is delicious, and shows your true conqueror's melancholy.

---

[318] The Tebicuari forms the northern boundary between the territory of Misiones and the rest of Paraguay. It is a large river, and in my time (1872-1875) was bridgeless, and had to be crossed in canoes, whilst the horses swam, or were towed behind the canoes with ropes.

---

[319] Yapeyú was the largest of all the missions. The name signifies a chisel in Guaraní.

---

[320] Bucareli, in a letter to El Conde de Aranda (Brabo, `Coleccion de Documentos relativos á la Expulsion de los Jesuitas', Madrid, 1872), says in reference to the perils by which he imagined himself surrounded: `El misero diminuto estado de la tropa, por el atraso de sus pagas y la falta que encontré de caudales en estas cajas, era una urgencia que me atormentaba.'

---

[321] This war, undertaken by a fool (Lopez) against enormous odds, served to show what a people even when in the wrong, and in a bad cause, can do when it believes itself to be fighting for national liberty. As a matter of fact, Paraguayan liberty was not threatened for an instant, and Lopez declared war against both Brazil and the Argentine Republic out of mere ambition to be a second Napoleon. His solitary qualifications for the character were that, like his prototype, he was fat and loved women. The war commenced in 1865 and finished in 1870, and left the country almost a desert. So lonely was it,

that I have often in those days seen tigers calmly walk across a road in mid-day, and a shout or a pistol-shot but little quickened their movements.

[322] *Capilla* was the name given in Paraguay to some of the smaller villages which had a chapel, the chapel (*capilla*) being more important than the houses.

[323] El V. P. José Pignatelli, in his `La Compañia de Jesus en su Extincion y Restablecimento', says that the Paraguayan Jesuits were all sent to Faenza.

[324] `Carta del Gobernador de Buenos Ayres (Bucareli) al Comte de Aranda'. Brabo, `Coleccion de Documentos Relativos a la Expulsion de los Jesuitos', p. 8, Madrid, 1872: `Les hice vestir a la Española asistiendolos y tratandolos de modo que conozcan la mejora de su suerte. . . .'

[325] Brabo, `Coleccion de Documentos', etc., p. 101. The letter is headed `I. H. T., Ore Rey Nitu Don Carlos Tercero'.

[326] Brabo, `Coleccion de Documentos', etc., p. 185.

[327] Ceremonies, no doubt, have their uses in enslaving mankind. A courtier once said to a Spanish King, `Your Majesty is but a ceremony yourself.'

[328] Letter to Aranda: Brabo, `Coleccion de Documentos', p. 196: `Y las mujeres en tal extremo, que es impossible demostralo sin faltar a la modestia.'

[329] `Semejantes tiranias'.

[330] P. 222: `Y teniendo presente que por lo que mira a este punto resulta de los informes que solo hablan estos Indios su idioma natural, pero que no es prohibicion de los PP. Jesuitos, sino por el amor que tienen a su nativo lenguage pues en cada uno de los pueblos han establecido esculas de leer y escriber en lengua española, y que por este motivo se encuentra un numero

grande de Indios muy habiles en escribir (dos de ellos etan copiando hora esto que yo escribo y de mejor letra que la mia).' Also pp. 223-225, etc.

[331] Brabo, `Coleccion de Documentos', etc., p. 200.

[332] `Y sobre todo, fuera de la America y libre de Secretaria y Consejo de Indias.' Brabo, `Coleccion de Documentos', etc.: Letter of Bucareli to Aranda, p. 231.

[333] Brabo, `Coleccion de Documentos', etc., p. 280.

[334] The alcaldes of Indian villages usually have a long cane with a silver head, like those formerly carried by footmen, as a badge of their office. In remote places I have seen them, with their canes in their hands, a battered tall hat upon their heads, a linen jacket and trousers, and barefooted, riding on an ox, and thought that they served to maintain the majesty of the law quite as well as if they had had stuff gowns, horsehair wigs, and had been seated on a sack of wool.

[335] Vol. iii., book v., cap. viii., p. 130 (`Ensayo de la Historia Civil del Paraguay', etc.): `Los Caciques y corregidores que acompañaban a Bucareli, habian sido alhagados por todos los artificios de sugestion. Esto á la verdad, no era mas que coronar las victimas, que se destinaban al sacrificio.'

[336] Chapter IX.

[337] Brabo, p. 304.

[338] Brabo, `Coleccion de Documentos', p. 320: `Y porque estoy informado que muchos Indios de los que se habian ausentado con las tropas Portuguesas, y que han residido por gran tiempo en el Rio Pardo, Viamont, y otras partes se han restituido a sus pueblos, ciudaran . . . de que todos estos con sus families seran traslados a los mas interiores o distantes de aquellas fronteras por no ser conveniente se mantengan en ellas o sus inmediaciones, y asi en lo sucesivo lo ejecutaran . . . con los Indios que se restituyan, sin dejar

alguno, para evitar todo motivo de communicacion que puede ser muy prejudicial.'

[339] `No conviene dejarles una entera libertad, que seria por extremo fatal y prejudicial á sus intereses pues la astucia y sagacidad de los españoles triumfaria facilemente de su rudeza.'

[340] Brabo, `Bucareli's Instructions', p. 327: `Que el commercio de los españoles ha de ser libre.'

[341] The Paraguayan Jesuits were allowed to take away all their personal property, and it appears that they did so.

[342] Cayetano Ibarguen had only two, P. Lorenzo Balda three, and so on (Brabo, `Coleccion de Documentos', p. 388).

[343] So late as 1818 Rengger, in his `Essai Historique sur la Révolution du Paraguay', etc., talks of arriving in Buenos Ayres `après un court trajet de soixante jours.' From thence to Corrientes he took seven weeks, but does not say if the passage was considered short or long.

[344] Funes, `Ensayo Critico de la Historia Civil del Paraguay', etc.; Don Feliz de Azara, `Descripcion y Historia del Paraguay', etc.; and also `Memorias sobre el estado rural del Rio de la Plata en 1801'.

[345] `Ensayo de la Historia Civil', vol. i., book ii., p. 341.

[346] Funes, `Ensayo de la Historia Civil', etc., book v., cap. viii., p. 133.

[347] Brabo, `Inventarios', Appendix, p. 669.

[348] Demersay (`Histoire du Paraguay'), writing in 1847, says of the mission of La Cruz he saw a few trees still standing in a miserable state.

[349] Funes, `Ensayo de la Historia Civil', etc., book vi., cap. viii., p. 395.

[350] Hudson, `Naturalist in La Plata'.

Milton Keynes UK
Ingram Content Group UK Ltd.
UKHW030740071024
449371UK00006B/700